FLAWLESS

FLAWLESS

~

Lessons in Looks and Culture
from the K-Beauty Capital

~

Elise Hu

DUTTON

DUTTON

An imprint of Penguin Random House LLC
penguinrandomhouse.com

Library of Congress Cataloging-in-Publication Data
has been applied for.

ISBN 9780593184189 (hardcover)
ISBN 9780593473801 (export edition)
ISBN 9780593184202 (ebook)

Printed in the United States of America
1st Printing

BOOK DESIGN BY ASHLEY TUCKER

While the author has made every effort to provide accurate telephone numbers, internet addresses, and other contact information at the time of publication, neither the publisher nor the author assumes any responsibility for errors or for changes that occur after publication. Further, the publisher does not have any control over and does not assume any responsibility for author or third-party websites or their content.

For Eva, Isa, Luna

I wonder if you are the pretty girl in question. I wonder what you do with a power which, though potent, makes you vulnerable to every probe, every demand, every infiltration? I wonder what you do with a power that turns you into an open atlas upon which any idiot can map their own route?

—ZADIE SMITH[1]

'To be born woman is to know—
Although they do not talk of it at school—
That we must labour to be beautiful.'

—YEATS[2]

CONTENTS

A note on romanization of Korean: Korean-language names and terms have been romanized using the Korean government standard system adopted by the Ministry of Culture and Tourism. Following Korean custom, surnames precede given names. Exceptions are made for those whose English names have been published with alternate transliterations or with English spellings that are more widely known and commonly accepted (e.g., Syngman Rhee, Seoul, etc.).

A note on Chinese romanization: Mandarin has been romanized using the pinyin system, except in certain place names, personal names, and other proper nouns that are standard in English in older forms (e.g., Taipei).

INTRODUCTION

~

I've seen the future, and it's poreless. In 2015, I moved from Washington, D.C., to a city I'd never previously stepped foot in—Seoul, South Korea—to be an international correspondent and the first-ever Korea and Japan bureau chief for the American broadcaster NPR. Almost immediately, I realized that by making the move, I had time-traveled forward and was face-to-face with the future of how we might live, look, and relate to one another.

South Korea's capital is an endless assault of images blasting in your direction on every street corner, at every hour. Many of them are faces. They tower above you on digital signage glowing from the sides of skyscrapers, flash by in subway stations deep underground, or whip past on cars topped with oversized screens. What I found after I moved there (with my journalist husband, toddler daughter, geriatric beagle, and two cats) was a city that felt like a living monument to conspicuous consumption, with upscale malls, blinding lights, and blinding wealth—everything hitting you with its height and size and newness. Looking at all the floor-to-ceiling ads featuring faces, I started to notice they had a uniformity to them, as if they were variations on a prototype.

In the bustling Myeongdong shopping district and along the supercool streets of Gangnam, there were so many skincare and makeup stores that I could stand on a corner and see a Face Shop across from a Face Shop across from a Face Shop. It was common to spot women walking around with silicone nose covers and medical tape, following cosmetic procedures. I sometimes spied even more dramatically bandaged bodies of tourists, with full-on Freddy Krueger–style post-op masks, moving about the crowded spaces of Seoul.

The obsession with appearance runs deep—you're expected to include a photo, height, and weight on résumés for jobs across various industries—and the country's wide and early embrace of digital technologies has turned its society into an overlap of selfie culture and "self-care" consumerism. South Korea is leading the way on bringing these trends to global consumers—South Korean cosmetics exports quadrupled from $1.6 billion to $6.3 billion between 2014, the year I got assigned to Korea, and 2018, the year I moved back to the United States.[1] Having gained a cultlike following around the world, the K-beauty industry is projected to be worth $13.9 billion by 2027.[2]

Korea's advancements include an enthusiastic embrace of consumer beauty, for everyone, and a look that's free of surprises—no blemishes, bulges, or hairs out of place. Equally embraced is support for the idea that digital filters can be less imperative if you perfect your look not with temporary cover-ups but with a more permanent alteration of the canvas—the body itself. That's possible thanks to developments in science and technology—skincare products, injections, and plastic surgery. But the sought-after result of all the beautification work is for it to appear like there was no work done at all. The future I glimpsed brought technological innovation to the surface of our faces and bodies, while promising consumers "choice" and self-expression for the whole process.

~

Within my first year in Seoul, I found that the flaws I only privately identified when I stood before a mirror were amplified constantly—either out loud through comments from strangers or through the incessant reminders of the criteria for what counts as pretty. At the same time, I couldn't, nor did I truly want to, escape all the beauty consumerism of the place. I went back and forth over those years on whether to give in and try a medical spa procedure or dip into Botox because everyone did it. At some point, it stopped feeling like a choice I wasn't making but instead a mandate I was refusing. Though I never could commit to injections and surgery, I did go all in on face massages, pore vacuuming procedures, and skincare products that lured me in with sumptuous packaging. Do I want an affordable eye cream so I can wake up looking fresh when I'm not? Yes. Or foot masks that get my feet to feel as soft as a baby's bottom? Get me that twelve-pack, please.

For those with the money to self-optimize, what kind of relationship with ourselves—and one another—are we ultimately pursuing? How do we reconcile the idea of self-care through consumer spending . . . and *actual* care? As technology and medicine make it possible to be more "beautiful," where do we draw the line on the work of improving our exteriors? Especially when upgrades require upkeep?

I wrestled with these questions for years and still do. But these pages reflect a shot at considering a topic that's overlooked as a transnational cultural force. It's a key lever in our relationships with ourselves and each other. South Korea, which rocketed to become a beauty product superpower, is a place where the dominance of the beauty industry and the dominance of an appearance standard feed off each other in an endless loop. But the pursuit of beauty is a tentpole of the modern female experience everywhere. It informs how we perceive ourselves and how we perceive others. Global consumers have nearly doubled their spending on beauty and personal care products and services in the past fifteen years, as beauty has moved into a phase of "total pop-culture domination."[3] Its impact on modern-day meritocracy, meaning-making, and the experiences of women, who bear the most pressure to look a certain way, deserves more examination and reflection.

We've all become more aware of our appearances these days because we can't escape our digital reflections and the many options available to improve them. We've grown accustomed to Facetune and features like built-in skin smoothing, jaw narrowing, and eye enlarging that now come standard with social apps like Snapchat or TikTok. But living in Seoul made me hyperaware of how I look and how others saw me on the surface. The availability—and expectation—of enhancements fuel an existing societal competitiveness in South Korea, where it seems the only way to boost social status is to spend more to become more "attractive" by industry-led, algorithm-fed standards. The winners look like K-pop idols, actors and beauty influencers who set specific aesthetic markers for the rest of us to follow. Their choices in fashion, footwear, skincare—even their signature selfie poses—are replicated in nanoseconds on the social web.

They are so successful in exporting aesthetics thanks to the strength of Hallyu, the Korean cultural wave that's spread across the globe and become part of South Korea's public image. The influence of Hallyu carried K-beauty products, services, and surgeries along with it, as they promise to help people get ever closer to reaching the reigning beauty norms of the day. Beauty, "in the form of cosmetics products and cosmetic surgery," researcher Sharon Heijin Lee writes, "is one of [Korea's] most profitable export industries, even economically outpacing its manufacturing and shipbuilding industries, the two industries upon which the Korean economy was first built."[4]

I would spend nearly four years in Seoul, from early 2015 to the end of 2018. During that time I observed the place with both a microscope and a telescope—examining the aspects of K-beauty that enchanted me up close, but also finding that sometimes it's easier to see certain realities from a distance. In Myeongdong and Gangnam and other commercial parts of Seoul, where a specific standard of beauty prevailed and consumerism dominated, I thought, *Wow. There's something that seems both strange but also familiar about this situation.* I wanted to better understand.

Through my research and interviews of hundreds of Korean women, ranging from age seven to age seventy-three, I have held close the notion of "speaking nearby," a concept brought forward by the filmmaker Trinh T. Minh-ha. She takes the "speaking nearby" approach when making art about a culture that's not her own: "Although you're very close to your subject, you're committed to not speaking on their behalf, in their place or on top of them. You can only speak nearby, in proximity . . . By not trying to assume a position of authority in relation to the other, you are actually freeing yourself from the endless criteria generated with such an all-knowing claim and its hierarchies in knowledge."[5]

My nearness is nuanced. I lived and worked in Seoul as an Asian woman, but as a Chinese and Taiwanese American and not a Korean native. That meant I could simultaneously feel the burden of expectation for Asian women and sometimes escape it, simply by switching into my "foreigner" identity. I felt no shame moving about the city having just rolled out of bed, not an ounce of makeup on my face. My Korean women friends would catch far more disapproval for doing the same. Because for better or for worse, the bodies we occupy affect our interactions with the world and the way the world interacts with us. The experience of occupying my body—long-limbed, feminine, but with a proud gait—is distinct from the experience of a Korean woman or a white European man.

So many outside observers who have written about Korea in English are European or American men. When I prepared to move there, I found that the vast majority of go-to, mainstream English language texts about modern Korea are written by non-Korean white dudes. By the time I came home in

2018, I could see the glaring blind spots my aforementioned colleagues did not interrogate: namely, the persistence of South Korea's conservative, patriarchal gender norms, including what these norms mean for the women there and how a strict gender binary shows up in insidious ways, for everyone. Discourse is useful—it's both a source of power and a means of exerting it, as the philosopher Michel Foucault has pointed out. It can reinforce the status quo, but it can also undermine and expose it. I craved a wider conversation about norms for women that became so embedded that they're nearly imperceptible.[6]

South Korea remains one of the most unequal societies in the world, despite being one of the richest. The gender wage gap, women's labor participation rates, and the number of women in leadership positions are the worst among developed nations, and the number of women CEOs in the country hovers around 100, total.[7] (Many of those women leaders are descendants of their firm's founders.) "Accounts of the nation's stunning pace of development and the millennial success of its culture industries as a dominant source of pop culture content . . . disavow this inequality," Korea studies scholar Michelle Cho writes.[8] Perhaps the punishing gender imbalance in contemporary Korea is missing in English-language books about it because they're written by those who don't have to feel the blunt end of it.

Today, Seoul remains a dynamic epicenter of global beauty innovation, leading the world in plastic surgery rates and churning out new products faster than its European or American competitors. At the same time, some young women in Seoul are divesting themselves from consumer beauty culture and redefining the ways beauty and power intersect. In 2018, hundreds of thousands of young South Korean women started the "Escape the Corset" movement, in which they spurned makeup, long hair, and tight clothes.[9] Women who once looked like the standard-bearers for East Asian beauty posted pictures of their crushed cosmetics on social media and now talk about how much mind space and money they freed up. These gestures carry a meaning and a weight that they wouldn't in the United States, because the rejection of basic appearance norms comes with punishing social sanctions for Korean women. These activists have become outcasts at school and at work. Sometimes they're even uninvited to their own family gatherings. In their activism, these women show us a competing vision of the future.

They're a fascinating community, challenging a self-care culture that tells us to fix problems we didn't know we had while putting profit in businesses' pockets. We're familiar with this exchange because it transcends East and West. As long as "women are broadly objectified, beauty will function as value, and its absence as lack," observes American writer Jia Tolentino.[10] Korea is a place where this tension plays out palpably.

⁓

What goes through your mind when you see yourself in the mirror? If I linger too long, I start noting where I could look better. Maybe smoother skin. A skinnier face. Shinier hair. If something is off enough about my reflection, my entire mood can take a hit. I know better than to conflate external appearance with self-worth, but a good hair day puts a bounce in my step and getting pampered at a spa *feels* good. The vacillating enthusiasm and unease I feel for beauty culture underlines the tension at play—skincare or spa services allow us to care for our bodies, finding ways to nurture ourselves in these turbulent times. But market-driven standards for female beauty are also tools of powerful systems. They sustain the idea that looking better—and spending energy and money to do so—is a worthwhile pursuit in the first place.

This complex, often contradictory relationship has nagged at me for as long as I can remember. In South Korea, I found a dizzying, dynamic place where looks matter in a way that felt exacting and extreme—but in the end, illuminating. Because I don't think I'm alone in struggling with where to draw the line on self-improvement, now that selfie culture and self-care culture collide. As the rest of the modern world develops into what Seoul already has been for years—an image-laden, social-media-driven landscape, where digital representations of us can be automatically filtered to have longer lashes or poreless skin, and digital makeup can be instantly applied before we show up on our video meetings—it makes clear Korea's looks-obsessed culture, where appearance norms inch further and further out of reach, isn't some anomaly. It presents a vision of a future that's already arriving. And it offers a lens through which we can ask the larger, thornier questions about the power we give commercialized beauty itself. It's reflected in systems: economics, the workplace, our home lives. As the old saw goes, the personal is political. Or it gets political once you look beneath the filters and the face masks.

Ultimately, it's not just Korean women but all of us who must wrestle with a system that sells us on the notion that we are insufficient and that consumption can cure it. What today's beauty imperative lays bare is how the core promise of capitalism—transformation through spending—can now be expertly and inexpensively carved on our faces. In South Korea's super-intense interpretation of "making something of yourself," that means remaking our very bodies with fast-improving technologies. Like everything else, it comes at a price.

~

CHAPTER 1

Beauty Is a Beast

Our new Seoul home spread across half the thirty-fifth floor of one of the tallest high-rises north of the Han River, which famously bisects the city. We never got a key to the place because every unit was fitted with an electronic keypad for entry. The door played a trill or a five-note ditty, depending on whether it was unlocking or locking. The first week, I padded around in my socks on gleaming white heated marble tiles that were warmed underneath by Korea's traditional ondol floor heating. My feet never once went cold in that apartment.

I learned you could un-press the elevator buttons to de-select destination floors, which saved me many times when my then two-year-old Eva would get trigger happy with all the buttons. I marveled at the central vacuum system, in which every room had a conduit to plug in our vacuum hose, so we'd never be bothered to push around a vacuum cleaner from room to room. Down in the underground parking garage, maintenance workers waxed and buffed the floors so often that when we eventually bought a used Hyundai to drive, the tires would squeak when we parked, as if we were backing up on the surface of glass.

In the comfortable confines of my tower, I lapped up my initiation to Seoul. From our apartment's floor-to-ceiling double-paned windows we could see everything, from the grassy patches of the U.S. Army base next door to the Lotte World Tower—Seoul's tallest skyscraper, a 45-minute drive away—to the numerous green-clad mountains that surround the city. Compared to most American cities, Seoul is first-world *plus*. It has all the advancements and conveniences of the world's most developed places, but shinier, sleeker, and more efficient. Ours was just one of the many buildings pushing high into the cloud of pollution above the city. Like the rest of them, it was mixed use, so we had access to a coffee shop, nail salon, convenience store, and restaurant right in our apartment building. Underground, subway cars come with heated seats from which I could stream my favorite shows on my phone, the Wi-Fi never interrupted. If I ever missed a bus, the next one reliably showed up two minutes later. And absolutely everything—everything—could be delivered straight to our door. Furniture, food, convenience items. Agencies even send actors to your doorstep if you need extra party guests—or a fake spouse—in a pinch.[1] The futuristic place and its on-demand, always connected consumer culture was the opposite of a hardship post. It felt like a vortex and a privilege.

I settled in by the summer of 2015 and spent the early weeks of June waddling around the apartment heavily pregnant with my second daughter, unpacking our clothes and housewares after they finally came off a container ship. At night I'd go live from Korea for NPR's *Morning Edition* in America, which was thirteen hours behind. Reclining on the slipper chair in my windowless home office, I used my belly as a handy shelf to rest my Comrex audio transmitting device on. The baby used my insides as a speed bag, doing nightly workouts on the lower part of my belly. Just enduring this was enough to wear me out.

That summer was sticky and smelly, as hot as Seoul's winter is cold. The humidity hung so thick that the barbecue smoke, diesel fumes, and steam from the sidewalk grates packed a pungent punch. Women scurried down the street hovering battery-powered pastel fans in front of their faces, and my husband Matt would come in from his commutes joking that he lost six pounds from sweat alone.

I eventually dropped eight pounds—and four ounces—when Baby Isabel Rock made her entrance in early July, officially kicking off my maternity leave. We gave her the middle name Rock partly as a play on the Republic of Korea (ROK) acronym that U.S. soldiers throw around. My parental leave allowed for eight weeks of nursing, sleeping in three-hour stretches to match the newborn's schedule, and altogether sweating a lot in my postpartum husk. I stayed at home as if I were quarantining, which made sense because that summer MERS, a mysterious respiratory virus, came in from an airline traveler and spread rapidly through the city.

In my reflection I saw all the nights of interrupted sleep and the heaviness from carrying a baby for nearly ten months. Dark circles parked under my eyes, and frown lines carved themselves between my brows. The hair on my head and body had grown thick from the hormones of pregnancy. A little patch of fur even sprang up somewhere it never existed, on the front of my neck. Pregnancy and postpartum are the only periods of my life I have ever had boobs, so I enjoyed that at least, though less perhaps because they constantly leaked milk.

Up until that point, my skincare routine consisted of a drugstore cleanser (thank you, Clean & Clear), followed by a moisturizer before bed. I had finally made myself at home in a skincare product mecca and suddenly had nowhere to go and a lot of time on my hands. I decided it was time to try all the goop I'd seen and read about.

When my unapologetically capitalist brother Roger came over to visit from Beijing, where he was also living as an ex-pat, I knew he'd be game to go spend money in the name of self-improvement. He particularly wanted to shop for trendy clothing "where the hot Korean girls are, in Gah-roh-soo-geel," purposely drawing out the Korean. He was describing a tree-lined shopping street in the glitzy Gangnam district (made famous by the eponymous song) that's a Korean equivalent to Rodeo Drive. I learned the phrase *one-minute bags* to describe luxury handbags so trendy that on Garosugil you'd spot one on someone's arm every minute or less. When Louis Vuitton was the most popular brand in South Korea, its handbags would flash by at an even quicker rate, earning them the nickname "three-second bags" because of their ubiquitous appearances.[2]

To wander these shopping streets, I brought along the two-week-old baby Isa. I strapped her onto me with one of those single pieces of stretchy cloth used to harness a sleeping baby onto your body, tangling myself and the baby to-

middle fingers and spread it over my face, standing over my sink with a stretchy terry cloth cat ears headband holding my hair back. For thirty minutes I left the surface of my face—everything but the eye area—blanketed by the thick sugary scrub. The sandy stuff sent my older daughter into screams and giggles when I approached her. "Momma aaaaaaah!!" she squealed, before bolting in a blaze of laughter. One night, out of curiosity, I reached my tongue over my top lip to taste the scrub, since it was brown-sugar-based, after all. Nope, not sugary sweet. It tasted more like a grainy hair pomade.

My clumsy product testing was strictly out of curiosity, since I was drawn in not as a reporter but as a woman who wanted to try these things and see what they might do for me. I was attracted to the promise of improvement and possibility that came with each series of bottles, to their colors and design. And ultimately, all the dabbling in the products helped me better understand what makes the Korean beauty industry unique. It also underscored just how little about skincare I'd absorbed until that point, probably because I grew up in America during a time when actively frying our skin in tanning beds was the thing to do. Tanning sessions came free with gym memberships in the late 1990s, and I remember tacking tiny palm-tree stickers on my hip to see how tan I got in those pneumatic-tube-looking UV-ray-blasting pods. It seems jaw-droppingly irresponsible now, like how our parents would let us ride bicycles without helmets or down two-liter bottles of Coke.

As I futzed around with my potions, the difference between my cultural understanding of skincare and that of native Koreans could not have been more pronounced. Most middle- and upper-class Korean women my age, in their mid-thirties, had practiced protecting and caring for their skin practically all their lives. My twenty-six-year-old assistant Haeryun, a K-beauty skeptic, shared with me the supposedly correct temperature of water that Koreans believed you should use to wash your face in the morning. The other moms at preschool, as well as my Korean Pilates teacher Soomi, all had go-to facialists for regular treatments and various oils and serums they could recommend off the tops of their heads. These regimens weren't about covering up blemishes, they were about caring for the canvas itself.

The cultural know-how is immense because consumer beauty matters more in Korea than in any other place on earth. South Koreans spend twice as much on skincare products as consumers in the United States, the UK, and France.[3] The entire country is small enough to fit in the space between Los Angeles and San Francisco, but its beauty brands number in the 8,000s.[4] Demand drives a geyser of cosmetic offerings, and a saturated market drives demand, and on and on it cycles. Beauty practices that only recently became common in the West, like microblading eyebrows or laser facials, were mainstream in Korea a decade or more ago. The Korean beauty industry invented the cushion makeup compact now emulated by more established brands like L'Oréal, Clinique, and Lancôme.[5] Same goes for the now widely desired effect of "glowy" or "dewy" skin—an ideal for Korean men and women alike. This is a country and a culture that knows its stuff when it comes to skincare.

Sales success is owed in part to a selling point the K-beauty industry carved out—heritage ingredients—"natural" or herbal product sources that represent a connection to a land's heritage. AmorePacific has staked its Innisfree brand on using plants and other sources grown in Korea—ginseng, fruits, certain herbs, and flowers—to advance skincare and its bottom line. Plantations on Jeju Island grow one such ingredient in abundance, helping sell millions of units and launching an entire product line.

~

Jeju is South Korea's southernmost island, a former volcano small enough that it takes only forty-five minutes to drive across it and a few hours to drive its perimeter. Koreans often refer to it as the Hawaii of Korea. Like Hawaii, Jeju impresses with its natural beauty, unpolluted air, and untouched patches of lush greenery.

I ventured to Jeju for the first time about a month after Isa was born, and only five months since our arrival in Seoul. This was a family trip, where the four of us were joined by the Yau family, fellow American expats and new friends we met in Korea. (They became such frequent travel companions that my daughters refer to their kids as their cousins.) I hadn't left my apartment in weeks save for my shopping trip with my brother. So the morning of the flight marked only the second time since Isa's birth I ran a brush through my bird's nest of hair. Isa was strapped to me in a BabyBjörn, her sweaty face pressed to my chest and the steady weight of her sleeping body resting on me for most of the trip.

In Jeju, humidity hangs thick in the air, and the sea breeze sends you the faint smell of the abundant shellfish from the ocean. I saw endless stretches of fertile fields as we whipped past horses milling by the roads that ended just before the shore. We visited a beach where everyone took off their shoes and neatly lined them up on the boardwalk before stepping onto the sand.

There is a vastness to Jeju. An emptiness. A few four-way intersections have no stop signs or traffic lights, leaving you on your own. And the attractions there are strange in their own way. I saw a UFO-themed restaurant in the shape of a silvery disk, with no patrons. I saw a rock formation labeled a waterfall that lacked falling water. My travel squad visited a completely empty—yet weirdly, open—theme park the size and scale of a large city zoo. Clerks and ticket punchers appeared when we passed through, but if you went back five minutes later, they were gone. The park called itself Psyche World until it changed its name to something equally puzzling: Ecopia. We wandered into a butterfly exhibit with only three butterflies. A castle-looking structure displayed a jewel museum featuring fake but famous jewels, like that blue one from *Titanic* that the old lady dropped into the ocean in the end. A giant marquee promised CSI: THE EXPERI-ENCE, but no showings were scheduled. A concert park with gleaming white seating in the grass was devoid of humans except for a display of two life-size crocodile statues. I am not sure what explains this total weirdness, though our not going as part of a group tour package probably had to do with it.

All these amusements obscured a key Jeju commodity,

growing right under our noses—green tea. I didn't know it at the time, but the beauty giant AmorePacific owns several tea plantations on the island, and most of its crops aren't used for drinking. They're for skincare.

In 1979, AmorePacific began cultivating green tea on a private farm for its products, claiming to be the first company to use the ingredient in makeup.[6] Green tea produces antioxidants that, depending on your skin, gently exfoliate, clear clogged pores, and fight the signs of aging. "Green tea's truly one of my favorites," beauty author and aesthetician Rio Viera-Newton told me. "It's a soothing and calming ingredient, but it's also so hydrating and helps with fine lines. People also believe that it helps with sun damage." Today the company owns four green tea farms across Jeju and, it says, produces a quarter of all South Korea's tea. Ongoing research has led to the expanded use of various parts of the plant—leaves, flowers, seeds, and roots—for skincare concoctions.[7]

Not content to rest on its tea leaves, AmorePacific developed its own green tea plant varietal—Jangwon No. 3— which the company says delivers "high levels of amino acids" for moisturizing and green tea seed oil for clarifying benefits to the skin. Even if you've never heard of Jangwon No. 3, you may have already tried it on your face.[8] The varietal is found in the Innisfree brand's entire Green Tea product line, whose standout is a sleeping mask you can get practically anywhere around the world. I bought my first green tea sleeping mask canister at the Incheon International Airport, sold on it because I am a sheeple. The salesperson said it was one of the hottest duty-free purchases for travelers to fly away with, so I gave it a go. The goop felt cool on my skin, and as a final step in a skincare routine, it seems to effectively hydrate my dry face by morning or by the end of a long flight. I still buy it and currently have two tubes of it on my bathroom sink.

The use of green tea—and before that, of other plant products like mung beans and barley—as a key ingredient in Korean beauty products tracks with a history of farm-to-medicine-cabinet skin therapies made with red ginseng, rice, or honey.[9] Korean beauty today continues to differentiate itself by leaning into this nature notion in making and marketing its products. The Face Shop plays up the "pure vegetarian elements" in its products. Skinfood markets products made of fruits and vegetables under the slogan "Feed Your Skin." In addition to its green tea, Innisfree is known for its product lines made from natural ingredients. "Tradition, culture, it really influences what we do and how we do it," said Jessica Hanson, AmorePacific's U.S. president from 2017 to 2020, and a former executive at L'Oréal. "The pride level went up for me significantly knowing where our brands come from, the stories that were developed."

Naturally, modern tradition and culture in Korea is often linked to the Confucian-influenced Joseon era, as it lasted for centuries, ending only in the early 1900s. An emphasis on harmony and appearing "natural" is evident in modern K-beauty ingredients and marketing. The "heritage ingredient" play works—it's now emulated by the growing Chinese beauty brand Pechoin.[10] But in K-beauty it's a both/and proposition, drawing on what seems "natural" about the olden days, while also maximizing on the newness of tech-fueled invention. So two opposing tropes about Asia are deployed simultaneously. On one hand are traditional, "heritage" laden products; on the other, K-beauty projects an aura of being on the bleeding edge of the research curve, with scientifically perfected, futuristic innovations. Companies roll out unique botanical ingredients discovered and perfected by R&D, one after another. Think snail mucin, bee propolis, or shark's liver oil. Korea's cosmetics industry is lauded globally for its churn in quickly retiring what doesn't sell and putting new products out into the market, unique among the world in its speed.

"It does have that kind of scientific, technical, marketing glaze," says Asian studies researcher Emily Raymundo. "It's like, 'Yes, we've developed the secrets.' But they're also *Oriental* secrets, you know? Of forever. So it's somehow both ancient and current . . . which is tied to how a lot of Asian countries are selling themselves and selling their exports in global markets. It's kind of like self-orientalizing, or using that discourse to their advantage."[11]

AmorePacific is a multi-tentacled conglomerate behind a parade of brands: its namesake AmorePacific line, the higher-end Sulwhasoo, the more accessible Laneige, Mamonde, Innisfree, and Etude House, all of them offering a never-ending bounty of beauty products. In Korea, AmorePacific competes in dollar value among South Korea's better-known exports of electronics, cars, and shipping. It's now the eleventh biggest beauty brand globally and remains the top Korean seller,[12] bringing in $5.3 billion in revenue in 2019, the last year before the coronavirus pandemic.[13] The quest for poreless skin drives impressive profits.

~

Skincare know-how among contemporary Koreans flows from skinfirst thinking handed down through generations, evolving to fit their contemporary high-paced, growth-minded society, which hinges upon consumers constantly, well, consuming.[14] Korea's domestic customer base is so accustomed to budget cosmetics brands competing for its loyalties that shoppers have come to expect a lot in terms of quality and innovation. The way K-beauty brands are forced to respond to the demands of their discerning customers gives K-beauty an identity wholly its own, distinguishing it from its industry counterparts in France and the United States.

Industry sources tell me since about the mid-2000s, the domestic market became so saturated with cosmetics and skincare brands that customers have grown not just savvy but super-selective. These days, the emergence and wide adoption of an app called Hwahae illustrates customer sophistication. Open it up on phones to browse or search for your go-to cream, essence, hair mask, etc., and every ingredient in every product, and sometimes even their formulations, can be verified by an always connected and knowledgeable customer base. Hwahae, on its site, boasts that it's had more than 10 million cumulative downloads, and it reports that eight out of ten Korean women in their twenties and thirties use the app.[15]

Hwahae compiles individual ingredient information and ratings of thousands of beauty products sold across the Korean market. You can check for potential parabens or dyes or other add-ins that might irritate your skin or for ingredients that you know your skin needs and responds to. You can also find extensive reviews of every product from users, and filter which reviews you see by skin type or what skin condition you're trying to solve. Hwahae's comprehensiveness has no parallel in any other skincare market, partly because no other user base demands this level of product transparency. That the app is so popular and widely used is a testament to the skin savviness of Korean consumers, whose tastes are monitored by cosmetic companies. Women are scrutinizing the cosmetic companies, who are in turn scrutinizing them.

"Korean customers are so well educated, and they move sensitively to the market," says Eddie Aram Baek, the cofounder of the direct-to-consumer K-beauty platform Wishtrend. He says the fact that Korean customers are extremely knowledgeable, discerning, and demanding gives the entire industry a leg up. "If we can jump over the hurdle of Korean standards, we can satisfy anyone worldwide."

They have to go global to grow. Because with the Korean market both small and already saturated, there is virtually no place left within it to expand. Brands have to create their future by growing into new markets outside the country, or by creeping into new demographics within.

~

Every Wednesday a private Korean-language tutor, whom I called by her first name, Unkyung, would show up at my apartment with a greeting I only pretended to understand

and a sympathetic smile. She stood just over five feet tall and wore minimal makeup, leaving visible a constellation of light freckles on both her cheeks. Unkyung was in her fifties and a mom to one college-aged son. It delighted her to come to my home each week and sneak a few moments with my young girls—the toddler Eva and the new baby Isa. Since we had virtually zero friends those early months in Korea, Unkyung was one of the first people to meet the baby.

My sessions with Unkyung lasted ninety minutes, which was more than enough time for her to work her magic with her other students, like the Australian and British ambassadors to Korea. But very early on, she could tell I wasn't "gifted at languages," nor was I inclined to practice between our sessions. In my defense, the Korean language is ridiculously difficult! Unlike English and Mandarin, the languages in which I'm fluent, in Korean the verbs come at the end of the sentence. So if I wanted to say, "I rode a taxi to the airport at ten o'clock," the language structure made it impossible for Unkyung to rescue me mid-sentence because the verb wasn't sliding in until the very end. (Feels like it should come earlier, no? Verbs are a communication linchpin! Maybe you can sense why I wasn't a good student of Korean.) So many times, she would sit next to me at my dining table, not correcting me as I flailed about, spouting out words in any order I pleased, until I reached the very end and tacked on the verb.

Being the exceedingly patient human she is, Unkyung would still try and get through to me, in some form. After an adequate amount of lesson time trying to teach me Korean grammar and vocabulary each week, she switched into talking with me (using some Korean phrases) about modern culture, social issues, and life in Seoul. This did little to improve my grasp on the Korean language, but it did prove invaluable for story ideas and consistently informed my coverage. Unkyung was the first to teach me about *bbali bbali*, which describes a sensibility that abhors waiting. Literally translating as "fast fast," bbali bbali is an ethos and practice of hurrying, rushing, and getting things done as quickly as possible. It flourishes in the country, and as a result, she said, Koreans can be pushy and expect everything on-demand.

In its most favorable light, bbali bbali means efficiency and is often described by Koreans as evidence of South Korean exceptionalism—the result of or reason for the country's rapid industrialization and development. A nationalistic need for speed, for instance, led the former military regime in the post–World War II era to push young girls to leave their homes and work in South Korea's textile factories, hurrying up to make more goods for the national economy.[16] The country came into its impressive wealth and modernity inside of two generations, a singular and astounding speediness known as the Miracle on the Han. Following World War II and the devastating Korean War, South Korea was poorer than sub-Saharan Africa.[17] Today it is the tenth largest economy in the world and has shifted rapidly from being a UN-aid-receiving nation to an aid-granting one. The swiftness of this economic development is something with which its society still grapples.[18] Going from a premodern society to a postmodern one took only thirty-some years, stretching from the early 1960s to the mid-1990s. That's a fraction of the time it takes other countries, transforming South Korea into the unapologetic celebration of corporate values and business culture it is today.[19]

The bbali bbali narrative underpins the cosmetics industry, which responds to market wishes faster than other places, for cultural as much as financial reasons. It prides itself on perpetually cycling in new things. Government data shows companies spend an average of 64 percent of their research budgets on creating new products. (It's hard to make direct comparisons to other countries, because the numbers are tracked differently from one place to another.)[20] This constant and rapid transformation even inside a single brand is another one of the K-beauty industry's defining traits and, combined with high consumer scrutiny, is crucial to Korean beauty's influential march across the world.

South Korea's industry landscape is dotted with giant R&D and manufacturing clusters that are fueled by a mix of private and public funds to maintain the industry's fast churn rates. At these Original Equipment Manufacturing (OEM) centers, entrepreneurs can bring a simple concept to a team of R&D professionals and get their product packaged and designed, with an initial order, all in one stop. OEM companies take over the entire process of development from R&D to production.[21] It helps explain how Korea's cosmetics industry keeps turning out new lines and products so fast— while OEMs can manufacture anything in this way, Korean ones are particularly experienced at cosmetics. There are several in Seoul, and other major OEMs in the port city of Incheon, the second administrative capital of Sejong, and in the central Korean city of Daejeon.[22] Most of the centers have decades of experience in making beauty potions and their packaging.[23] It's not unusual for a product to go from conception to the sales floor inside of three months, said Eddie Aram Baek, who cofounded Wishtrend. Tonymoly, the brand known for its hand and facial creams packaged to look like tomatoes and bananas, brings products from development to production as quickly as six weeks, a pace similar to that of fast fashion.[24]

For as little as $20,000, you can have a cosmetic product created, bottled, and (ballparking) a few hundred units of it packaged, says Hellen Choo, who started Swagger, a haircare and cosmetics line in 2009. "They have labs, they have everything. So you go and have a meeting, say this is what I want. You go to their factory and ask them, 'Hey, I want to make a product that's exactly like this one.' They'll make it for you, and you just give them that design. That's how fast and easy it would be."[25] Many of today's K-beauty start-ups are helmed by individual cosmetics researchers who branched out of established companies.[26] Connections to the OEM clusters helped solo entrepreneurs or smaller companies start their own brands without much friction.

Twenty-nine-year-old Park Jeong-eun experienced this near-overnight pace of product development—and success—with LUOES, a line of vegan lip balms.[27] (LUOES is Seoul spelled backward.) She came up with the idea based on time abroad during grad school in the UK, where she saw "vegan everything". She told me she had a gut feeling that a vegan beauty product could set itself apart in the Korean market. In 2019, she went on Wadiz, the biggest Korean crowdfunding site, with her idea and raised enough money to go to

Hangkuk Kolmar, a well-known Korean OEM, to design, make, and package the product.[28] In seven months she had 5,000 lip balms in each of her three starting shades. By 2021, LUOES had caught the eye of Olive Young merchandisers, who are power players in domestic Korean beauty, and her line of lip balms got picked up for the retailer's online emporium. Park, who remains Seoul-based, has since expanded her line beyond lip balms, to masks, face rollers, and tone-up cream. "The merchandisers are gatekeepers. Their preference is really important," Park says.

Rapid manufacturing helps boost Korea's two largest cosmetic conglomerates—AmorePacific and LG Household & Healthcare. They consistently beat out the world's dominant players—French beauty companies like L'Oréal or Lancôme— in releasing new products and lines, even if these are just remixes or packaging changes. In turn, the world's larger players, recognizing K-beauty's promise, have bought in. After Unilever, a massive British consumer goods corporation, acquired the parent company of the Korean beauty brand AHC in 2017, the iconic Estée Lauder followed suit, acquiring the K-beauty skincare brand Dr.Jart+ in 2019.[29]

In recent years, Korea has competed with U.S. and European companies to become one of the top cosmetics exporters in the world.[30] The fast rise is due in large part to the experience of Korean manufacturing centers, which these days are also trusted to produce and package products for non-Korean brands like the wildly successful American beauty start-up Glossier.[31]

To reach customers across the region and world, the Korean government subsidizes export-focused beauty start-ups.[32] Government records show that in 2006, only about 350 Korean beauty brands existed. By 2012, the number climbed fourfold, to more than 1,000. In the following decade, more than 7,000 Korean beauty brands were launched, making up the vast majority of the now nearly 9,000 Korean beauty vendors in existence by 2020.

The Korea Health Industry Development Institute (KHIDI) works with the Korean Ministry of Health and Welfare to help the Korean personal care industry expand overseas. In the 2010s,[33] Chinese consumers were the major market for growth, but in 2020, the resurgence of Chinese nationalism and an increasingly sophisticated Chinese beauty industry coincided with the pandemic. After the Chinese market closed off, industry pivoted. At a 2021 Korean government-sponsored convention promoting K-culture, the KHIDI and Health Ministry promoted a slew of beauty brands to seven targeted growth markets: Chile, Russia, Mongolia, Singapore, Indonesia, Vietnam, and India. According to Kim Mihee, who oversees the KHIDI makeup team, the agency supports K-beauty companies holistically—everything from global market analysis, to running incubators for start-ups that want to expand into exports, to connecting them with buyers in the target countries, to financially backing pop-ups in those markets to see whether brands are catching on. The K-beauty support program started in 2012, and "every year, the funds increase," Kim says.

Beauty editors say when it comes to invention and innovation, South Korea's industry is not just a little bit ahead, but typically at least a decade ahead of the rest of the globe.[34] Jessica Hanson, who led AmorePacific's U.S. business after several years as an executive at L'Oréal and Sephora, told me the difference between Western and Korean beauty giants was that, in L'Oréal's case, it was "about domination, market share, a specific way of looking at business." French companies wanted to be the best, she said. But from AmorePacific's standpoint, "it's about being the first." The challenge, she said, is sticking with that commitment, because the drive for newness is relentless. "We didn't just look at red ginseng and say, 'This is a great ingredient, let's use it.' [Instead] it's 'Let's study it. Let's be the first to say what this does.' Then we have product development like . . . we just debuted the 3D mask at CES [Consumer Electronics Show]. So it's about being the first."

Customers are so accustomed to speed and newness that they expect product lines to appear and disappear as quickly as fashion brands create new looks for each season. Charlotte Cho, a key player in bringing K-beauty to the American masses with her direct-to-consumer K-beauty brand Soko Glam, said K-beauty is about "skincare innovations, whether it deals with packaging . . . formulations and textures, ingredients and format."[35]

Take a cleanser, for example. Let's say that for your whole life whatever cleanser you used for your face came in a tube. Korean beauty companies would say, "Let's take a cleanser that originally came in a tube and turn it into a stick form." They might then offer the tube and the stick, and suddenly it's called a cleansing platform. "They're always kind of pushing the envelope in terms of innovation," Cho says, whether it's the product itself, its delivery method or form factor, or the packaging around it.

A couple of years ago, the push from AmorePacific's

Laneige line was "cream skin," with which the brand decided to try and combine two of the steps of a typical skincare routine—toning and moisturizing—into one product. It ended up looking curiously like skim milk. The "cream skin" two-in-one came in a frosted glass bottle with a white cap, and then packaged in individual milk cartons in shades of pastel, with cartoon animals on the outside. The company called this twist "skip care," subverting the idea of a multiple-step skincare routine (itself an invention of media and marketing) to allow users to skip steps and combine them.

The childlike, whimsical cuteness of products and packaging is another point of distinction for K-beauty. Cute animals on sheet masks. Cute animals on head wraps to keep your hair out of your face when you're washing it. Be it pandas on eye sticks, or lip balms that come in true-to-size plastic peaches, or face stamps and inventive form factors, packaging both helps K-beauty stand out and be emulated by competitors.

Sleepless from all the overnight infant feedings of that first summer in Korea, I think Tonymoly's Panda's Dream So Cool Eye Sticks kept me looking somewhat rested. The sticks come in lipstick-like tubes, but thicker, with black bases and a happy panda face lacquered on the caps. The marketing copy calls it a "little burst of cooling eye cream." As I would with lipstick, I popped off the cap and twisted the base to push out the baby-blue treatment, which had the consistency of a less-greasy ChapStick. I wrote on my under-eyes with it multiple times a day, whenever I was bored or walked past a mirror. That summer, it was just one of an entire line of panda-packaged products from that Korean brand.

Store experience matters, too. At a three-story Olive Young, the cosmetics superstore you can find on most corners, I came across a giant conveyor belt smack-dab in the center of the first floor, slowly circulating with skincare, cosmetics, and beauty tools you can grab like it's all-you-can-eat sushi. Olive Young, like Sephora, is a one-stop shop for Korean skincare and cosmetics. These days it's supplanted many of the individual brand-name shops that used to dot Korean streets. In 2020, there were 1,259 Olive Young stores in South Korea,[36] roughly twice the number of Sephoras there are in the States.[37] Accounting for the population differences between the two countries, that means Koreans are roughly six times more likely to encounter an Olive Young than an American is to encounter its equivalent. While stand-alone cosmetics stores were closing shop during the pandemic, Olive Young saw steady growth.[38]

~

As I reached the end of my first year in Seoul, my skincare experimentation stayed just that, never morphing into a routine. The occasional nights I spent perched on my bathtub ledge wearing plastic socks did pay off for my feet. Those booties were foot peels to leave on for thirty minutes, letting the chemical concoction seep into your skin, and a day after treatment, the dead skin on my heels would start sloughing off. I announced to my entire household that my feet were as soft as a baby's bottom. My husband got into it, too, and made foot peels a regular practice, the only one of us to begin a lasting skincare practice after all of my guinea-pigging.

I'd dipped my feet figuratively into consumer K-beauty formulas, too, but as a woman, not as a reporter. I didn't train my journalistic eyes on the beauty industry or appearance standards at all in that first year. I was just a happy participant. As 2015 rounded into 2016, when I went on *Morning Edition* to fill a two-minute segment on settling into Seoul, I launched into a tale about our apartment's fancy Japanese toilets, and the last big story I covered in 2015 featured the experiences of Korean women, but those from a century before. Korea and its early twentieth-century occupiers, the Japanese, had brokered a deal in which the women Japanese soldiers took as sex slaves would receive an apology and $8 million in restitution from the Japanese government.[39] The other stories that took up my time: Korea's technological forwardness, geopolitical tensions between South Korea and its neighbors like China, and domestic social stressors—an all-work, no-play attitude burning out young people. I didn't realize then how beauty ideals intersected and informed all these narratives in consequential ways.

~

CHAPTER 2

The Birth of K-Beauty

C *hok chok* is a Korean term meaning moisture or wet-ness but it is used most commonly as a way to describe "that girlish glow," which is the primary objective for Korean skin. Another way to praise skin is to say it has *gwang,* or radiance. The globalized term for both is "glass skin." That is, fresh skin without visible makeup, which means either great genes and/or a dedication to skin-care maintenance that at the very least exceeds my ability. "It's when your skin is so healthy, even-toned, and plumped with hydration that it's almost translucent, like a shard of glass," Christine Chang, cofounder of Korean beauty brand Glow Recipe, told *Vogue.*[1] Since its mid-aughts introduction, the glowy skin trend has evolved into specific subtypes, or looks—"radiant glow" (*yoon gwang*), "honey glow" (*kkool gwang*), and "moist glow" (*chok gwang*).

The look appears dewy, or even greasy, if you're accustomed to matte finishes. But as Soko Glam's Charlotte Cho recalls, "the more time I spent in Korea . . . the more I realized that their foreheads weren't oil slicks, just glowingly moist." Cho had the foresight back then to see that this was a "permanent future of skin and not just a passing fad."[2]

Glass skin is a notion fairly new to the States. In Asia, a barrage of commercials and print advertisements emphasize that "good skin" is smooth, young, poreless, line-free, bright, transparent, white, and full. "Bad skin" is referenced in ads as skin with wrinkles, aging marks, and dryness.[3] While Korean marketers have promoted the glowy glass skin concept since the mid-aughts, skin that appears white and smooth as glass is an ideal that can be traced back even further, to the Joseon Dynasty, when Confucian thought ruled the day.[4]

To claim something is "Confucian" immediately makes me cringe; it's so overused that it feels like a lazy catchall for stereotypes about East Asian culture. All the same, it cannot be disputed that Confucian influence has had a long tail. A quick summary: Master Kong, or Confucius, was a man who lived during chaotic times during the deterioration of China's Zhou Dynasty, circa 500 BC. His philosophy was focused on societal harmony, as his followers noted in the *Analects*. Crucially, he believed harmony could exist among the people only if they knew their place and stayed in it.[5] Three centuries later, when the new rulers of the Han Dynasty came in, Confucian philosophy about deference and duty aligned with their project of uniting China. Thanks in large part to the way Han Dynasty rulers nationalized these ideas (making Confucian texts the cornerstone of schools, for instance),[6] Confucius's ideas emphasizing harmony over individuality have reverberated for centuries and had "profound implications for the way the East Asian self experiences reality," writes *Selfie* author and historian Will Storr.[7]

The operative thing to understand about Confucianism—or in these days, neo-Confucianism—and its influence on beauty standards is that it is also a form of patriarchy with a focus on piety to your elders. And during Confucianism's heyday under Korea's Joseon Dynasty, which lasted from the fourteenth century until 1910, the Korean people came to understand their bodies as hereditary gifts.[8] A son's body belonged to his parents, and any kind of self-harm—which included tattoos and cutting hair—was seen as disgraceful.[9] The filial piety of daughters was less important, because a woman was expected to join another family and bear male offspring. But historians cite the Joseon period as the foundation for a Korean beauty standard of "looking natural" that is, in crucial ways, still with us.

For women, beauty was equated to being dutiful to your elders, serving your husband, and spending time with your children—activities that took place indoors and out of the sun. Clear, bright, flawless skin was valuable back then, too. Under the Confucian system, women's bodies needed to reflect "purity," and that meant a fair complexion. Blemishes were considered unappealing because they disrupted the "original" state of women's bodies.

Materialism conflicted with the pure and simple ideal, so middle- and higher-class women wore minimal makeup and never cut their hair during the Joseon period. Only the lower-class *gisaeng*, courtesans akin to Japanese geishas, wore makeup. The idea that makeup was only the domain of the gisaeng dominated mainstream culture into the twentieth century. Though the Joseon days are long over, shaming women for their nonconforming beauty practices lives on. Women who wear too much makeup or appear outside the norm of acceptable beauty are shamed for looking like streetwalkers, a social sanction that has reverberated across time.

Beauty culture in the West had risen out of the mid-nineteenth century emergence of photography, which heightened the importance of image-making and performance in everyday life.[10] America's mass-market beauty industry sprung out of that cultural change by the turn of the twentieth century.[11] It transformed the nascent industry from a hodgepodge of local druggists tinkering with creams to a uniform market for beauty. American and European beauty products started flowing into Korea at the end of the nineteenth and beginning of the twentieth century as a result of two Japanese actions: the Japan-Korea Treaty of 1876 and Japan's annexation of Korea in 1910. Korea had isolated itself for centuries from international trade, but as part of its 1876 treaty with Japan, it was forced to open three commercial ports. Then in 1910, Japan annexed the Korean Peninsula and brutally occupied it for decades with executions, forced labor, and near-total repression of Korean culture. It remains the source of deep emotional scars for Koreans and a foundation for ongoing tensions between the two nations.

Foreign beauty products flowing into the Japanese colony of Korea through trade, competition and influence from the West led to the 1916 introduction of the first mass-produced Korean cosmetic, Pakgabun (which translates as "powder made by the Park family"). This OG K-beauty product, a makeup powder, successfully marketed itself through word of mouth, marking a turning point in which everyday

Korean women—not just courtesans—began putting powder on their faces. "Culture tends to spread from top to bottom," Chung Ah-young wrote in *The Korea Times*. "But cosmetics and fashion codes are mostly the opposite. The elite and upper-class women tended to mimic the fashion of *gisaeng* (female entertainers) during the Joseon era."[12]

At first Pakgabun didn't come as a powder at all. Its earliest forms existed as a white block, like chalk, which you could rub onto your palms before patting the powdered residue into your face. In a really early parallel to one of modern K-beauty's defining traits, changing the product's form factor catapulted it to mass-market success. Once the owners broke down Pakgabun into a powder form and packaged it in a canister, it grew so famous that the family reportedly sold 10,000 units per day, irrespective of its astronomical price point—$90 US per canister, in today's money. Despite its popularity and how many Korean copycat products it inspired by the 1930s, there's a reason Pakgabun is on history's sidelines. The powder was made with kudzu, barley, rice, and—wait for it—lead.[13]

In 1934, a customer sued the Park family, saying she developed a serious skin problem from using Pakgabun, heralding its ignominious fall from grace. The Parks tried to resurrect their namesake powder's image, bringing in a Japanese expert to reformulate the ingredients, but customer trust had been lost and the business was shuttered. Still, the episode had taught Koreans an indelible lesson: you shouldn't wear lead on your face. To this day, many Korean cosmetics include a disclaimer on the packaging saying, "This product does not contain lead."

In its heyday, Pakgabun benefited from changing social mores of the early twentieth century and the emerging concept of the Modern Girl. Analogous to flappers in the United States, Modern Girls were young women who rejected traditional standards of beauty. They cut their hair into bobs, even though it represented a break from familial ties. They ditched traditional clothing for styles seen in New York and Paris and presented themselves with a visibly made-up look—arched eyebrows, face contouring, and dark lips. Korean intellectuals (all men) frowned on the makeup-adorned Modern Girl, considering these women frivolous because they spent time, energy, and cash on their appearance while more pressing political issues, like the actual freedom of their own country, were yet unresolved.[14]

Looking back, however, researchers have found that wearing the Modern Girl look was actually a flex for women at the time. Clear class distinctions in Korean society were represented in women's clothing and adornments. But making themselves up and choosing individualistic cosmetic expressions allowed Modern Girls to "disguise" their class, gender, and ethnicity (which was key during Japanese occupation). The subversion—makeup—gave them a mobility and a fluidity of identity that they would have otherwise not enjoyed. Was the Modern Girl really frivolous, or was she using the tools available to her to subvert a confining patriarchal system? Similar debates continue to shape the discourse about K-beauty today.

AmorePacific, one of Asia's most powerful cosmetics empires and the grower of all that green tea, officially came on the scene in 1945. The conglomerate established itself at an inflection point for the Korean Peninsula. World War II came to an end, and with it, the Japanese occupation. In that vacuum, Americans and Soviets cleaved the formerly unified Korea arbitrarily at the 38th parallel as part of an arrangement between two warring world powers. The division created a socialist North Korea (backed by Soviets) and an authoritarian South Korea (backed by the United States). The Pentagon deployed American troops and stationed them throughout South Korea to help stabilize the new country, and American forces fought alongside the South in the Korean War, a clash that lasted from 1950 to 1953. With the U.S. military presence came such influences as animated entertainment, many cans of Spam, and the Western gaze. Today, tens of thousands of American forces remain, and so does AmorePacific, which lays claim to being the oldest K-beauty company in the nation.

The roots of the company spiritually trace back before 1945, when founder Suh Sung-whan's mother, Yun Dok-Jeong, started concocting camellia-based hair oils and creams from her home in present-day North Korea.[15] Strong packaging made her products stand out. She blasted the name of her store, Changseong Sangjom (Prosperous Store), on every product.[16] The matriarch, Yun, created the products and taught her son Sung-whan how to make her creams when he was just a boy. But his key role in the early operation was collecting bills from customers and riding his bicycle down south to Seoul to pick up bottles and labels before hauling them back, making a fifty-mile round trip trek multiple times a week. When Suh grew up and eventually took over the company in 1945, he changed Prosperous Store's name, calling it Pacific Chemical

Industry (now AmorePacific) because, with the world war over, he had ambitions to sell his products across the Pacific. Suh moved the entire business south to the capital by 1948.

In 1954, the family opened the nation's first cosmetic laboratory near its Seoul headquarters.[17] The lab sent researchers to Germany to study cosmetics, and eventually Suh's company produced Melody, the first hydrating cream of decent quality in Korean history.[18] The company also released ABC pomade, a hair cream for men, and it became an instant domestic hit. Still, these early products couldn't compete at scale with dominant American and European imports. Years of war had devastated Korea and all its industries, so during the 1950s, as the U.S. military committed to maintaining a presence, American influence and products spread across South Korean society. Through the 1950s, it was Pond's Cold Cream you wanted, not Melody.

All the fresh Western influence and local trends among the middle and higher classes merged in a bustling commercial district called Myeongdong, the home of Seoul's first beauty parlors and fashion boutiques.[19] Over fifty years of growth and innovation, it would become the modern-day makeup mecca, the first place I ever stayed, and shopped, in Seoul.

~

AmorePacific statistics show that in 1960, 80 percent of the cosmetic products consumed in Korea came from outside the country.[20] But General Park Chung-hee, the militaristic dictator who came to power in a coup and led the nation from 1961 to 1979, would change that. Park remains infamous in modern Korean history for his ironfisted grip on the country, and his obsession with investing in the rapid industrialization of South Korea throughout the sixties and seventies. Under his authoritarian rule, Park poured state investment into South Korean industries and banned the sales of foreign products inside the country.[21]

Restricting the consumption of imports effectively booted foreign cosmetics from Korea. Domestic cosmetics brands sprang up to fill the void, fueling the flourishing of then-fledgling Korean cosmetics brands, which is why several scholars I talked to situate the birth of the Korean beauty industry to this period—the 1960s and 1970s. Even still, Korean customers were not heavily spending on their own serums at that time. They tried to get their hands on cosmetic products smuggled out from the American army bases or pressed overseas family members to bring them in. Korean American writer Katherine Yungmee Kim's family immigrated to the United States in the 1960s, leaving behind the extended family in Seoul. "When I was growing up in the 1970s, and we would go to Korea in the summer, the majority of our suitcase would be smuggling Western items. We brought jars and jars of Estée Lauder. My mom would just stock the suitcase with Estée Lauder and money and things they couldn't get, because it was really black market [back then]."[22]

On top of that, for many Korean women, there wasn't much opportunity to splurge on makeup. A government-decreed *gansobok* Simple Clothing Movement was the order of the day, as legions of young women were conscripted to work inside factories dedicated to South Korea's industrialization.[23] In 1973, the Park dictatorship also declared fashion shows illegal and banned men from having long hair and women from wearing skirts shorter than 17 centimeters (6 to 7 inches) above the knee.[24] Under this regime, beautifying yourself was seen as distracting or counter to the goal of national development.

And yet, much like the subversive Modern Girl had made her mark in the 1920s, the makeup-adorned Factory Girl came forward in the 1970s as a figure of defiance and resistance.[25] Movies were still accessible to the masses, and women passed each other beauty magazines at salons and department stores. It inspired different ways of expressing themselves through the fashion and cosmetics that were available. New trends emerged—or in Instagram parlance, new "goals." Working-class women, who spent their days in government-issued uniforms cranking out textiles on assembly lines, would wear colorful makeup on their faces. Their bodies might have been conscripted by the government, but the makeup on their faces was a measure of autonomy.

The Factory Girls took some cues from Western beauty culture, using bright lipstick and flashes of femininity that kept with trends of the time and contrasted with the drab clothing mandated by the government.[26] Their consumption of foreign cosmetics, perfumes, "and lavish textiles such as velvet" allowed them to show off not just femininity but modernity and the freedom through expression that fashion can offer. Their displays became a way to "challenge and resist the top-down hegemony," writes UCLA researcher Kwon

Hye Kyoung, whose work focuses on Korean women's historical beauty practices.[27]

Even under Park's watchful authoritarian regime, the Factory Girl look spread one by one and made its way into visual culture.[28] This informed Korean cosmetics companies, which would use the Factory Girl influence to create a corporate-driven K-beauty identity as they entered the 1980s.

The country began to change politically and economically after the assassination of General/President Park in 1979. In the aftermath, the strongman Chun Doo-hwan stepped in as a de facto leader until cementing his leadership, also with a military coup. South Korea then endured martial law under Chun, who also led as a brutal dictator, from 1980 to early 1988.[29] Chun was the most unpopular Korean leader in postwar Korea and is best known for ordering troops to attack and massacre his own people to stamp out pro-democracy demonstrations. In his effort to distract Korean citizens from the struggle for democracy, he launched what's known as the "three S" policy—sex, sports, and screen—to encourage the development of Korean media and entertainment industries, as a kind of diversion.[30] He also followed the guidance of two celebrated economic advisers in opening Korea's doors to foreign companies in 1983.[31]

Student activists struggled against Chun's dictatorship throughout the 1980s and eventually, in 1987, a year before Seoul would host the Olympics, they drove a mass movement to sweep aside a quarter century of dictatorship and usher in Korean democracy. In this new national environment, Korea experienced a sociopolitical shift. The state had stopped its strict restrictions on how Korean women should look and instead became interested in growing new sectors of its economy and upping its international image. When South Korean cosmetic brands began competing against foreign names, they used the heritage play—Korean traditional ingredients like green tea and red ginseng—as a point of distinction. Individual Korean cosmetics brands began cropping up in the 1990s. Mamonde launched in 1991 and Laneige in 1994, and with the help of some government investment, they began to flourish. When AmorePacific's founder, Suh Sung-whan, died in 2003, his cosmetics company had saturated the Korean market. As of 2006, it was selling 90 percent of its products domestically and was beginning its outreach across Asia.[32]

It was a half century of light-speed cultural change, especially for South Korean women and their interactions with beauty via fashion and cosmetics. First the Modern Girls and then the Factory Girls were fomenters of a rebellion, as scholar Kwon Hye-kyoung has noted. Both types of women were viewed with suspicion by the establishment, sparking judgment. Both groups obscured or transcended their class status by playing with their presentation. In doing so, they won a kind of freedom from strict appearance regulations. Hair and makeup bought these women some cover from societal perceptions. They used makeup as a form of protest and as an equalizer.

Later, their signature looks—the way they adorned themselves—were swallowed up and appropriated by the mass-market consumer beauty industry. And these days, consumer beauty culture is, in its own way, regimenting appearance from the top down once again. Japanese colonial governments once dictated how women should look. Later the militant Park Chung-hee regime decreed it, with efforts ranging from censoring certain "flashy" styles from state TV to imprisoning men with long hair.[33] By the 2000s, however, popular culture and market interests wielded a certain control and power of their own. In showing and repeatedly setting examples of a standard Korean beauty ideal, media and marketing pushed an appearance regime that consumers learned to enforce on themselves. These days, consumer beauty culture has a way of convincing us that the reigning look is what we wanted all along. Women can conscript our bodies all on our own, no state intervention required.

~

CHAPTER 3

Hallyu Has No Borders

Near the turn of the millennium, Korea's government and corporate power centers were no longer satisfied with their swift manufacturing of consumer electronics via Samsung, televisions via LG, and mid-priced cars by Kia and Hyundai. They joined forces to diversify exports beyond their mainstays, and not totally out of choice. Hit by a currency crisis in the late 1990s, the International Monetary Fund (IMF) gave South Korea a $57 billion bailout—the largest ever at the time—and the government had to rebuild its economy to pay back the loans.[1] Korea was barred from making lucrative defense infrastructure by a postwar peace treaty that required U.S. approval of any military technology Korea developed on its own.[2] So the country carried out a deliberate *soft* power strategy to get back on its feet, throwing its subsidies and support behind a highly visual entertainment culture, not just manufactured goods. Soft power entails using nonmaterial exports—positive persuasion—to level up in international relations. Instead of hard power, such as military force, or economic payments or sanctions, soft power is all about building networks and communicating compelling narratives to grow influence. As Korean British artist Sammy Lee described it in a visual essay, Korea's "forms of spectacle . . . are their arsenal."[3]

A Korean government council report in 1994 signaled the potential cash cow in exporting image. It suggested that making just one blockbuster on the scale of *Jurassic Park* could single-handedly equal the value from the sales of more than a million Korean manufactured cars.[4] The national financial crisis had created an imperative for Korea to get back on its feet, and it managed to pay back its IMF loans in four years. Socially, focusing on the upbeat vibes of Korean pop culture helped put aside the national trauma of its economic woes. The newly elected Korean president Kim Dae-jung teed off the beginning of national support for this new strategy in 1998, saying: "We must pour our energy into globalizing Korean culture . . . Tourism, the convention industry, the visual industry, and special cultural commodities are a treasure trove for which a limitless market is awaiting."[5] As South Korea modernized and emerged from the decades of tight government control over culture, so did its cultivation of commercial pop culture.

Samsung, the country's largest and most influential firm, began to invest in visual culture—filmmaking—through the creation of its own CJ Entertainment division, separate from the main conglomerate. CJ launched a multiscreen movie theater chain and would go on to finance and make blockbusters that could compete with Hollywood films.[6] Entertainment companies, auteurs, and music producers pumped out content that first caught on in neighboring Chinese-speaking areas in the 1990s. K-dramas, or Korean soaps, were the first biggest export, featuring rags-to-riches tales about Korea's hierarchical social landscape. After President Kim lifted a historic ban on cross-cultural content with Japan, K-culture infiltrated neighboring Japan.[7] It swept into Southeast Asia next, growing a fan base and giving rise to that notion of a cresting wave that eventually hit the West.

K-culture kept expanding its reach after it gained a foothold, due in part to continuous support and subsidies from the Korean government. After the IMF crisis, the government made it its responsibility to finance and promote film, TV, and music. President Kim's government passed a law to bolster the arts, and it allotted $50 million of bailout money to create the Korea Culture and Content Agency.[8] Today the office has an annual budget of $400 million. More recently, during the years I lived in Seoul, President Park Geun-hye created a $1 billion for-profit investment fund aimed at making high returns on South Korean cultural exports. It turns out, those exports are exactly what audiences wanted, as K-dramas amassed fans around the world.

The Culture and Content Agency explicitly focuses on how fashion, film and TV, comic books, animation, and Korean music—in the form of the global behemoth of K-pop—can boost economic growth by exporting culture. Its stated aims are straightforward: "facilitate promotion of popular culture" and "support spread of the Hallyu." It helped build concert arenas, open cinemas and theaters, and fund the Busan International Film Festival in Korea's second largest city. South Korean embassies and consulates throughout the world have helped organize foreign K-pop concerts. K-pop stars became unofficial ambassadors and the faces of the South Korean tourism industry, resulting in a successful co-production of culture and place. K-pop has become so associated with the South Korean state that the sounds of Big Bang and GFriend were blasted into North Korea on loud-speakers blaring democracy propaganda along the 151-mile North-South border.[9] In recent years, the K-pop group BTS was even named by former South Korean president Moon Jae-in as special envoys for diplomacy before they appeared together at the UN General Assembly.[10]

Beyond that, extensive market research eats up the rest of the budget. The government goes to great lengths, writes global business strategist Martin Roll, "to understand which Korean Wave products would have the best probability of success in different markets. The secret is that no one understands these markets better than Korea."[11] I do worry that the conflation of cultural industries with the state flattens complexity and analysis, because as Korea's pop culture influence grows, so has the degree of *kkukbong,* fanatical national pride, that comes with it. "They like to equate their identity with the public image of the nation," South Korean dermatologist Hae Shin Chung observes. "Kkukbong can make people lose their objectivity, just as an overbearing affection can turn people blind to reality." Since Korean industry or cultural productions are rarely separated from their home country, sometimes sources I spoke with would stop short their musings about the beauty industry or Korean society, saying they didn't want to "diss their own country."[12]

There was a dip in K-culture's popularity, however. The original pan-Asian Korean Wave came at the start of the new millennium, but by around 2010, K-dramas were recycling stories and the wave was falling. "The wave was about to die, crash and burn," says Sharon Heijin Lee. "Then in 2009, 2010, that intersection of young people and digital media, nobody could have predicted. The government didn't do that. That was just the sort of really serendipitous thing that brings us to this moment."[13] Digital media sparked a second wave and Hallyu went supersonic. Ultimately, it was this second international wave of Korean cultural exports that helped usher K-skincare to the global masses.

Through K-pop, K-drama, Korean cinema, video games, and the myriad other forms of storytelling it has embraced, South Korea has succeeded in transforming itself into a global giant of image, exporting untold units of "cultural technology." The term was coined by a legendary K-pop entertainment mogul, Lee Soo-man, who founded SM Entertainment and in the mid-1990s made a prescient, sophisticated observation, which he recalled in a 2011 address: "The age of information technology had dominated most of the nineties, and I predicted that the age of cultural technology would come next . . . I see culture as a type of technology. But cultural technology is much more exquisite and complex than information technology."[14]

Disseminated on film and television and in K-pop (since K-pop is a visual genre as much as it is musical), the look seen on Korean entertainers also eventually became state-championed. "As soon as [women] get put into the matrix of selling the nation, it's good," Michael Hurt, a Korean and Korea-based sociologist, told me.

Now it's everywhere. Within the past decade, the Hallyu

wave has surged into an all-encompassing force—the idea of a "global Korea."[15] Korea officially adopted the phrase in 2008 to support its objective to make Korean culture not merely cultish or regionally popular, but globally relevant. By 2011, K-pop groups first "crossed over" with tours in Europe, and in 2012, Psy's inescapable earworm, "Gangnam Style," took off and turned into a worldwide sensation, introducing K-pop to billions. The nation's commitment to image production that rose at the turn of the century ultimately did work like a giant wave, carrying the K-beauty industry with it. And the industry itself fueled signature innovations that have since sprung multiple copycats. One of these was the development of high-quality "budget" cosmetics. Another was a revolutionary product called BB cream.

Game-Changing Budget Cosmetics

Korea's lower-priced budget beauty brands that emerged in the 2000s contradicted the long-standing truism in cosmetics that more expensive products sell better.[16] Typically, luxury brands carve out a class segment by making their products appear "exclusive" via higher prices.[17] But the Korean brand Missha made itself competitive in the way Two-Buck Chuck worked for wine—through its super-low prices and selling at high volume with low unit profit margins. Missha launched in 2000 exclusively online, on a digital beauty platform called BeautyNet, known for its engaged community of reviewers. When it emerged, it offered all its skincare products— lotions, toners, essences—at 3,300 won (about $3).[18] In doing so, Missha highlighted how the actual production cost of cosmetics is small, as the scholar Oh Youjeong has observed, and invented the concept of budget K-beauty cosmetics. It simplified the "previously complicated" distribution process, lopped off packaging costs by commercializing cheap but well-designed containers, and emphasized marketing and advertising instead.

The site BeautyNet was a proto-Hwahae, which allowed for a lot of two-way communication between customers and brands. By 2002, Missha had developed a large enough customer base to open a physical store. Its first brand store is what Koreans dubbed a road shop, a stand-alone, tailored retail store that sells only one cosmetic brand's products. Before the advent of these, cosmetics were sold only in department stores or in shops such as Olive Young, where several different brands are available. In just two years, the number of Missha brand shops passed 200, and by 2015 it had reached 696 retail stores across the country.[19]

Missha's success popularized an entire market—low-priced cosmetics sold in their own retail locations, a now-defining aspect of the K-beauty industry. Its success led Korea's giant conglomerate, LG Household & Healthcare, to follow by taking over a low-end brand, The Face Shop, which opened its first store in Myeongdong in the late 1940s but was perfectly suited for this 2000s trend of low-cost cosmetics. By 2015, The Face Shop was operating 1,190 road shops across the country.[20] As retail moved online, the number of shops dropped, dipping to 598 by 2019, but their dominance in budget cosmetics persists.[21] You might know Face Shop for its wall of rows and rows of sheet masks. These one-sheets have been global bestsellers and come in avocado, honey, chia seed, acai berry, aloe, cucumber, green tea, and more. AmorePacific also got in on the road shop game by establishing Innisfree, which carries all that AmorePacific skincare made with green tea. The total number of low-end cosmetics brands has since proliferated, not only lining streets but occupying stalls at subway and train stations. Among them are the brands Skinfood, Aritaum, It's Skin, Banila Co, holika holika, Too Cool for School, Tonymoly, Etude House, and Nature Republic.

BB Cream

K-beauty's "ten-step skincare" and "double cleanse" practices are sweeping the globe, a kind of reach that underscores how far the industry's come from the days of lead-laden Pakgabun powder. Yet it wasn't powder but a smooth cover-up called BB cream that really put K-beauty on the map across the region. It's unclear what BB actually stood for to begin with, but depending on the person you ask, it's short for "beauty balm," "blemish balm," "blemish base," "blemish blocker," and "beblesh balm." A German dermatologist developed it back in the 1960s to help patients cover up the redness of swollen facial skin after undergoing chemical peels or cosmetic surgery,[22] but Korean cosmetic companies have taken this medical product to another dimension.[23] They transformed the once-cakey medical cream into a fluid and silky daily moisturizer with a light, sheer texture and usually some SPF. It glides on for natural-looking coverage. Korean BB cream was first developed by Korean manufacturer

Costree in 2006, and after its introduction, global sales were so brisk that it quickly exceeded the sales of foundation in Asia.

"It went to the Japanese market, and then [the] Chinese market, which was the explosion," says Eddie Aram Baek, whose years in the K-beauty export business bookended the astronomical global growth of the industry between 2010 and 2020. BB creams swept the regional Asian markets, crossed Europe, and finally arrived in the U.S. cosmetics market in 2011. In recent years, formulas have improved and moved right down the alphabet, from BB to CC and DD creams. But BB cream was the first K-beauty product to become famous worldwide. Then the attention moved to the cushion.

The cushion is a delivery system for BB cream that AmorePacific's IOPE brand introduced in 2008, forever changing the way Asian users apply the much-loved BB cream.[24] Before it, the cream came in a tube or bottle, like liquid foundation or sunscreen. AmorePacific researchers, noting the inconvenience and messiness of that kind of application, reacted by dreaming up a BB-cream-soaked sponge encased in an airtight compact, which made the cover-up portable and easier to apply. Inside these compacts, the fluid foundation is drenched into a flat sponge—the cushion—which spring-loads onto a makeup round (or your fingers) when you press into it. Within a few short years, the cushion compact found a permanent place inside women's makeup bags across Asia. As with the original cream, the air cushion was received with open arms in China, Hong Kong,

Singapore, and the Southeast Asian markets first, then subsequently introduced in the European and U.S. markets.

By 2013, seven out of every ten Korean women said they carried a cushion compact with them.[25] Since then, the product has become immensely popular all over the world, and non-Korean brands have taken note. Lancôme has released a product of the same concept, and Christian Dior partnered with AmorePacific and released the Capture Dreamskin line using air cushion technology. Today, not only are Korean products copied by European brands but MVP products either made in or conceived in Korea can be found across the Pacific, just as the AmorePacific founder envisioned. The AmorePacific brands Laneige, Innisfree, primera, and its namesake AmorePacific products are easily found in U.S. stores. (Before the pandemic, the company planned to open a hundred American branches of its retail chain Aritaum, similar to Sephora,[26] but fell short of the hundred store goal when the coronavirus pandemic throttled everything.)

The philosophy of Korean skincare, one that includes copious sun protection, double cleansing, and multiple types of moisturizers to keep a dewy, radiant glow is the standard across Asia and popular with Gen-Z skincare enthusiasts across the developed world. This is the beauty culture that gave us sheet masks, cushion compacts, oil cleansers, experimental essences, and ampoules. These Korean beauty innovations are now go-tos, sold everywhere from dedicated cosmetics stores like Sephora to discount giants like Costco.

The ways in which appearance ideals influence how we see our own identities and how we relate to one another may be hard to measure but are having an impact. "People didn't pay attention to K-beauty for the longest time. But K-beauty is the ten-thousand-pound gorilla in the room that Hallyu studies scholars bent over backwards to ignore," Korea-based sociologist Michael Hurt says. Why? Discourse about the influence of Korean culture is often measured in album sales, YouTube views, and other quantifiable metrics. But it's difficult to track and verify in a scientific way the regional or global transmission of wearing hair or makeup a certain way.

"When you think about what's actually spreading around the earth, young people know Korean style is one of the memes that spreads," Hurt says. "Red shadow around the eyes, for instance. That's a recognizable Korean style that goes around through music videos, Instagrams, YouTube tutorials. But there's no way to put a number to that. It's like, 'Oh, that's in the background.' They get ignored. And these cultural transmissions [aren't taken seriously] because, they're seen as 'what women do.'"

The success of this consumer beauty industry would have been impossible without an exacting commitment to what made Korean culture look and feel unique, the result of very intentional branding. Alongside its government, Korean conglomerates played a big part in supporting Korea's cultural exports and packaging them for a global audience. Samsung and Hyundai have sponsored BTS, the biggest music group in the world. As I write this, BTS holds down its reign, tying the Beatles for the most chart-topping albums in a single year (three). Koreans have also, in recent years, broken previously stubborn barriers of cultural achievement, like the Academy Awards, with back-to-back wins for *Parasite* and *Minari* in 2020 and 2021. The South Korean survival drama *Squid Game* became Netflix's most streamed show in ninety countries within two weeks of its release[27] and, at the time of this writing, has been bested only by another Korean series, *Hellbound*, as the most watched series in the platform's history. Korean gamers dominate e-sports globally. In 2021, the *Oxford English Dictionary* added *hanbok*, the traditional Korean dress, along with twenty-five other Korean entries, including *kimbap* (similar to sushi), *mukbang* (binge eating on live video), and of course, *hallyu*, defined in the dictionary as a boom in the international consumption of Korean culture.[28]

It's all wildly profitable. Government and industry have enjoyed huge returns on their investments. BTS alone is estimated to contribute $5 billion to the Korean economy each year.[29] "K-dash" culture draws in tourists wanting to visit the filming locations of their favorite K-dramas or to see the city that gave K-pop artists inspiration. The proactive efforts to use the Korean Wave to cultivate positive images of the country and develop new markets created fans not just of the entertainers but of Korea itself. Borderless K-pop fan bases are activated at the speed of a single post, given their loyalty to K-pop "idols," as they're called. BTS fans are known as the ARMY and can be activated and coordinated like one. The ARMY has notably operated as a netroots political force in recent years, humiliating Donald Trump during his 2020 reelection race and supporting the Black Lives Matter movement by drowning out online attacks against it.

Taken together, these cultural exports create a kind of fantasy place, spreading to the world an aspirational version of Korea, based on "Korean Dreams," as Korean cultural researcher Sharon Heijin Lee calls it.[30] She says Korean Dreams flow from the American Dream as an idea of mobility, cosmopolitanism, and consumption—where you can "buy all the things and look the way you want."[31]

Hallyu story lines show it. "It's all money, money, money, and it makes sense, given Korea's history, where the rich became rich very quickly," Lee says. K-dramas are dominated by stories featuring protagonists from chaebols, Korea's dynastic conglomerates. "Want a melodrama about a love triangle that bridges a poor family and a snobbish rich one? Korea can deliver," notes British writer Madeleine Spence.[32] Hallyu's fantasy version of Korea symbolizes the glittering new money the country came into so fast. But that version belies the complex domestic reality, which has been increasingly reflected in Hallyu productions. Psy's "Gangnam Style" satirizes the gaping wealth chasm in contemporary Seoul. Korean auteurs, who represent the country's id, hammer home the themes of everyone losing, while capitalism wins. *Squid Game,* for instance, is an obvious metaphor for late capitalism's harms while being the most profitable Korean television export ever. It's amazing to me how easily capitalism absorbs its own critiques.

This is where the timeline of K-beauty's ascent and my time in Korea begin to intersect. I didn't know the context at the time, but when I moved there in early 2015, Korea had become a neoliberal dream state—a place of "unquenchable consumerism," to borrow scholar Kwon Hye-kyoung's phrase.[33] But class fissures and the precarious situation of the middle class, especially for young people, created a constant hum of anxiety. My tutor Unkyung taught me about bbali

bbali early on, and not long after, she explained the "dirt spoon/silver spoon/gold spoon" distinctions in South Korean society, too. In January 2016, *The Washington Post* encapsulated class anxieties this way:

> *It's a place where, according to a growing number of 20-and 30-somethings, those born with a "golden spoon" in their mouths get into the best universities and secure the plum jobs, while those born with a "dirt spoon" work long hours in low-paying jobs without benefits.*
>
> *This Korea even has a special name: "Hell Joseon," a phrase that harks back to the five-century-long Joseon Dynasty, in which Confucian hierarchies became entrenched in Korea and when a feudal system determined who got ahead and who didn't.*[34]

Now a hyper-capitalist ethos determines who gets ahead and who doesn't. The ideas even show up in the lyrics of K-pop's golden boys. One BTS song, "Baepsae," has "Silver Spoon" for its English title, while their hit "No More Dream" urges the listener to rebel "against the hellish society." The lyrics continue with the call to "Ask yourself what is your dream's profile. / Become the subject of your own life that's always been suppressed."

You can see modern anxieties about who's a silver spoon and who's a gold one in the advent of Doenjang Nyo, or Soybean Paste Girl, a derisive moniker for women and girls that emerged in recent years. Doenjang is fermented soybean paste much like a Korean miso, and in a stew called doenjang jjigae, it's considered a cheap dinner or side dish (and it is delicious). The Soybean Paste Girl, then, describes a woman so vain and materialistic, so preoccupied by expensive, consumerist pursuits (such as luxury handbags, makeup, and cosmetic procedures), that she scrimps on her meals, eating only cheap soybean paste soup to get by.

The similarities between the Soybean Paste Girl and her predecessors the Modern Girl and the Factory Girl abound. They are all in "damned if they do, damned if they don't" situations. Each type is a flattened caricature of a Korean woman. For all these types of "girls," makeup invited derision from male critics but simultaneously gave the women who wore it a fast pass to travel beyond class borders. There's something empowering in the way these women blur rigid socioeconomic boundaries of their time and challenge "class immobility and the static economy, by creating . . . ambiguity" through their appearance, as researcher Kwon Hyekyoung put it.[35] As far-fetched as it may seem, "Confucian understandings of gender, class, and femininity continue to actively inform notions of national womanhood," writes Kwon.[36] The tenets that constrain women have withstood the test of time.

With legions of consumers drawn to K-drama and K-pop stars, beauty products are ushered into ports around the world. Television dramas don't just transmit stories, Oh Youjeong notes in her book *Pop City: Korean Popular Culture and the Selling of Place*. "They represent and lead trends in fashion and lifestyle. Since K-pop is recognized more for its visual appeal than musical offerings, the images of K-pop idols also contribute to notions of 'Korean beauty ideals.'"[37] The popularity of the people representing the face of South Korea creates demand for K-beauty's skincare rituals, products, and looks. "K-Beauty wouldn't be able to sell itself without images of beautiful Koreans," Emory University researcher and professor Jenny Wang Medina says.

Korea now sets the bar for visuality, cultural trends, and appearance norms. These are especially worth understanding, as Korean beauty norms are exported across the world, notably in Southeast Asia, where more than 50 percent of the population is under the age of thirty-five.[38] Cosmetics companies capitalize on the Hallyu connection, directing symbiotic marketing strategies.[39] The biggest K-pop and K-drama stars are spokespeople for K-beauty brands, further linking Korean cultural exports with its aesthetic standards and its beauty industry. Among many other K-pop idols, Nichkhun is the face of It's Skin, G-Dragon for the SAEM, SHINee for Etude House, Super Junior-M for Tonymoly, and NCT 127 for Nature Republic.

Thanks to the internet, South Korean aesthetics are not just distributed, they're emulated and reproduced by influencers, wannabe influencers, and their followers. The drama *Descendants of the Sun* was *the* must-see K-drama during my time in Korea, and star Song Hye-kyo's Laneige's TwoTone lipstick sold out in the weeks after it began airing.[40] Just as the full, peach-looking butt seen across social media has led the so-called Brazilian butt lift to become the fastest-growing cosmetic procedure in the world, the facial transformations available in Korea and seen on Korean idols set trends and invite copycats, further embedding Korean beauty trends as desirable, not just domestically but everywhere.[41]

International fans set up websites and podcasts to introduce K-beauty linked with K-pop idols, posting articles like "How to Look Like K-Pop Idols," "K-Pop Star Tiffany Young's 18-Step Beauty Routine," and "K-Pop Star Jessica Jung's Korean Skin Care Secrets, Revealed."

Across the Asia region, South Korean stars are credited for establishing Korean ethnic features or locally grown trends as part of a definitive beauty standard. Chinese actress Zhang Yuqi reportedly underwent plastic surgery to look like Song Hye-kyo, one of the most popular actresses in Korea.[42] Across the globe, celebrity style and streetwear fashion now commonly have roots in South Korea, especially for fashionable Gen-Z men.

When the Hallyu wave had already spread across many other places in the world and finally reached the United States, the diaspora played a role in juicing South Korea's soft power success. California—particularly Los Angeles—has the largest concentration of Koreans outside Korea, trailed by New York. "[Hallyu] comes in as a niche kind of thing, as a subculture to white spaces. But it was already consumed in America by Korean American communities in large urban areas," says the Emory University professor Jenny Wang Medina. "This global Korea brand couldn't have happened without the proximity to the U.S. and the Korean diaspora. The immigration and the transnational migration of Koreans created . . . spaces for cultural importation."[43]

K-pop aesthetics have proven that while highly specific to Korea, they're also legible enough to be gobbled up everywhere. By 2020, South Korea became the third largest cosmetics exporter in the world, behind only France and the United States, and K-beauty exports reached 160 countries.[44] "If the argument about cultural globalization has been a concern about its flattening and homogenizing impacts, then this approach is 'No, we're absolutely specific in our cultural principles, but we produce something that is legible and desirable everywhere,'" says Michelle Cho, whose research at the University of Toronto focuses on K-pop.[45]

Sure, you can't quickly measure beauty culture's influence in the same way rankings-obsessed Korean media like to enumerate Olympic medals, Oscar nominations, or the GDP. But how we look—how we're expected to look, how much we prioritize looks—is reflected in the way we live.

To me, the diversity inherent in the extension of K-beauty's global reach offers a refreshing shift. Growing up in white suburban America as the only Asian girl in my classes, I often felt ashamed of my differences and desperate to fit in. K-beauty's ascendance means my three daughters experience a culture in which West finally chases East in some aesthetics and pampering rituals, inverting the previous power dynamic. Crossover sensations used to mean crossing over only in one direction. Now Asian beauty—so often exoticized by the West—has become a transnational standard-bearer of its own, allowing culture crossover to flow back and forth. But as Korea's soft power flex continues to pay dividends, with its growth center moving on from China to Southeast Asia and most recently the West, the business and geopolitical stakes to keep it humming grow ever higher.

~

To keep K-beauty exports moving and the international market share climbing, government agencies go beyond support of cultural content: they give huge tax breaks to export-only companies like Wishtrend, the Korean beauty company that sells only to the United States. You can buy its popular Klairs line online, or you can find its products at Urban Outfitters stores across America. And Wishtrend doesn't have to pay corporate taxes in South Korea at all. "For instance, if the corporate tax in Korea is 10 percent, we would pay it but then get all of that payment refunded once we proved we sold our products overseas," Wishtrend cofounder Eddie Aram Baek explains. He called it an invaluable boost to the survival and growth of these export-based cosmetic companies. Five years into its founding, the company said it had doubled its sales every year since opening its doors.

A few notable hypewomen have further given the industry a lift in the US and Europe in the way sometimes awkward government-driven marketing efforts could never have done. Government agencies are bafflingly incoherent in their marketing of South Korea. To wit, the city of Seoul's cringeworthy "I Seoul You" campaign or a 2008 national tourist slogan, "Korea Sparkling." Yikes. Contrast this to the brand-building of entrepreneurs like Charlotte Cho, Glow Recipe founders Sarah Lee and Christine Chang, and Peach & Lily's Alicia Yoon, who are among founders in the Korean diaspora. Ace marketers all, they leveraged their lifetimes of toggling between Korean and Western cultures to effectively promote K-beauty concepts in the U.S. Glow Recipe started out as a curation site for other K-beauty brands, amassing more than a million social media followers and earning itself credibility as a tastemaker, which then helped the brand sell products of its own. When Cho founded the online Korean beauty shop Soko Glam in 2012, educational content about Korea's skinfirst philosophies came free via their website, but all that teaching also marketed her brand. Cho is credited with coining the 10-Step Skincare Routine, understood widely today as a pillar of K-beauty.

Charlotte Cho's 10 Steps
1. oil cleanser
2. gel cleanser/water cleanser
3. exfoliator
4. toner
5. essence
6. serum
7. sheet mask
8. eye cream
9. moisturizer
10. sunscreen[46]

Cho's success in bringing K-beauty knowledge and products to the uninitiated led her to launch her own skincare line, Then I Met You. In 2012, Yoon founded the Korean beauty emporium Peach & Lily, and has since created her own skincare line under the same name. Cho and Yoon's companies were among the first to make K-beauty products available and accessible in the United States. For many American consumers, Soko Glam and Peach & Lily introduced them to the notion that Korean beauty is synonymous with skincare. It's also likely how they became familiar with the double cleanse, sheet masking, and essences. Lee and Chang's Glow Recipe launched a K-beauty-inspired brand in 2017.[47]

Cho, Yoon, and other entrepreneurs opened up K-beauty to a side of the world that hadn't encountered it before. They act as guides to wider K-beauty offerings, which can mystify on first encounter.

"I would never have imagined Korean beauty trends, products, and brands that were relatively foreign and unknown would become so trendy and hot," Cho says. "People get so enthused by learning these techniques and tricks from Korean culture. And I'm very pleased to see that. That's why I find my work really rewarding."

Once you learn some techniques and tricks or find products that work, it's hard not to keep trying and buying them. The risk is, the more you buy, the more you want.

~

CHAPTER 4

Skinfirst

In the heart of Seoul's Myeongdong makeup district, Korean beauty brand AHC opened a flagship store called the Future Salon. AHC's parent company was acquired by Unilever for $2.7 billion in 2017, marking the first—and still the largest—foreign acquisition of a Korean cosmetics firm.[1] Its Myeongdong flagship marries robots with skincare, underscoring the futuristic selling point of K-beauty. Walking into the store feels like entering a giant Apple AirPods case— gleaming white acrylic walls, glossy white floors, mirrors for ceilings, screens that envelop you in a tunnel. Instead of ads on the wraparound screens, like the ones lodged in my brain from *Minority Report*, these screens glisten with kaleidoscopic patterns on which the store projects customers' faces. I stopped by a console somewhere around the eye cream packaged in plastic syringes and lined up my face to fit in an outline drawn on the mirror. Then a "face scan" supposedly read my skin type in seconds. I reached my hand into a small opening in the mirrored wall and an automated device spit out a dime-sized dollop of clear serum into my palm, purportedly tailor-made for my face. Out of a different slot came what looked like a receipt. On it was a "prescription" for products available in the store for my specific skin needs, based on the scan.

We were on a break between interviews for a story, so my Korean translator and friend, Se Eun, joined me in this leisurely shopping journey through Myeongdong. I remained as curious about the 10-step skincare routines as I'd been during my early days in Seoul and as unable as ever to keep them straight. But the air of scientific certainty presented by the face scan and the "prescription" for my skin seemed to sell me precisely what I needed.

The AHC salesgirls could speak pretty good Mandarin. (In the mid-2010s, it was often easier to communicate in Mandarin instead of English, owing to all the extensive Mandarin training that shopgirls received to cater to Chinese customers.)[2] Still, I had to rely frequently on Se Eun to translate the details. When I went in, bewildered, the saleswomen pitched the new "booster" of moisturizer in the syringe-looking dispenser, a push release emphasizing the "injection" of moisture this would give you. A literal shot of extra hydration! They also sold me a bottle of Eye Cream for Face, which is exactly what it sounds like and a product so popular that a tube is supposedly sold every three seconds in one of their stores.[3] After collecting my prescribed products, I proceeded to quiz the clerk about how to use my new wares.

Elise: So I'm gonna do cleanser first, then booster.
Clerk: Cleanser, toner, then serum. Moisturizer.

Me: Then moisturizer, then after that I'm gonna add Eye Cream for Face? So that's only like, six, seven steps?

Se Eun, my translator: Six.

Me: Well, this booster is new. I also use that Time Revolution, from Missha. Is that toner? When is it?

Clerk: It's essence.

Me: So when is essence?

Clerk: Toner, essence. Then Eye Cream for Face.

Se Eun, the translator: So it's gonna go cleanser, then booster, then toner, then serum or essence which are pretty much the same thing, then moisturizer, and or cream. Then the Eye Cream for Face goes after the serum.

Me: So how many times a day?

Clerk: Two times a day.

Me: When is my sheet mask?

Clerk: Sometimes, last. That's the last thing you use.

[Se Eun and I walk out of the store and back out onto the street.]

Me: Okay, how confusing was that?!?!

SeEun: Oh yeah, oh my god. Why would someone need that many steps?

Me: Why *would* someone?

The so-called 10-step Korean skincare routine has neither ten hard-and-fast steps or a routine sequence to it, but dermatologists and brands do recommend a general order of operations. The first few steps are usually an oil cleanse and a water-based cleanse (hence a double cleanse), then optional exfoliation and toner. The back half of the steps are all variations on moisturizing, and throwing on a sheet mask is last. Products that moisturize include the following but are not limited to essence, serums, boosters, ampoules, eye cream, face cream, and anything called, well, moisturizer. You can't come close to ten steps of skincare without at least a few variations on moisturizing.

Korea's "skinfirst philosophy" undergirds all of this. As the dermatologists like to point out, skin is the largest organ of our body, accounting for about 15 percent of our total body weight(!),[4] so it makes sense that skincare should be part of our overall wellness routines. Especially when treating skin well can be a preventative of future ills and it can feel restorative, too. While it's possible to spend a great deal of money on your skin, some protective measures (like wearing a hat or sunscreen) are low cost.

Where many of us in the United States and Europe might have first come to skincare because of teenage acne, pesky eczema, or in my case, mosquito bite scars, Koreans treat skin as a fundamental part of the body that needs regular care and maintenance, like brushing their teeth. (I should note that Koreans are THRICE daily brushers of their teeth. It's not uncommon to see a line of office workers in the bathroom mirrors after the lunch hour, brushing their pearly whites.)

That there are this many steps to skincare routines reinforces how South Koreans have long cared about intricate skincare practices and treating the root of skin conditions, but also says something about Korean beauty standards. When "perfect" blemish-free skin is expected, working for it is an accepted part of a person's regular daily routines.

Growing up in America, I thought of spa days or facials as special treats. Among my friends and family, we bought spa packages as gifts or reserved them for bachelorette parties or holidays. And it wasn't until the past decade that YouTube influencers, such as the pioneering Michelle Phan, helped makeup and skincare to explode as a subculture on social media, turning skincare into an aspirational lifestyle priority on the level of fashion.[5] In Seoul, facials are considered more like exercise, but for your face. Regular people get them as often as three times a week. Facial massage, extraction, skin treatments like whitening or hydration—they are a middle-class norm within the reach of everyday citizens, not just the provenance of the rich. Coupons for my favorite type of facial, a suction-focused session of pore vacuuming (known in Korea as an aqua peel and in America as hydrofacials), abound on various apps and are available for less than $50. Eyelash extensions, which can run $250 or more in Los Angeles, are a quarter of the price in Seoul and, in my experience, far more expertly applied. The real eye-opener for this American is the casual and widely accepted practice of facial injections—Botox, filler, skin boosters, and new classes of injectables that are available only in Korea. Many middle-class women (and increasing numbers of men) begin neurotoxins or filler while still in their early twenties as a preventative practice, which requires getting their faces jabbed at least two or three times a year. But more on injectables later.

Staying Out of the Sun

Skincare as self-care starts with skin protection and preventative maintenance. Koreans take sunscreen more seriously than do people in any other place I've ever been on earth. "The people of the entire nation wear sunscreen all year round with a devotion bordering on religious fervor," writes Korean dermatologist Hae Shin Chung.[6] On average, 90 percent of Korean women and 56 percent of men apply sunscreen at all times, compared to the 30 percent of women and 14 percent of men who wear sunscreen in the United States.[7] Chung came to the United States to advance her experience specifically because it's rare to encounter skin cancer patients in Korea. In the U.S., skincare—compared to makeup or haircare—accounts for 20 percent of the beauty market; in Korea, it's 50 percent of the market.[8] And prevention—in the form of sunscreen and its various form factors—is the biggest segment.

It's not unusual to see men and women carry sun umbrellas to shield themselves from the sun on bright days. Staying out of direct sunlight is culturally and even governmentally supported. During the muggy, sun-drenched summers in Seoul, the city puts up giant umbrellas or sun shade sails over the sidewalks at intersections, helping block pedestrians from being in the sun while awaiting a traffic light change. Going to outdoor pools felt like entering a weird vortex, because no one seemed to wear swimsuits to swim. Koreans covered their bodies by wearing rash guards as swimsuits, sometimes with full-length pants, giant sun visors, and a thick coating of pasty white sunscreen.

Whiteness

Along with *glowy* or *dewy, milky white* and *porcelain* are terms thrown around when describing K-beauty. Glance at any number of K-beauty products and you'll spot *whitening* on the label. (*Whitening* does not mean skin-bleaching agents. Usually the word *whitening* on products is a poor translation for *brightening*.[9] Korean regulators define whitening ingredients as those which prevent melanin pigmentation in the skin or those that help fade it.)[10] Korea's whitening substances and procedures make up 63 percent of global sales. That's the lion's share of the global market for their definition of whitening.[11]

The preference for milky white skin does land K-beauty into controversy, given Korea's history of being invaded and colonized. It kicks up especially over the common practice of using visual effects to make stars look even lighter than they already are. Skin is the "alpha and omega of racial difference," as the scholar Brenda Dixon Gottschild put it, so seeking to "whiten" skin draws due scrutiny.[12] It is painfully true that historically, across the planet, those with fairer or lighter skin have been prized, and Western inflows to Asia starting in the late 1800s influenced appearance norms. But as researchers Sojeong Park and Seok-Kyeong Hong have observed, "It is difficult to explain this only from the imperial perspective of direct Western influence."

That's because the white skin preference also has a culturally specific context. Local historical preferences for porcelain-white skin predate Western colonization in Northeast Asia. Class-related preferences and beauty practices for white skin date to Korea's Gojoseon period (which ended in 108 BCE), because white skin suggests "that one has led a labor-free life."[13] In premodern Japan (prior to the 1860s) the nobility of both genders would use chalky white powder on their faces for the same reason.[14]

Heated debates have sprung up over the years about K-pop idols getting "whitewashed"—lit in certain ways or Photoshopped whiter than their natural skin color. I certainly spotted a difference when I saw photos of the original K-pop boy band, Seo Taiji and Boys, whose members' skin appeared darker, and compared them with modern groups like EXO or BTS. But when I'm shopping and see *whitening* on product labels, I know it doesn't mean bleaching agents but ingredients such as vitamin C to promote brighter, not literally whiter, skin.

Double Cleansing

Another striking differentiator in the K-beauty skincare routine is the concept of double cleansing. For a long time, double cleansing—removing makeup with an oil-based cleanser, then washing your face with a water-based cleanser—has been standard in Korea. It's finally caught on with a cult following in the West, even though putting oily stuff on my face in order to clean it still feels counterintuitive to me. Maybe I was misguided by reading too many *Seventeen* magazines in my youth, but I grew up believing that oil on your face would just make you oilier.

It's the opposite in Seoul. "That makeup products cannot be removed properly by ordinary soaps or water-based

cleansers alone became a deep-rooted faith," wrote dermatologist Chung of growing up in Korea.*[15]

Ironically, this idea—of using an oil to remove makeup
first, and then a cleanser to wash the face—started with the
use of an American product, Pond's Cold Cream. Yes, *that*
Pond's Cold Cream, the inexpensive drugstore moisturizer
dating to the early 1900s and used by your grandmas and
Hollywood beauties like Marilyn Monroe and First Lady
Jackie Kennedy. American women followed the company's
literature using it as a moisturizer to wipe off with a tissue
and leave the rest on overnight. Korean women developed
double cleansing as a hack, by using Pond's Cold Cream as a
makeup remover, aka an oil cleanser, to wash makeup off
with, and following it up with soap cleansing.[16] The practice
stuck.

Exfoliation

Korean skinfirst culture includes not just the face but the
whole body. Products to slough off dead skin cells range
from facial scrubs and peeling gels to a variety of body scrubbing tools, foot files, and callus removers that employ mech-
anical and chemical methods like the foot peels my husband
Matt was devoted to.

But exfoliation at the hands of Korean *ajumma*s (older,
authoritative aunties) is an unmissable part of a Korean spa

---

* For just getting the makeup off, it seems like no one seriously disputes
that soap and water are the most effective thing, though some dermatologists do recommend double cleansing because the oils help hydrate the skin.

experience. In Korea, public bathhouses are inexpensive and accessible, and most Koreans visit them every week, using a coarse washcloth to manually exfoliate every corner of their bodies. These spa facilities, called *jjimjilbangs,* are also available in some parts of the United States, concentrated around Korean communities. As is true of a Japanese onsen, you strip down naked and wash off the day, then join others of your sex in alternating hot baths and cold baths to your heart's content. After you're robed or dressed in the standard-issue shirt and shorts, you can veg out in various co-ed saunas.

I tried my first jjimjilbang soon after moving to Seoul. I lived a couple of blocks down the street from Dragon Hill Spa, a jjimjilbang open 24/7 and frequented by locals and visitors alike because of its location near Seoul's bustling Yongsan train station and the longtime U.S. army base, the Yongsan Garrison. My fellow expat friend Amy sold me on a visit by sharing all the fun she had getting naked and alternating between hot baths and cold baths, before baking in dry saunas.

Man, I didn't know what I had been missing. After the cleaning and alternating baths, you can take advantage of the full-body scrub, where a worker manually exfoliates every inch of your body. They use a coarse washcloth known as an Italy towel, a rough-textured bath mitt for body scrubbing, originally from Italy but widely made in Korea for these exfoliating purposes. These scrubs hurt so bad when those mitts are taking off that top layer of dead skin cells that Conan O'Brien yelled during his televised jjimjilbang visit, "That's skin that's been on me since Jimmy Carter was president!"[17]

Other optional jjimjilbang services include vagina steaming, where you sit or squat over a steaming brew of traditional herbs like mugwort, which is believed to help heal several ailments, from menstrual pain to vaginitis.[18] I brought it up with a mom friend at a playdate after learning about it, and she promptly whipped out her phone to reveal a photo of her and a girlfriend smiling widely, wearing strapless towel dresses and their hair tied up in white towels, sitting down beside each other on what looked like giant buckets, getting their privates pampered with vapor.

~

Here are some "problematic" things about my skin. It gets super dry and flaky in various patches. Winter is the worst, because the skin over my knuckles inevitably gives up, breaking and bleeding. It overreacts to bug bites, making them irresistible to scratch, so my legs and ankles are perpetually a constellation of bites and scars. And this is the worst part, at least in an Asian country: I have freckles.

Freckles!

The freckles that dot my cheeks never troubled me once in my first three decades on earth. I thought they were innocent. Cute, even! But during my initial months in Seoul, I learned that those freckles might as well have been puss-oozing boils when noticed by cosmopolitan South Koreans. Upon encountering my freckled makeup-free face, South

Koreans might utter any of the following reactions or a combination:

> Ohhhhhhhhhhhhh, *jugungae*! (Freckles.)
> We have ways to take care of that.
> Do you know [insert name of dermatology clinic]? They
>   can remove.
> You said you like your freckles? That is not a Korean way
>   of thinking.
> [No comment at all, just automatically Photoshopping
>   out freckles after snapping my picture.]

I should have expected this, given all that I absorbed from my Asian mother. She's Taiwanese and indoctrinated in a wider Northeast Asian hegemony against freckles. Growing up, my mom hated her own freckles and was always trying various whitening creams or newfangled light therapy to lighten those suckers or blast them off entirely. She wears embarrassingly wide-brimmed hats and visors to avoid the sun and recoiled when I spent money on tanning beds in my teenage years to be as dark as possible. (I later developed a precancerous mole for my troubles, so yes, mistakes were made.)

In a country where beauty is synonymous with clear, smooth, and blemish-free skin, freckle-phobia is inescapable. Freckles will get you ridiculed by your peers and downgraded by potential partners. Extend this across any number of perceived imperfections, like moles. Or frizzy hair. Or not enough hair. For the first time in my life, to avoid the discomfort of comments from strangers, I stayed out of the sun to keep my freckles from getting darker. And I started using my first-ever Korean makeup product—what else? A BB cream cushion—to cover them up.

But freckles were just one thing to be fixed. After only a few months in Seoul, I felt that whether I was trying to be lighter or smoother and firmer, somehow nothing about me was just right the way it was. Every part was a foundation on which to improve and then maintain. The comments and judgment I faced in Korea loosened up calcifying memories, reminding me that the quest to erase perceived imperfections was introduced to me in my childhood and adolescence, leaving an early and lasting imprint.

As a sixteen-year-old in Dallas, Texas, I started working as a commercial print model, showing up on the pages of cheesy teen magazines and appearing in nationwide department store signage and inside thick JCPenney catalogs. (This was the late 1990s and early 2000s, when mail-order catalogs still existed.) It all happened accidentally. My friend Prairie lived down the street from an advertising creative who asked for candid pictures of her high school friends. I showed up in the stack she showed him, and six of us were cast in a national 7UP campaign. The Dallas-based Campbell Agency signed me a month later.

When I look back on this period twenty years on, modeling is still the easiest money I ever earned. I got paid nearly $2,000 a day to show up at a studio or on location, then let other people dress me, glam me up, and take my picture. I learned about new music (or old music, as was often the case) from the photographers and about makeup and clothes from the stylists. They treated me like an adult even though I had just gotten my driver's license. I constantly got lost trying to get to warehouse-turned-studios in the run-down but hip areas of South Dallas. At my other high school job, server at Souper Salad, I got paid in sexual harassment and minimum wage, plus tips. On these relatively relaxed photo shoots, I earned hundreds of dollars an hour for not doing much of anything.

But gosh, I was just sixteen. My getting introduced to this industry so young meant I learned early on that my value to the economy was not my ideas or skills, nor my willingness to work eight-hour shifts at a fast-casual restaurant gig, but only how I looked on-camera. I'd rarely felt self-conscious about my looks until this point. But that appearance matters is not an abstract notion when you work as a model; it is the central operating principle. Especially in that fatphobic crucible of the 1990s, objective notions of beauty were enforced. Runway modeling was out for me because at five-nine, I was an inch too short. I didn't have a unique enough look for editorial spreads in magazines, because as the agents said, I was "classically beautiful," which relegates you to commercial print (read: store posters, advertisements, and catalogs). For a model or a mere high school student, the beauty ideals back then were the same that we broadly still aspire to now: thinness, firmness, smoothness, and youth.[19] If the body positive movement in fashion has been able to widen the standard on one aspect—say, thinness or youth—the other ideals have stayed firmly fixed.

Absorbing constant judgment and rejection over my appearance became the order of things. I ran mental checklists of what was wrong with me: Wide "birthing hips." Check.

Perpetually dry skin. Check. One of my too-thick eyebrows was longer than the other. Check. Hair too flat. Check. Chest too flat, another check. The stylists would stuff my bras with flesh-toned silicone inserts that looked like chicken cutlets, and I think they're actually colloquially known as . . . chicken cutlets.

Rushing to an endless series of castings after school or sometimes during school hours, I'd encounter other girls in the waiting rooms who inevitably had fuller lips or shinier hair or actual breasts. We'd sit there with our books, short-hand for our portfolios, silently sizing one another up. From my seat, everyone else looked prettier. Every time.

When I started, my hips measured a slightly too wide 36 inches, prompting my agent, Peter, to drop into a *Growing Pains* dad voice to say things like "Are you working on your body?" It was the only nudge I needed to begin restrictive di-eting. Being an overachiever, eventually I learned to limit my-self to 800 calories a day and ran six miles each morning the summer before college. I surpassed my goals of losing weight and inches off my waistline, but my body started breaking down. I became so underweight by the start of my freshman year at the University of Missouri that I stopped having periods and frequently felt cold and dizzy. When I would lie on my back to do sit-ups, the bones of my spine would grind against the floor. I felt simultaneously satisfied and scared.

Those photo shoots were fun, but the pursuit of landing shoots didn't feel like fun and good times anymore. All my energies were directed at an invisible master, one I sensed that I'd never satisfy. So after I took notice of my hunger one ordinary morning in the basement kitchen of my sorority house, I just . . . stopped starving myself. But (still an over-achiever) I stopped starving myself with flair. I reached into the open trash can and scooped out with my bare hand a chunk of a just-discarded chocolate sheet cake, left over from a lunch for two hundred girls, and shoved it in my mouth. During one semester, I gained far more weight than I'd lost, and after a time of searching and therapy, I also gained perspective. I became possessed by and then exorcised an energy-sucking, damaging fixation on my looks and weight, all before I was old enough to drink.

Once I stopped competing in the rigged game, I never tried competing again. My position on beauty work, or body work, was set in place as one of nonengagement. To this day I resist any food restrictions, wear little to no makeup, and can go days without showering.

But to say my relationship with beauty standards ended when I was twenty is too neat a narrative. It obscures the complexities baked into self-perception, and it gives me a pass I haven't earned. When I shut down the efforts to meet the thinness standard in my own life, I started actively ignoring beauty's larger machinations and stopped thinking about important questions concerning how beauty intersects with sexist power structures. I excused myself from noticing the effect on all of us when we enforce beauty mandates and from considering who benefits when women expend so much energy enhancing ourselves. Perhaps because it seems impossible, we have yet to meaningfully change the way things are, at scale. I let myself stop wondering about this for nearly two decades—and then I moved to Seoul and had to start all over again.

In retrospect, my lesson in the downsides of chasing impossible beauty standards inside an explicitly looks-based industry is as on the nose as possible. The beats of my story are so common that they make up a recurring arc called the therapeutic narrative. Autumn Whitefield-Madrano recounts the template, as applied to beauty: "Prepubescent girl with well-adjusted bodily esteem meets world; world (in the form of mother, father, media machine, thoughtless dance teacher, etc.) implies she's too fat/gangly/bulb-nosed/narrow-featured to be considered beautiful; girl embarks on rampage of disparaging her looks; girl comes to terms with her appearance and goes back to a place of well-adjusted bodily esteem."[20]

In Seoul, I was suddenly surrounded by products promising paths to look more "beautiful," which produced twinges of insecurity that stirred somewhere deep. Until then, I had obscured the idiosyncratic experience of beauty for the sake of fitting my individual arc, which mapped neatly on that therapeutic narrative, one of "hobbled to healed." Once I was plopped into a society of appearance conformity, fatphobia, freckle-phobia, and beyond, I realized I had a lot more to think through.

~

By my second year in the cosmetics capital, the beauty imperative felt omnipresent and overwhelming, with an eerily familiar ideal female face following me wherever I went. This visage is inescapable: milky white, smooth, glowing, with a narrow nose, anime-sized eyes, and a small, delicate jawline that meets at a V. It's the Asian variation of a global ideal: the It Girl. The girl's face is always dewy, unblemished, and unwrinkled, her eyes perpetually bright, her forehead uncreased.

My perspective widened when I was settled in and was, finally and refreshingly, not pregnant. I moved around town faster, developed reliable sources, and got my sea legs as a Korea correspondent. I could observe Seoul without the panic and overwhelm of a total newbie. I found myself able to pay more attention. With it, I felt increasingly unsettled by the unwritten rules, the mindset—and the work—required by my external appearance. I also felt uneasy about being looked at, not because I drew attention but because it felt like everyone in South Korea was always judging everyone else, comparing themselves to one another, relentlessly.

Korea is a real rankings-focused culture, which means Koreans discuss one another's "rankings" regularly, whether it's on their looks, test scores, external wealth, or most often, the whole package. "It's not about finding your own path or your own self as it is about doing better than those around you. It's in many ways a zero-sum game," Tom Owenby told me, for one of my first stories in Seoul. He spent five years in South Korea, teaching Korean high school students.[21]

It made me self-conscious. I rarely understood what Koreans were saying with their voices thanks to my stubborn inability to pick up the language well, but that only made me more sensitive to what I could pick up from people's gazes. I felt constant judgment, at best. Straight-up disapproval, at worst. I grew less comfortable in my own skin. On all the judgment and comments about one's appearance, the beauty entrepreneur Hellen Choo said, "You could look at it as being negative. Or you can look at it as a very interesting and creative side of Korea, and it makes the industry grow faster."

In some ways, Choo is correct. The cultural distaste for "imperfections" does set off a flurry of invention and commerce. Many of the cool new K-beauty products we love came online and found a mass market because they purported to cover up or make perceived flaws disappear. But as multiple steps to skincare became more widely accepted and our individual differences became viewed as problems to solve, I wondered: Where does all that obsessive work get us? What does consumer beauty culture lead to, if left unconsidered and unchecked? It was already swallowing up some of my money and time, more than it ever had before I moved to Seoul. But the bigger risk was that along the way, it would cannibalize my sense of who I was.

Eventually, I saw how Korea's conflation of appearance maintenance with self-care puts other beauty work—haircare, chemical peels, laser treatments, injectables, and even invasive surgery I might have considered drastic in my pre-Korea days—on a continuum of self-improvement labor. The continuum moves from low cost to high cost, and from simple to complex: everyday maintenance, to routine beauty work performed by professionals, to medical procedures performed by dermatologists and surgeons.

When I began seeing things from this perspective, the shine from my fun foray into skincare dulled. The persistence of a clear-cut standard of Korean beauty opened a window to the culture that drives K-beauty itself. Because sure, we're talking about steps of skincare, but another way I began thinking about "steps" is as a stand-in for gargantuan amounts of appearance cultivation, decoration, and performance, and not just with beauty products. It extended into how women and girls are expected to behave, dictating how much autonomy we have over our bodies and how much time we have in our days. Viewed this way, it's not ten steps, but hundreds or thousands. The steps are never done, the labor never complete.

CHAPTER 5

~

Lookism

In retrospect, I began to understand the monumental labor of appearance work while I was in labor.

On the morning of Isabel's birth, I was crouched over my eldest daughter, Eva, tying her hair into a ponytail for school. A sharp pain radiated across my midsection, an unmistakable contraction. I grabbed Eva's backpack and tucked a water bottle inside it before taking our building elevator down thirty-five floors, rushing past the dessert place on the ground level and through a small playground to hail a taxi at the curb.

We used public transportation and taxis to get around that first year, since both reliably showed up the moment you needed them. The cabbies' driving skills? Not so reliable. I'd been in cabs where the drivers straight up fell asleep at the wheel and started veering off the road more than once. On that morning, my laboring body climbed into the cab of the most extreme stop-and-go, herky-jerky, brake-pumping driver yet. Did I need to throw up before getting into the car? No. Did I need to now? Yes. "I don't think I can stay in here,"

I said to Matt, my eyes widening in panic. He looked amused and annoyed, and agreed we had to exit. But we were crossing the Han River by then, hurtling over a kilometer-long bridge. As soon as we reached the other side, I yelled for the cabbie to stop, jumped out, then spent a few minutes enduring at least one contraction on the side of the road as Matt hailed another cab. We took the second taxi to drop off Eva to school, and then finally rode on to the birthing center.

The midwife, randomly assigned to me for the delivery, spoke only a few words of English, so Matt wound up as my doula. We rode out contractions together in a spacious suite bathed in sunlight from the third-floor window. In my downtime between contractions (which ranged from five to ten minutes), I tried to take mini-naps, or we read tweets and news links on our phones and cracked jokes about the various birthing apparatuses in the room—ropes hanging above a bathtub, the tub big enough to fit a Prius, exercise balls of different sizes, a waterproof cover over the mattress as a reminder of why we were there in the first place.

The staff fed me constantly. At lunchtime, and again for a teatime snack and then at dinner, I would get a menu to review. They offered "Western" options like fast food, or the "Korean menu" of congee or grilled mackerel, and a bevy of banchan side dishes. When the contractions came more often, I got on all fours to make the excruciating labor pains more bearable and Matty snapped a picture of me eating a cheeseburger in that position. (I had ordered the Western option.) It's a memory I'm proud of and embarrassed about in equal measure.

Surely, there was air-conditioning in that birthing suite,

but I couldn't feel it anymore at the pushing stage. The sun had come down, sending long shadows into the room. My hair dripped with sweat. I wanted all my clothes off and stripped down to only my bra, out of a primal instinct to be naked. But the midwife kept covering me up with a blanket. Modesty in the delivery room?! No one was there besides the midwife, Matty, and eventually my ob-gyn, Dr. Chung, who had seen about 80,000 vaginas by then, given his line of work. I'd toss off the blanket the midwife draped over my lower half; she'd cover me back up. This back-and-forth continued a few times, even as I could feel the excruciating pressure of a small human emerging from between my legs. Finally in desperation I shouted, "*Stop covering me up!*" And she relented.

Later, I would come to see that unpleasant standoff as emblematic of a prevailing attitude about women's bodies: that in their most "natural" state, when bodies are naked and not prettified, they should be hidden.[1] The idea that femininity should be cultivated and our bodies somehow cleaned up for presentation is something I'd already been picking up from Korean beauty culture. But our bodies at their most naked can already come with confusion or shame. Having to wage a battle to be naked during an experience shared by women across time and space? I gotta say, it registered as wrong, even as I winced and wailed through the last few moments of labor.

In the weeks and months after we brought Isa home, I learned to censor my postpartum body. Isa's early summer birth meant that during the first few months of her life, my skin beaded with sweat every time I stepped from the steaminess outside onto the air-conditioned subway. The extra heat that comes with nonstop lactation didn't help. One September morning I let myself don a sleeveless V-neck red-orange knee-length dress to wear as I took Eva to school via subway. It proved to be a quick and demeaning lesson on how not to appear in public. My nursing breasts meant I was naturally bustier, and the dress revealed a hint of cleavage. (Though not much—even my nursing breasts don't fill more than a B cup.) I remember stepping onto a subway car and finding a spot standing next to the metal pole near the doors. But between that stop and the next one, the subway car's entire middle area had cleared away from me. Those in the seats along the sides shot me looks of disapproval and puzzled disdain. People had moved so far away from my modest cleavage that I might as well have been loudly farting on the subway. Or naked.

Bare arms were a no-no—you'll notice that Korean women wear cardigans over their camisoles or tank tops even in the height of summer—and cleavage seemed to scare people off. These norms were among the countless invisible appearance rules I didn't know about until I broke them. My Korean girlfriends later told me that it's frowned upon to so much as duck downstairs to the convenience store without makeup on. For most, it's not worth flouting such rules because they're enforced with open discrimination. There's even a name for it: lookism.

In Korean, the term is *oemo jisang juui*, which translates to "looks are supreme." Lookism describes the stubborn social prejudice against those who fail to meet certain appearance standards. William Safire used the term in a column in

2000, but he traces it as first appearing in a *Washington Post Magazine* article in 1978, when the fat acceptance movement used it to describe what their members experienced.[2]

Despite lookism being forbidden in Korea by a 1995 law which says you can't discriminate against anyone on the basis of sex, marital status, family status, or "without any other due reasons," appearance-based discrimination is a cultural norm.[3] "When you meet someone, the first things you say is about their looks," says Hellen Choo, a Seoul-based Korean beauty entrepreneur. "Like, 'Oh my god, look at your eyes.' Or, 'You have nice eyebrows.' 'Look at your skin.' 'Wow, you're so thin.' It's something that people can't really understand when you're from overseas and you get offended. But it's very, very common here. And it's competitive, too."

Lookism is prevalent in the professional sphere. A 2017 South Korean poll found that nearly 40 percent of respondents experienced discrimination based on their appearance when applying for jobs.[4] South Korea's job boards are filled with listings that instruct applicants to attach photographs. A survey of more than 900 businesses by a job website called Incruit found that about 60 percent required a head shot on a résumé.[5] Passport photos are heavily retouched, by default, as they are often used for official job applications, giving rise to numerous passport photo studios that specialize in taking your picture and digitally smoothing out hair, wrinkles, and any other perceived imperfection. The National Human Rights Commission of Korea studied 3,500 recruitment posts in 2015 and found discriminatory questions on a host of different topics, including candidates' age, appearance, and gender, as well as birth region, marital status, religion, military service records, and pregnancy.[6] The average number of such questions per post: four. Often, job listings will use terms like *neat* and *beautiful* to describe ideal candidates, and mustaches and tattoos are explicitly prohibited. One advertisement that drew media attention specified C as the ideal bra cup size.[7] Meanwhile, a post on a jobs blog said that big firms prefer "pretty eyes" and that government bosses like "high noses."[8] Even the Ministry of Employment and Labor once shared a link on Twitter, encouraging job seekers to mind their looks, suggesting "cosmetic surgery has become one of the seven credentials needed for employment," and asking what type of face companies preferred for its applicants.[9] (It's since been removed.) That head shots and often height and weight stats are required for employment that doesn't involve acting or modeling at all is a practice unthinkable in the United States unless you're daring people to sue you.

Looks matter in South Korea, irrespective of gender. But institutional sexism and gender divides in the country make lookism harder on women, since men are the deciders, dominating positions of power within the hypercompetitive workforce. Not being able to find a job is a real possibility: during my time there, the unemployment rate among young Korean workers hovered around 10 percent.[10] Among the twenty-seven countries in the Organisation for Economic Co-operation and Development, Korea ranks last where gender pay equality is concerned, with few women in management positions despite equal educational attainment among the sexes.[11] The oversupply of women in the hiring pools compared to the demand—since men are considered first for positions—means women must compete fiercely not just for social capital but for economic capital, too.

In 2018, television news anchor Yim Hyun-ju decided to wear her glasses while hosting the morning news program for the first time despite the unspoken rule against women wearing glasses at work, because her daily application of fake eyelashes had dried out her eyes and she was going through an entire bottle of artificial tears a day.[12] Daring to wear glasses on television was so noteworthy that Yim became the news. Viewers complained, her producers scolded her, but a groundswell of women thanked her, online and in person. "If I could act freely, I would apply makeup less," Yim told *The New York Times*. "But I'm stuck between my mind and heart, which says one thing, but there is the reality of my job."[13]

In my interviews, women who were just entering the job market or in the early stages of their career told me repeatedly that they simply can't afford *not* to improve their looks, for financial and social reasons. Their families insist on it. Their prospective employers expect it. At high school graduation time, just after the national college entrance exam, students are commonly given cosmetic surgery gift certificates by their parents and grandparents. Hair and makeup salons offer college graduation packages for young people entering the job market. Dermatology and plastic surgery apps offer discounts to recent high school grads of 50 to 70 percent in a "three-pack" of the most popular procedures for young Koreans—eyelid surgery, nose jobs, and Botox for facial contouring of the jawline.[14] Korean women get Botox by their early twenties, because looking "pretty" (as defined by that youthful glow) isn't just important, it's the price of entry in the labor market.

It's not hard to draw a line from unchecked lookism to the rapid ascent of the most extreme beauty culture in the world. For a cocktail of reasons, many Koreans today believe beauty work—the work you do on your outer shell—is the same as self-improvement. Consuming makeup and skincare, as well as availing yourself of cosmetic services and procedures, is understood as a matter of self-respect, personal management, and respect for the community. The surface of the body, writes University of Hawaii professor Sharon Heijin Lee, is "a space of modernizing labor in and of itself, a site where buying and selling, loving and coercing, freedom and power all coalesce."[15] The body is an instrument you take to work in order to earn a paycheck. It is also a worksite of its own, open 24/7. Whether it's work we do to our bodies or the work performed by our bodies, it's a whole lotta labor.

~

Writer Lee Min-kyung wears an unfussy, cropped boy cut and no makeup on her milky white face. Her dark clothes hang loose, obscuring her figure. At twenty-nine, she's part of a movement of young women who have rejected beautifying themselves in order to focus on their ideas and activism. Lee grew up in Seoul, where at the age of ten she began waxing her neck, arms, and legs after boys teased her for her "hairy" neck and nicknamed her "Monkey." Like many I interviewed, she points to the first decade of the 2000s, when she was in elementary school, as a pivot point in the culture. K-pop was going global and the Korean cultural industry was on the ascent. It was then that parental priorities for children shifted, and beauty came to be a push point. In 2007, the prototypical K-pop girl group Girls' Generation debuted, along with Wonder Girls and Kara. The start of You-Tube's global expansion was happening at the same time.[16] Korean cultural observer T. K. Park notes that in the era of music following the debut of Girls' Generation, "the strategy of turning female artists into a carefully curated product" was perfected.[17] Lee Min-kyung recalled: "Girls' Generation appeared. And I was a student. On television the girls were so much thinner. They were never that thin before then. From then on, it started."[18]

Value to the labor market through education was what mothers used to impress upon their daughters, at least in the decades following South Korea's rapid modernization in the 1960s and through the dictatorships that ruled Korea until 1987. After the nation emerged from decades of war and dictatorship to become a market-based democracy, beauty's inextricable link to Korea's cultural ascendance led good looks to become a dominant ethical ideal. To be beautiful was to be good, and vice versa.

"Family members would praise me for acts of kindness by telling me I was pretty," Korean American Hojung Lee wrote in an essay. She moved to Seoul to train at a K-pop academy and eventually became a backup dancer for the group Wonder Girls. "This fused together my desire to be a good person with my desire to be beautiful. In order to be morally good, I had to be pretty. In order to be pretty, I had to be morally good. Korean society taught me that these two concepts are one and the same."[19]

Surface presentation became tied to the very notion of the self. But there's more. In the competitive labor market, middle-class Koreans are judged as "good" not only due to their looks but for the work they put into staying that way. Appearance management is self-care. Skin improvement is self-improvement.

It's not that beauty and adornment haven't been considered a plus for millennia, and in cultures around the world. The ancient Greeks even had a word, *kalokagathia*, that combined *kalos*, meaning beauty, and *agathos*, meaning good, to capture the idea that someone's body is a way to understand who they are.[20] But the Greco-Roman idea of beauty "seemingly had less to do with the surface and more to do with the soul," beauty writer Jessica DeFino notes.[21] Other researchers have found ancient societies such as the Egyptians using makeup and adornment for spiritual purposes—to emulate and communicate with the gods.[22]

In the West, a deep dive into the journals of American girls reveals that before World War I, girls sought moral behaviors as the ultimate virtues, not looks.[23] They desired qualities like goodness through honesty, kindness, duty to family and the community. But priorities underwent a change during the rise of film and the birth of television, in which women and girls became more valued for how they looked than how they thought or behaved. Society ascribed good qualities to them just for looking pretty, and women internalized beliefs conflating beauty with moral superiority.

Something similar happened in Korea in the aughts as

the Korean Wave spread via entertainment culture and digital media. The wide availability of the internet, with its capacity for image distribution, and high-definition television screens—manufactured in Korea and exported around the world—made intense the pressure for poreless *chok chok* skin and the products to maintain it. In a highly visual, media- and tech-saturated time, surface appearance became the goodness signifier, not what was underneath. The constant bombardment with beautiful faces and bodies to inspire our consumption and our emulation tightens the link between physical appearance and one's value as a human being.

So Korean moms who previously prioritized educational and intellectual achievement in their children started emphasizing their looks as well. Lee and others I interviewed say spending so much time, energy, and money on beauty products wasn't a priority among Korean consumers until the first decade of the 2000s. "The idol thing, K-beauty and cosmetics expanded, and the road shops mean cheaper cosmetics than the department store [so young girls can afford it]," Lee Min-kyung says. "The parents' generation has changed. They don't believe studying hard is everything. They're looser. And this generation of parents thinks that beauty is a kind of freedom. [Because] beauty is very important. It's the value of women."[24]

Sexism and Lookism Intertwine

After I'd been in Korea for more than a year, I knew to preemptively begin conversations with strangers by saying *chunguk-keh, miguk-saram-imnida*—I'm a Chinese American.

When I slid into a cab, nine times out of ten the Korean cabbie (usually a man in his sixties or older) would respond with
a throwaway line about how my Korean was pretty good
(something they say to all the foreigners), then ask me one of
three questions, in his native tongue:

Why are you in Korea?
Do you like Korea (and/or) Korean food?
Do you have a husband?

I could barely understand Korean but heard the key vocabulary words repeated enough times that I could respond
by heart. One night I slid into the back of a cab of a driver
who presented me with new vocabulary: 처녀, *chaunyau*. He
started yelling it.

Chaunyau? Chaunyau?! And I responded with "I don't
understand."

Exasperated, he yelled it in English: "VIRGIN?? You,
virgin??"

"*Moh?* [What?]"

"Virgin?!"

I chuckled, uncomfortable and stunned, then said in broken Korean, "No, I have two daughters!"

Later, still mystified, I recounted this incident to my Korean friends, who laughed uproariously and explained, "Oh,
that's because he was using the word for single, which is
interchangeable with virgin."

The episode encapsulated a lot of my experience as a giant (at five-nine), non-Korean, Asian American who ultimately spent the entirety of her four years in Seoul either

pregnant and/or nursing. All their questions had other questions behind them: What was I doing there? What was my value in relation to a man's? My differences—as a woman and a foreigner—relegated me to second class on two levels, with my postpartum or pregnant body emphasizing my femaleness in an unmissable way.

It wasn't just in cabs. The bureaucracies and business world that I entered in my capacity as NPR bureau chief reminded me of my outsider status again and again. There were separate sections at ticket booths or government offices for foreigners, an endless series of lost-in-translation moments, expectant questions like "Who is your bureau chief or boss?" And failing to compute when I said, "I am the bureau chief, I am the boss," because I didn't look the part. (The foreign news bureau chiefs at that time were mostly British or American white men, older than 33 years.)

When I didn't back down from pushing for access to press conferences reserved for only domestic reporting *kija* "clubs," the mansplaining would come with condescension so thick that it needed no translation. Men patronized my husband for giving up his job to support mine, calling him "Superman." They constantly cut in front of me in line, drivers asked me to get out of their cabs because they didn't feel like taking me where I wanted to go, and men physically took up more space on the buses and subways. (That last one happens just about everywhere.) One winter I went to see NANTA, a popular live cooking theater performance, and in the entranceway, a poster of the cast and roles hung with each actor's photos: Manager, Head Chef, Hot Sauce, Sexy Guy, Nephew, Woman. Men can have multiple roles. Women? One.

Being a woman was problematic always, but sometimes being a foreign woman allowed for a little leeway. It occasionally gave me an excuse to slip from the appearance rules of Korea. Foreigner status meant Koreans overlooked my sloppy-for-Korea appearance and spared me social retribution for it. Either that or I just didn't quite understand when it came.

~

Today, on a single shelf display at a gift shop in Seoul, you can find the following products to improve yourself: A posture corrector. A toe aligner. A modern-day corset. Push-up pads to create the perfect cleavage line, which, according to the marketing on the box, should form the letter Y. A jawline slimming tape to "Fix your face." And lots of packages of what appear to be adhesive patches, because you can give the sheet mask treatment to any part of your body, whether it's common trouble spots, such as inner thighs or lower abdomen, or places with sagging skin, like maybe your neck. All this on one shelf in one store of the near-exponentially growing Korean appearance improvement industry.

When lookism reigns, good skin is a surface-level indicator of wellness, morality, and work ethic. Seoul is not a place where "accepting the skin you're in" is de rigueur. The mantra here is more akin to the glowing billboard advertisements in the subway, whose messages promote "harmony of the eyes, nose and jawline" and "touch-up surgery" over lunch. They all promote various versions of "Be you, but prettier."

As we've seen, you need "beauty" to secure a job. Beauty

is also how you obtain a husband. And the marriage market is a minefield of expectations. Heterosexual men expect women to look feminine by specific standards like long hair—without it you're immediately assumed to be a lesbian or tagged as a "radical feminist," a nasty slur in Korea. And the market overflows with matchmaking firms who take height, weight, and even facial proportions into account in their compatibility algorithms.

Haein Shim, twenty-seven, recalls being in middle school when her father started showing her Miss Korea pageants on television. She grew up in Gwangju, a metropolis in the southern part of the country. For nights on end, she says, she sat in her living room after dinner as her dad played on repeat a video of pageant contestants walking in their bikinis and high heels "to teach me how to walk," she says. "Then I had to walk in front of my dad, with this video, every night, to be a good daughter." *What if you refused?* I asked. She said she feared her parents would have shamed her and starved her had she disobeyed. "They kind of were starving me already. I remember every morning, my mom and dad would talk about how big my legs were, how big my stomach was. Saying, 'She's not going to get picked as a wife later.'"[25] Her example is not unusual for her generation, with the emphasis on beauty as an instrument to both social and economic success playing out inside many families.

Disciplining your face and body comes to be considered a necessary means to an end. Until Korea, I didn't think deeply about all the work and the rigid definitions of femininity promoted all around me. But as I considered the interplay of these expectations, I realized that Korea is not so unusual, is it? The K-beauty industry enjoys outsize influence and intensity. But it operates on the same ideas as the beauty industry writ large:

1. That your appearance is not good enough, and you should fix it.
2. That you can empower yourself if you spend energy and money to compete.

Korean women who partake of the beauty culture are doing what it takes within a constant push-pull between the traditional values of filial piety and South Korea's hypermodern neoliberal pull of individualism—trying to "win" a game of self-determinism and growth. After the 1997 Asian financial crisis, South Korea's unemployment climbed to as high as 20 percent, and the government decreased spending in social services at the same time, leaving many Koreans to fend for themselves, piecing together part-time work, relying on family members, or just barely scraping by. Observers believe the precariousness of that time fostered neoliberal mandates to increase your own "human capital" in an endless competition for work and material success.[26] As feminist scholar Cho Joo-hyun writes, "the most successful self-entrepreneurs . . . will be those who faithfully internalize the neoliberal logic [of] subjugating themselves."[27] This describes a kind of social Darwinism incited by market competition. "The idea of competition becomes the new norm of life in postwar capitalism," turning South Korea into a "neoliberal machine," according to Alex Taek-Gwang Lee, a cultural studies professor at Kyung Hee University.[28]

"In traditional society, a woman's body was completely controlled by male-centered society, especially because of the ideology of staying a virgin, which was a strict controlling tool of women's bodies. But now, lookism has replaced that ideology," wrote Kim Sang-hŭi, then the executive director of the country's largest feminist group, Womenlink, in a 2003 op-ed. She argued that appearance pressures exert a form of control over our bodies, but with a consumerist, can-do twist. "In a lookist society, it is not just about self-maintenance, it's that unbeautiful women are seen as lazy and as incapable.[29]

Koreans have a term for their work requirement: *kkumim nodong*, or "display labor"—their outsides must be embellished for display, and work must be undertaken to make women displayable. "It's the perfect sort of manifestation of neoliberalism," says Jenny Wang Medina. "You are laboring with your body and also consuming at the same time."[30]

Cultural Conformity

Beauty work is uncomfortable. It's hard work. It's expensive. It's time consuming. So why don't more people resist? In South Korea, the social costs of sticking out aren't worth the isolation. It can mean banishment or estrangement from the only family or community that you know. Societal harmony is valued over individualism, a cultural reality that showed up in myriad ways when I lived there.

More often than not, I found South Korea's communal culture quite refreshing compared to a very "Live Free or Die" America that I grew up with in Texas, which happened to be at the apex of a "no apology age" when I lived abroad. Koreans show a social responsibility to one another that I appreciate. This way of relating to one another is part of a wider cultural conformity, a holdover from the relatively recent days when a communal agricultural economy undergirded the country. As Korean American writer T. K. Park has noted, many premodern, agriculture-based societies were made up of tight-knit communities whose members cooperated to earn a living (as a current-day example, think of the Amish). Homogeneity is an outgrowth of such societies, a mode of survival.

So is a shared social contract of trust among strangers. When I accidentally left my purse in a Seoul Baskin-Robbins, it remained there tucked under a table untouched for three and a half hours, despite dozens of customers cycling in and out. Later I learned putting your most expensive personal item down on a table in a coffee place in Seoul is actually how you save the table. The unwritten norms there extended to trusting other adults with your small humans. When I was short of change to pay for my snacks one afternoon, a convenience store clerk was perfectly happy to watch my preschooler for five minutes while I ran up to our apartment to grab extra money. I came back down and found my then-three-year-old sidled up on a stool behind the counter, playing on the clerk's phone. I spoke so little Korean that the clerk and I communicated wordlessly when I picked her up, but the social contract transcended language. I found comfort and trust in being able to predict how people will behave.

This sense of social contract is part of a wider, national willingness to think as one—and another way it plays out is in how quickly everyone (I mean, *everyone!*) will fall in line to try the cool new thing. I've never seen people queue up to follow the hottest trends faster than in Seoul. One summer, Taiwanese castella cakes were in vogue, and I kid you not, three of those shops sprang up on the main drag near my house inside of a month, each one with long lines in front of them. (How do you even secure loans to open shops that fast?) Before castella cakes, it was churros. After castella cakes, it was coated almonds. The pervasiveness of a trend in Korea, once it's taken root, is undeniable. So when a popular trend develops, Koreans seem to follow the trend without thinking twice about it. "Everyone else is doing it" is a big energy.

It's a tremendous market advantage to have the whole country's buy-in, at scale, when there is something that demands national-scale cooperation, like fighting a pandemic or building for the Olympics. Unlike what happened in other host countries as they undertook the mammoth task of preparing to host the games, preparations for the 2018 Pyeongchang Winter Games went smoothly. In 2020, South Korea's already world-class healthcare system mobilized with impressive speed in response to the coronavirus pandemic, following lessons learned from its 2015 battle against MERS. When the COVID-19 vaccine became widely available, 90 percent of Koreans were vaccinated within seven months.[31] Through this and other types of responsiveness, casualties in South Korea have been a tiny fraction of the devastating losses experienced elsewhere, with cumulative deaths per capita forty times lower than in the U.S. and the UK.[32]

The other side of these achievements is the unrelenting

pressure to look and behave like everyone else, illustrating how even as Korea pushes to the forefront of modernity, its culture can hang on to priorities of conformity from the tight-knit communities of its agrarian days. Sociologists believe compressed economic growth also adds to the pressure of constantly caring about what other people think. So when something brings you individual shame, it can feel as if you've brought shame to your entire community. A former South Korean president[33] and a recent Seoul mayor[34] both died by suicide after misconduct accusations surfaced—corruption allegations and sexual harassment allegations, respectively. CEOs and others in positions of leadership have also died by suicide after learning they'd be publicly shamed. And these kinds of ends are not limited to people in power.

In my first month on the ground in Seoul, a demographic researcher tried to explain to me why teenagers killed themselves in South Korea at a rate that leads the developed world.[35] Suicide is the leading cause of death among teens, and eleven- to fifteen-year-olds report the highest amount of stress out of thirty developed nations.[36] The researcher blamed it on a society that just hasn't fully grown up, or perhaps grew up too fast—skipping a crucial period of transition, of "societal adolescence." After all, South Korea went from a developing state to one of the world's top ten economies with staggering speed, and much of that growth was spring-loaded from the top: state infrastructural investment, nationalization of key industries, and public spending on education. Humans simply may not adapt that fast. "It's kind of alarming, actually," Kim Mee Suk, the researcher at the

Korea Institute for Health and Social Affairs, told me. If the country couldn't guarantee the young people's happiness when they reached adulthood, then the future, he predicted, would be "really dark." During the time I lived in Seoul, I grew accustomed to people who made mistakes going on TV and bowing deeply (the most deferential kind of bow), apologizing to the rest of the country for not "doing their best" (that's the literal translation).

It makes sense that the simultaneously forward and backward birthplace of K-beauty is a place in which beauty norms are the most potentially punishing. They exist within a fast-paced collective culture that emphasizes harmony and not straying from the mean. In the effort to keep up with everyone else—in education, with wealth, with status—acceptable appearance is a minimum. And something, apparently, completely within an individual's control.

"What choice do they really have? When you are rewarded for your appearance and also punished if you have a poor appearance," says Heather Willoughby. Since the 1990s, she has taught at Ewha Womans University, an elite all-girls university considered to be the Wellesley of Korea. She's guided generations of girls who have come through her classes. Each year, she notes, the number of female undergraduates who say they've already had plastic surgery has gone up. "Young women do not have any confidence in themselves and are not pleased with themselves as they are—their personality or their accomplishments in school or any other level of achievement. I was working with one of my classes, to find [the students'] patterns of success. What are they good at?

What are they accomplished at? And some of them at first had a really hard time thinking even of just, like, little things."

I listened to Heather and thought, *Doing the work to keep up, to fit in, and to compete?* Those *are* accomplishments. A series of them. They're just so expected that they don't count.

~

CHAPTER 6

Selfie-Surveillance

I n the years just before I moved to Korea, I covered technology and culture, exploring how our modern-day tools were transforming the way we live and who we are. It was the early 2010s and I reported on a then-newfangled dating app that commodified people by letting us swipe left or swipe right on images of potential partners.[1] Another time, I experimented with wearing a camera on my lapel that shot surreptitious photos every two minutes, providing a real-time log of everything I encountered throughout the day, unbeknownst to the people being captured.[2] I wondered aloud, on the radio and online, how our brains were being modified as we relied more on smart virtual personal assistants powered by machine learning.[3] Sometime during my tech reporting years, a couple of tourists in Australia followed GPS directions on a road that turned to gravel, then thick mud, then right into the Pacific Ocean because they over-relied on the glitchy device.[4] I can picture it: the water, cold and glinty, and their car, glugging into it.

That's the thing, isn't it? We casually adopt new tech

tools without considering how they might end up altering our lives in the years ahead. By the time we do, it's often too late. We're hooked. I know the legacy platforms of Web 2.0—the social internet—are extractive and destructive, yet I have trouble opting out of the ones that rule my days now—they're too ingrained in my daily life. I keep up with news and encounter new ideas from my Twitter feed. Facebook groups are the primary means by which my elementary school parent community keeps in touch, while WhatsApp (another Facebook product) is the communications platform of choice at preschool. The problem is fundamental. "The only solution to make the internet better is to prevent companies like Facebook from getting quite so big in the first place," the internet culture writer Rebecca Jennings has observed.[5] Awareness and forethought on the front end was the way to avoid present-day predicaments, and it didn't happen.

Could the same be said for other technologies, like the ones designed to augment—and alter—reality and humans? When I repatriated to Los Angeles in late 2018, I created a new beat for NPR: The Future.[6] I intended it as a response to how news cycles were mostly concerned with only the short term. On the future beat, we'd explore reality, but from the year 2050. This led to lots of ribbing from my fellow NPR teammates. *Elise Hu, reporting from . . . The FUTURE*, my colleague Nate would say, in a deep Voice of God. My editorial team ultimately tried to be in on the joke ourselves, naming a video series about the way our brains and bodies were changing with an eponymous rhyme: Future You, with Elise Hu.

Computers have already migrated from our desktops into

our pockets and into our homes. Increasingly they're moving into our bodies. So to consider the future, I spent a year as a human test subject, eventually wearing several hundred electrodes on my head over that period to try out various brain-assistive devices. I wore electrodes and slept in a lab on the campus of the University of New Mexico so scientists could analyze my sleep, to see how our memories can be enhanced with something called transcranial direct current stimulation.[7] In a Houston lab, I wore electrodes so I could power robotic legs, an exoskeleton, using my thoughts.[8] For weeks, at home in California, I wore different electrodes and zapped myself in the motor cortex with tiny bursts of electricity to see if I could improve my vertical leap.[9]

The goal in guinea-pigging was to demonstrate the various technologies that might be mainstream and integrated thirty years from now, as part of augmenting our corporeal selves into cyborgs. Or at least faster, better, stronger, boosted humans. And more crucially, to consider the thorny ethical questions that flowed from these developments, wrestling with them now rather than later. Technologies allow us to chase that humanist goal of being more godlike, but whose hands control those technologies and their data? We asked how businesses or governments or other powerful interests might co-opt what usually begins in research labs to help humans, with inventions originally created for therapeutic purposes, and distort them for their own moneymaking purposes. We framed the work on a spectrum of potential change. Upgrades tend to move from ideas that assist our bodies to those that augment our bodies, to those that outright alter the fundamentals of what makes us human.

Korea Is Hypermodern

It didn't occur to me until writing these pages that the medicalized beauty industry of South Korea was promising—and delivering—human augmentation already, and at scale. In the same way we normalize expectations for faster internet or more fuel-efficient cars, Korean culture accepts the upgrading of our specs on the outer surfaces of the body. In America, we typically hear about specs when describing a new laptop or gadget. Modern South Koreans use the term in that way, too, but they also understand *specs* as a shorthand in conversation about people. It's a way to compare one another and talk about your own improvement work. Specs was originally a term for the criteria used to judge a potential spouse, popularized based on the categories Korean matchmaking firms use to evaluate single people.[10] For a woman, examples of specs that define "womanliness" include but are not limited to being under 50 kilograms (110 pounds), wearing at least a C cup bra, exhibiting a thin body and a small and white face, always wearing makeup, being hairless under your arms and on your legs, and possessing *aegyo*, or cuteness.

"Korea is the first country to enter a truly unapologetic state of hypermodernity," Korea-based sociologist Michael Hurt told me. "In hypermodernity . . . you have different kinds of things that are replaceable." In the context of the human body, "You can mix and match yourself, like your avatar." Half ethnically Korean and half Black, Hurt argues that his birthplace, the United States, tends to enter hypermodernity in fits and starts. "It still does this 'No, Photoshop is bad, be yourself, don't fall into the trap.' But you can't escape this shit! Korean society says, 'Fuck it! You look better, so go do that.' If I can make my meat face look like the better, hyper-Photoshopped digital version of my face, why wouldn't I do that? It's not THE FUTURE," he says, affecting the exact same deep register my colleagues previously used to poke fun at me. "It's right here in Korea today. Koreans get beat up for looking fake, they're body-shamed, but basically Korea is doing what everybody will be doing very soon."

In the process of becoming a "hypermodern" society, two types of technology feed off each other in a self-reinforcing loop. One is surveillance technology. Think ubiquitous apps tracking and inhaling data about us from our mobile devices, or the CCTV cameras standard in Korean public and private spaces. The second type comprises the technologies of self-improvement, be it skin smoothing, hair removal or transplants, or the upgrading of body parts. Appearance ideals and the labor required to meet them are taking shape at the nexus of those two forms.

Instagram and TikTok guide us on how to look and even how to live. Dermatologists, surgeons, and beauty workers shape us into the looks we seek. In Korea, we see how the long-established heteronormative notion that women chase beauty to appeal to the male gaze can be overshadowed by something more complicated: a technological gaze.

Technology of Surveillance

South Korea is a land of superlatives: the highest educational attainment in the developed world,[11] the most working hours per week,[12] and the most wired place on earth.[13] Its world-leading internet speeds and wide broadband penetration were early on the scene and remained unsurpassed for years. South Koreans spend an average of four and a half hours a day on their phones.[14] Among eighteen- to twenty-four-year-olds, smartphone penetration is 98 percent.[15] Internet addiction rehab centers first sprouted in South Korea.[16]

The country's advanced internet began with long-term thinking. In 1994, the birth year of the World Wide Web, the Korean government began investing in something the United States still lacks—a nationwide broadband network, instead of a patchwork of networks from private companies.[17] That kind of longtermism meant Korea could fully deploy said network by 1998. The government's top-down IT strategy turbocharged investment and bureaucratic heft toward an expansion of fast broadband speeds, while aggressive competition among private internet providers drove down prices. Korea has built-in advantages in this quest for connectivity, too—it's a relatively small country with high population density. This allows for a lot of households to be clustered within close range of internet providers' infrastructure.

By 2000, Korea's broadband penetration rate was the highest in the world, remaining so until 2006, and still outperforming more affluent countries today.[18] Getting online in those early days meant you could flirt or fight or connect with anyone else online without regard for how you looked or how you sounded—we were not represented by our images, we were made-up handles in chat rooms. But increased speed became the substrate for a visual digital media explosion at the start of the new millennium. Korea's capacity to handle high-bandwidth video and apps fuels a rich online life and culture for everything from PC gaming (Korean gamers are international celebs) to digital organizing to online shopping. The country's internet blasts digital imagery at its populace faster and better and with greater ubiquity than I could really even comprehend, so accustomed was I to mediocre broadband speeds in America.

The visual reinforcement system of beautiful people in K-culture and advertising runs nonstop when you move about the city. Seoul recently installed the largest LED screens on earth in the Gangnam district, wrapping them around a mall.[19] Our "primitive" brains are "under constant assault and control by our culture," wrote psychologist Judy Scheel, not specifically about Korea, in an essay straightforwardly titled "Culture Dictates the Standard of Beauty." "Culture and media do succeed at deciding what is or ought to be visually desirable, regardless of our own intuitive draw or what we really want or find attractive."[20]

These screens give a sense of surveillance, but there are cameras doing *actual*, near constant surveillance, too. Security cameras can be spotted in every elevator, outside every building entrance, on the street corners, on the dashboards of cars. Seoul is the fourth most-surveilled city in the world, outside of China, as ranked by number of CCTV cameras per square mile. Each square mile of Seoul has 333 CCTV cameras installed inside it, on average.[21] And this says nothing of Seoul's ubiquitous *hidden* camera problem, which I'll get to later.

Long before cameras and the internet played their surveilling function, beauty served as a gatekeeper. Since beauty is so conflated with goodness, societies use it to decide who's good, who's in, and who's bad, who's out. Repeatedly seeing what's considered beautiful has its way of burrowing the way we are supposed to look into our subconscious. It launches cascading judgments—of ourselves and others.

For example, psychologist Nancy Etcoff found we tend to exaggerate even minute fluctuations in our own looks, to our detriment.[22] As physical beings, we vary in tiny ways from day to day or even hour to hour. We bloat. We sag. We flake. We get blemishes. These may be small impermanent alterations, but in our minds, those changes can undermine our confidence in ways an equally minor fluctuation in mental agility or strength do not.

Conversely, when we look at others, we make real-time judgments of their appearance, always sizing them up. Our innate beauty detectors scan the environment like radar: we can encounter another person's face for a fraction of a second and rate its perceived beauty.[23] An experiment Etcoff recounts in her book *Survival of the Prettiest: The Science of Beauty* showed that respondents gave someone else's face the same rating after a longer inspection as they did in an initial half-second encounter. And long after we forget many important details about a person, our initial response to their appearance, our judgment as to whether they are beautiful or not stays in our memory.

The digital era ushered in a heavier barrage of images, social media feeds channeling our desires and setting desirability standards. "A crowd-pleasing image becomes a mold, and a beauty is followed by her imitator, and then by the imitator of her imitator," writes Etcoff.[24] Social platforms, driven by ad-based business models, are exceedingly good at blasting us with the imitators of imitators of crowd-pleasing images, teaching us what to find beautiful—and then enforcing and reinforcing those standards. We then, crucially, turn that critical eye on ourselves.

Panopticon is shorthand now, but it describes experiencing social control from the inside due to the constant *possibility* of surveillance. Picture a prison circular in nature, with each individual cell separated from the other. A guard tower looms in the middle of the ring of cells. First introduced by English philosopher Jeremy Bentham in the late 1800s, the idea is that from his perch the guard can see every cell. The prisoners, meanwhile, can't see each other. Because the individual prisoner has no relationship to anything else, she relates to the guard tower whether there's someone there or not. Even though he can't possibly watch everyone at the same time, the prisoners *could* be observed at any time; therefore, she always behaves as if she's being observed. That's all that is needed for control. The result is, we are constantly watching each other, aware of how we're seen, and judging ourselves as we judge one another.

French philosopher Michel Foucault advanced the panopticon beyond the prison system, considering it a symbol of social control that extends into our everyday lives. In *Discipline and Punish*, he argues that we internalize the tower guard's authority. Since the prisoner believes she is always being surveilled, she obeys laws because she self-imposes them. For example, we stop at red lights even on an empty road where there are no police, cameras, or other cars present.[25] The phenomenon is a "cruel, ingenious cage" of surveillance, a mechanism that disciplines even in its absence.[26]

Feminist scholars used the Foucault framework to explain the way beauty ideals are inculcated in women. Even at an early age, women are feminized—imbued with beliefs about what it is to look like and behave as a "girl." Since these expectations often ask women to prune away the natural, and maintain a perfect softness, hairlessness, and prettiness, they can alienate us from our bodies. As British art critic and documentarian John Berger observed in his 1972 work, *Ways of Seeing*: "She has to survey everything she is and everything she does because how she appears to others, and ultimately how she appears to men, is of crucial importance for what is normally thought of as the success of her life. Her own sense of being in herself is supplanted by a sense of being appreciated as herself by another."[27] We learn our femininity, internalize it, and behave accordingly to maintain it. And whether someone is watching or not, we're conscious of how we appear to adhere to this expectation.

Celebrities, whose livelihoods rely on their public image, have long been the standard-bearers of performed femininity. Korea's celebrity fascination is said to be stronger than Japan's or China's, fueling fierce followings and mimicry. Attractive Korean celebrities are referred to as *wanpan* stars, a term referring to how they can single-handedly drive brand sales. Actress Gianna Jun's look from the 2014 TV soap *My Love from the Star*, for example, is credited for Saint Laurent's Rouge Pur Couture No. 52, a coral-pink shade of lip tint, selling out across South Korea and China after a rumor spread that she wore that shade on the show. It turned out she hadn't actually worn that shade at all.[28] I wonder if the intensity of idol worship in Korea itself could be an outgrowth of Korea's status as the first truly wired nation. Technology may bring us together digitally, but it also distances us from one another physically. It can create a sense of dislocation. Are more young people growing up feeling unseen due to the distance created by technology? Does this lead them to project their dreams on distant entertainers?

An unspoken precedent seems to exist in which the rich and famous, by virtue of profiting off their fame, are less entitled to privacy than the rest of us regular people. But in the digital age, we've all come to occupy a weird quasi-celebrity niche. All of us are potentially in front of cameras as much as we want—and even when we don't want. On social networks, or what the Koreans call SNS (social network services), feedback from the audience is immediate. Viewers are also producers, and the boundary between subject and object is easily blurred. A social web makes up multiple mirrors. Beauty has a theatrical aspect in which we perform ourselves, critic Mimi Thi Nguyen observes, which suggests its "fundamentally social character," and appearance norms get set and reinforced at every step, on our addictive social comparison platforms.[29]

The human tendency to compare ourselves to one another drives feelings and behavior. It says, "Be like everyone else, but better."[30] Evolutionary psychologists believe comparisons are adaptive behaviors important to our survival and can foster the human need to belong.[31] It's helpful for the species to self-evaluate so we can, say, share how a newly discovered food should be eaten. Or so we as a group can find access to resources and mates.

Social comparisons, for most of human history, happened among far smaller circles—those in our immediate, in-person groups. In the social media age, the comparison pool potentially includes everyone and anyone, and a body of research has found social media comparisons generate feelings of inferiority[32] and envy and correlate with depression, anxiety, and lower self-evaluations.[33] This is especially true for people who use social media the most.[34] On the omniscient social web, our phone cameras, TikTok, and Instagram act as the guards in the tower. The internet becomes the ultimate panopticon.

I'm an elder millennial, or, as I like to introduce myself in Konglish, a millennial ajumma. My adolescence happened without social networking and then my adulthood became defined by constant visual self-surveillance. There is my digital "representation" via my online presence, and my actual self, the person I am when I'm alone in my car or in the quiet of the night, unseen. The digital avatar doesn't have to look quite like me—it can look a lot better. Constant technological improvement means ever more ways to filter our digital projections. Capabilities have advanced from the olden days of Photoshopping still images to real-time filtering of videos, snaps, and selfies. Even live video conferencing software, like Zoom, offers to "Touch Up My Appearance" with subtle skin-smoothing glam filters.

The way these two different selves interact is evolving as cyberspace merges with meat space; the line between our digital filters and real-life makeup already blurred. In

2021, an artificial intelligence and augmented reality company teamed up with Zamface, a popular South Korean video platform, to launch a new service: a virtual lipstick try-on powered by artificial intelligence. The technology uses machine learning to allow users to try on dozens of shades in seconds. The company is called, fittingly, Perfect Corp.[35]

Bodies and technologies are also informing our identity formation in ever deeper and more complex ways. In the social web's early days, construction of the digital self would follow the lead of the authentic self, trying to present a facsimile of it. By the 2010s, a decade into Facebook and Twitter and in the early years of Instagram, tech-forward, appearance-obsessed Korea exemplified the opposite approach. Online identities were primary. And their primacy wasn't confined to young people. Adults also privileged their online personas over their meat-space selves. A friend of mine in Seoul met her girlfriends for lunch in a tony Seoul neighborhood, and afterward, the ladies got together for a group photo to share their lunch online, as people do. Because my friend came to lunch unkempt, the other women asked her not to be in the photograph at all. Her appearance passed muster for sharing a meal in real life but was considered unacceptable for the photo documenting said meal.

On the internet, we are encouraged to LARP (live action role play) our lives. If metaverses take off as anticipated, we could start our relations with the aesthetic of computer animation and skip over the step of an authentic human model entirely. For example, one of Korea's buzziest influencers, Rozy, is not a human at all. She's entirely computer generated, with an uncanny likeness to a real human being.[36] Like so much technology, computer-led standards carry potential pitfalls. Will aesthetics that begin in the world of imagination overturn the status quo or reinforce it?

～

The relationship between sexual desirability and beauty ideals dates back millennia. And it has nearly always come with some form of constriction for women. In aristocratic China, young women had to earn the privilege of disabling themselves into having three-inch feet, because it was a show of status and also of sexual desirability. In pursuit of an impossibly narrow waist, Victorian women laced themselves into tight corsets that restricted breathing and could permanently damage the skeletal structure of the wearer. The long and convoluted history of the corset didn't come to an end until the 1920s. The feminist writer Sandra Lee Bartky argued in the 1970s that appearance ideals for the perfect feminine body reflect society's obsession with keeping women in check so men can appear more powerful. "The . . . project of femininity is a 'setup,'" she argued. "It requires such radical and extensive measures of bodily transformation that virtually every woman who gives herself to it is destined in some degree to fail."[37] Before her, Karl Marx introduced "false consciousness," the idea that under the right exploitative conditions, people will unconsciously go along with value systems that don't serve them. They'd perceive their world and be in denial of its oppressive aspects. Originally applied to the labor force, the theory goes like this: The ruling class manipulates the working class into believing their value lies in financial productivity. Workers then become invested in their own oppression. They might avoid rest or fail to prioritize non-money-earning interests, even if those things would improve their lives. Feminist writers such as Bartky have applied that to beauty, arguing heterosexual women are essentially "duped" into making ourselves sexually appealing to men. She believed if we ever saw the programming, we'd reject it.[38]

But . . . would we? Especially in a beautyscape like Korea, women are not deluded about the rewards of beauty. In a capitalist hustle culture, there actually are tangible rewards. By beautifying themselves, women are making economically rational choices to turn the self into an investment opportunity. Beauty work can be separated from sexual desirability, as this is not a wholly sexual pursuit. It can empower, economically, or as a form of self-protection and expression (notably for transgender women, or among former North Koreans who lived under a repressive government regime). It can also offer promise, as we work to transform ourselves and attain our aspirational imagined selves. Remember Modern Girls and Factory Girls who used then-radical beauty trends as a tool of resistance and a way to transcend class and economic condition? Self-objectification happens all the time, bringing us benefits beyond having sex appeal. Things like "a positive sense of self, a moral payoff (as the beauty ideal becomes an ethical ideal), and many practices have social goods attached to them," British Philosopher Heather Widdows notes. "These are not simply narcissistic pleasures, or the false pleasures of man-pleasing, but are real wins."[39]

No one can realistically live up to high appearance standards, but we may want to pursue them all the same, as part of the human striving toward betterment, on the one hand, and the human need to belong. Our striving and our reaching for ways to feel connected are wonderful human behaviors. But as with so many of our desires, business interests are quick to co-opt them, capitalizing on this striving or our fear of not fitting in to sell us more stuff. When so much of appearance-related labor is cloaked in self-care or "self-empowerment," it makes it difficult to separate external changes from soul-nourishing betterment of our minds and spirits. And if we can't tell it for ourselves, then critiquing anyone else's pursuits presents a trap. If a choice is freely made, we tend to grant it presumption against critique. Who are we to criticize someone else's empowerment?

The paradox, then, is this: The financial and psychological drain created by the beauty industry is, for many of us, exhausting. But working to get to our ideal self or even just temporarily getting closer to it is alluring and psychologically affirming, at least in the short run. The pleasure and feeling of power that we derive from improving our outsides may be deceptive and fleeting, but they are also very real.

Whose Gaze, Anyway?

To the extent modern Korean beauty standards flow from entertainment culture, men dream up the worlds and women they want to see. They are the power brokers and producers of K-pop and K-drama. They are coming up with "cultural technology" commodities, whether they are the triangle dance formations of K-pop groups, concert tours, or the ideal length of skirts seen onstage and in videos. Men remain the people with power in every corner of Korea's entrenched patriarchy.

But as we settle into this hyperconnected hyper-visual future, the technological gaze is most worrying to me. This gaze is an algorithmically determined set of ideal traits for our facial and body parts that social platforms feed us through the content we scroll.[40] It represents a power shift from an external, male-judging gaze to a self-policing narcissistic gaze, something noted by Rosalind Gill in her book, *Gender and the Media*.[41] The self-policing tech gaze creates demand for what we should look like and also feeds it, thanks to the attention economy that drives competition among the biggest tech companies.

Profit-driven platforms are optimized to pick the right content to get you to spend longer on their platforms so they can serve you more ads, since their revenue models rely on advertising money. Their algorithms use their vast amounts of data—how long you look at certain images, with which accounts you have the most engagement—to design ways to capture and keep your attention. The machine learns from the data and then builds on itself to keep giving us the content that lures us in. As tech ethicist Tristan Harris says, the concern is not that artificial intelligence overwhelms human strengths, it's that it overwhelms human *weaknesses*. So much data is available and machine learning is now so advanced that it's beyond what the humans who made it can fully understand, unsure exactly why they serve up what they do.

The wild success of social media companies in constructing our self-surveillance is well known, and not effectively regulated or resisted by users. In September 2021, *The Wall Street Journal* got its hands on leaked internal documents from Instagram parent company Meta (Facebook's new name) describing Instagram's harmful effects on young people. "Thirty-two percent of teen girls said that when they feel bad about their bodies, Instagram made them feel worse," the documents revealed. "Comparisons on Instagram can change how young women view and describe themselves." Instagram created a suffocating economy that rewards users in likes for their appearance and presentation, fueling a need for approval for how they look, and alongside it, feelings of anxiety.[42]

It is not a human gaze making them feel that way. It's in the design of our tech platforms.[43] This feeling represents a "deeper form of exploitation than objectification—one in which the objectifying male gaze is internalized to form a new disciplinary regime. In this regime, power is not imposed from above or from the outside, but constructs our very subjectivity," as Gill, the British scholar, puts it.[44]

The prevailing beauty ideal is etched by showing what's possible and what we can do. Then it's normalized as people attain it digitally or physically. After that, the ideal can be narrowed again, since not everyone gets to be beautiful. Standards for what's in can dynamically evolve in order to keep others out.

On the apps, filters that soften photos or smooth blemishes used to be opt-in. Gradually, companies "are in an arms race for who can beautify the image that comes back to you in the mirror," Tristan Harris told CNN.[45] And to keep their hold on your attention, apps from China and some others are now adding a subtle beauty filter by default, without asking if you want them to first. "They have an incentive to plump your cheeks, plump your lips, plump your eyes so you have a nicer self-image," Harris said. So "let's say Instagram realizes this is bad for kids' mental health. They can't—they won't stop that unless the other companies stop as well . . . TikTok actually beautifies photos without even asking users about it. They beautify by just two or three percent—invisible—and that's the kind of arms race that we're in."

Ultimately, the technological gaze "is inhuman, unforgiving, critical, clinical, and cold."[46] It also never stops demanding. It creates problems we were previously unaware of and suddenly require technological help to fix, be it thighs that touch or skin that's too uneven/wrinkled/dark/[insert issue here]. "For all its talk of 'connecting people,' image-based social media has done more to disconnect us from ourselves, from our essential nature, from true beauty," beauty critic and writer Jessica DeFino writes.[47] True beauty is not something we can buy off a shelf.

What happens if a "technological gaze" becomes dominant? Present-day social media already places a new pressure on everyone to remain forever photogenic, forever young, forever thin and fit, forever wrinkle-free. Our bodies would be projects to be worked on, forever. Depending on our biology, achieving the "ideal" can often only be achieved at the hands of outside technology, like a filter or a scalpel. It's a surreal, self-perpetuating cycle. Cameras get sharper and the places we can "perform" on the internet and the time we spend on our devices are increasing, alongside the technologies to surgically enhance our appearance. Theoretically, the standards of beauty could be constantly intensified, the bar of "perfection" continually raised, exacerbating the appearance improvement arms race. The more we collectively work to look a certain way, argues Widdows, the more the range of acceptable appearance narrows.[48]

So much self-discipline and technological enhancement is already expected of our bodies. Eventually we could become "a collection of disparate body parts to be endlessly worked on or even replaced as part of the plenitude of consumer choice," in the words of Estella Tincknell.[49]

Speaking of choice: The same young people who spoke of Instagram's degradations also kept returning to the service, the leaked Facebook data showed. "They often feel 'addicted' and know that what they're seeing is bad for their mental health but feel unable to stop themselves," the company's documents explained. After all, Instagram is where they are expected to be seen. Having a visual social presence online "is both a choice and not a choice at all," in the words of culture writer Megan Garber.[50] *A choice and not a choice.* The same can be said for the entire continuum of beauty work that comes with being seen. From shaving our legs to shaving our jaws.

~

I wrestle with these ideas for the same reason I wanted to cover THE FUTURE when I came home from Seoul. If hypermodern Korea is the direction we're going, what should we know now that we will wish we did later? The near future will take as a given the idea that self-improvement is possible and bodies and brains are malleable with the aid of ever-improving science and tech. K-beauty brands show off their wares at CES in the Las Vegas Convention Center alongside the Korean electronics brands you'd expect to be there. While Samsung's unveiling curved televisions and LG's making dry cleaning devices for your home closets, AmorePacific is right there with them, showcasing wands to give yourself at-home laser or UV light facials. Just as I found with brain-enhancement devices during my year of guinea-pigging the future, the quest to augment human bodies tends to move from bulky external tools, to extensions or implants, to actual adaptation of our physical "specs."

The technological gaze keeps feeding us an ever-evolving, ever-narrowing beauty ideal. With enough money, we can use ever-improving artificial implants, injections, or surgery to look however we want, fueling a filter-to-filler pipeline. What happens when the aesthetic enhancement technologies are so mature that realizing our "perfect" visions is made possible? South Korea's "improvement quarter," a square-mile district in Seoul, points the way.[51]

CHAPTER 7

~

The Improvement Quarter

C rossing south over the Han River, which bisects Seoul, will land you in Gangnam (*Gang* means river, *nam* means south). A little smaller than the island of Manhattan, it's the Seoul district that many of us know thanks to Psy. In Gangnam, streets widen to ten lanes and are lined with glossy multistory mixed-use towers, almost always with a franchise coffee shop on the ground floor. Gangnam includes abundant high-end residential properties, to be sure, but that's not all. Apgujeong, perhaps its wealthiest ward, has so many luxury retail and fancy car showrooms that it resembles a city-sized mall. At night, some of the buildings look like elaborate art installations, their facades changing colors every ten seconds, putting on free light shows for the crawling traffic out front.

Gangnam's posh Apgujeong and Sinsa wards are also home to an astounding concentration of South Korea's world-leading plastic surgery businesses. This has earned it nicknames like the Beauty Belt, the Improvement Quarter, or simply, Plastic Surgery Street (a misnomer—the area reaches far beyond a single street). In 2020, according to the National Tax Service of Korea, there were 1,008 total plastic surgery clinics in the country. Of them, 538 were located in Seoul, and around 400 of those were in Gangnam. Signs on the sides of Gangnam buildings list different plastic surgery practices, often occupying every floor of fifteen-story buildings. Their English names sound like promises: Elevate. Solutions. Reborn. Feel So Good.

Elevate is apt enough. For most of us the only way to even get close to the unachievable ideals set by visual culture is through digital filters or actual *fillers*—straight up changing the physical body. Korea's hypercharged industrial and biomedical sectors have responded to the comparative, competitive tendencies amplified by social media by making enhancements to the surface of the body—improving your specs—more affordable, expansive, and attainable than anywhere else.

American plastic surgeons and dermatologists coined the term *Snapchat dysmorphia* to describe young patients who want cosmetic fixes so they look more like they do in filtered selfies. These apps "are making us lose touch with reality because we expect to look perfectly primped and filtered in real life as well," physicians warned in the *JAMA Facial Plastic Surgery* journal.[1] Korean surgeons say they had been doing this for their patients for years, without pathologizing it as a syndrome. As the line between smartphone fantasy and reality blurs, one self tries to become more like the other—the synthetic version.

When it comes to cosmetic surgery in Korea, it's "not

even a moral question [of] is it good is it bad, it simply is," said Heather Willoughby, a professor at Korea's Ewha Womans University. The promise here is that your physical self can continually incrementally improve or retain its youth, gravity be damned. In a time of ever-expanding pressure to correct new areas of the body, Seoul is where you can go to get your armpit colorized, your asshole bleached, even your forehead or the back of your skull shaved down to be rounded just as you like. The city's surgeons are expert at applying the principles of incrementally improving tech specs to the body. South Korea can correct everybody, down to features you wouldn't even think anyone would bother altering.

It is probably not surprising that the journey to correction often begins on a screen. GangnamUnni, like a rival app, Babitalk, is an elaborate online emporium to shop for cosmetic fixes and get connected to discounts and doctors. It's like a car-buying app, but for surgery and injections. First you choose an icon of the body part that's not satisfying to you:

Face
Skin
Hair and hairline
Nose
Eyes
Forehead
Mouth
Breast
Waistline and stomach

Genitals
Eyebrows and lashes and body hair
Teeth
Ears
Etc. (though I can't imagine what isn't already covered
here)

Each area then has subcategories, not unlike what you'll
see in car buying, with all the makes, models, and features of
cars. Or going to wine.com and having to choose between
regions and endless varieties. Let's say you choose *face*. This
part of the body is then broken down into a dizzying kalei-
doscope of highly specific regions. They prompt you to complete a sentence: "My problem is . . ."

Cheek fat
Double chin
Jawline
Forehead volume
Temples
Cheekbones
Too little cheek fat
Overbite
More specific cheekbone areas (too high or too low)
Chin
Frenulum length
Swollen face
Head shape
Dents in the back of skull

"None of the above" is not an option, naturally.

On the day I downloaded the app, it was offering a post-Korean SAT promotion for high school graduates. "Special prices for 18-year-old men and women!" All you have to do is provide proof that you'd taken the high-stakes national exam, the Suneung, on the day it was most recently given.

The array of options reminded me that self-improvement technology is really no different from other consumerist apps we use to work faster or live more "optimized" lives—online retail apps, grocery apps and the like. Or any other place where you're invited to choose from a slew of options in order to make yourself better, or your life easier. As technology improves, so does the ease with which we buy things and the ease with which we can fix ourselves. Cosmetic offerings are getting less expensive and less invasive—more micro—as surgeries and cosmetic engineering advance. What used to take plastic surgery to adjust can now be changed with injectables, lasers, or "threading" instead of a knife.

In late 2016, on a day the air turned a biting cold, as South Korean winters often are, a cab dropped me off in Gangnam at Oracle Clinic, one of Korea's most well known dermatology and fix-up destinations. I had finally found a way to work my K-beauty curiosities into my NPR reporting, nearly two years into my stint in Seoul. A team of whimsical co-workers had helped me develop a travel video series called "Elise Tries," a perfect journalistic excuse to try something newfangled at that time: pore vacuuming. I'd yet to visit a dermatologic mega-clinic, or a medical spa of any kind, and my face maybe needed it. The pollution and the dry air of

Seoul had given me a persistently ruddy appearance and dry patches on the sides of my nose. For both my face and my body, this was an ideal time for my visit, because I was pregnant again, but at seventeen weeks, I'd fought past the intermittent hurling of the first trimester. I was ready for a bit of pampering.

A few weeks earlier, I had met a fellow Texan named Joyce when we were seated beside each other at a wedding reception. It had taken me nearly two years in Seoul to establish strong enough bonds to even be invited to weddings at all, and these friendships were making life in Seoul feel cozier, more like home. A Korean American, Joyce wrote about beauty for the site Refinery29 and talked up her skincare routine during the reception. Intrigued, I followed up and she agreed to bring me along to try the facial called an aqua peel in Korean, which she more accurately described as pore vacuuming. I hoped the procedure would magically clear and even out my skin tone without a twice-daily multistep routine like Joyce's.

Oracle is a three-story labyrinth of cosmetic enhancement in a space that used to be a Kinko's. As a dermatology clinic, it specializes in injectables and laser therapies rather than surgeries. Hundreds of people cycle in and out every day for touch-ups and treatments with the nonchalance of someone stopping by the nail salon for a mani-pedi. While I was there, a manager told me that many of their domestic patients come in weekly, if not more often.

Oracle Clinic's lobby bustles like a popular restaurant on a Saturday night. At each of the six or seven faux-wood tables in the lobby, a potential client sat across from a business-like woman, the two of them huddled over forms and pamphlets offering the menu of available procedures. The Oracle staffers are "consultants" or "coordinators" who conduct patient intakes and discuss treatment options after you fill out your initial form. As was true of the other beauty clinics I'd later visit, Oracle's intake form includes a black-and-white outline of a face and the outline of a body. You simply draw on the face or body the areas you'd like to fix. It reminded me of a persistent rumor about a sorority house's hazing in college, in which the upperclassmen took Sharpies to the bodies of the freshmen pledges and marked on their bodies the spots they needed to tone up.

My services at Oracle that day didn't fall under anything requiring a doctor or a nurse, but more medicalized cosmetic procedures were happening all around me. Women sat on benches along the marble-tiled walls, their hair pushed back with plastic headbands and their faces covered in thick cream, covered by a layer of Kirkland-brand plastic wrap. A staffer explained the white stuff is a numbing cream that is applied before injections such as Botox or filler.

Oracle is a known hub for medical tourism, surgery tourism, or what I'd describe as aesthetic enhancement vacations. Seoul's cosmetic surgery clinics were shutting their doors in the early aughts due to oversupply—too many surgeons, not enough patients. But in 2007, the Korea Tourism Organization sprang into action, establishing medical tourism as one of its focus areas for growth and one of the country's "strategic products."[2] Touting Korea's advancements, the skill of its surgeons, and competitive pricing of cosmetic surgery as a way to lure in medical tourists, the effort transformed

Gangnam's Improvement Quarter into a thriving attraction for aesthetic upgrades. Today, a Medical Tourism Support Center greets visitors at the Incheon International Airport, the entry point for the hundreds of thousands who visit South Korea for procedures each year.

In 2009, about 60,000 foreigners visited Korea for medical procedures.[3] By 2019, the number of medical tourists reached nearly half a million—an eightfold increase in a decade, after climbing steadily each year, according to numbers from the Korea Health Industry Development Institute.[4] Tourists made up an estimated third of all the plastic surgery business in Korea in 2014, a percentage that continued to climb until the coronavirus pandemic hit in 2020.[5] Oracle, like many other clinics, has previously partnered with hotels and restaurants to offer packages for tourists who came in for beautifying, much like how high-rolling gamblers get their accommodations comped in Vegas. Premier packages include perks like stretch limos for the ride from the hotel to the clinic.[6]

Just as it does for K-cosmetics and skincare, Korea's enormously popular entertainment industry serves as a running advertisement for its plastic surgery industry. Hallyu fans travel across the world to Seoul to get surgeries that will leave them looking more like their favorite Korean actors or pop stars, then embark on Hallyu tours during recovery. This "connection between popular culture, beauty, and marketing is not lost on South Korean governmental agencies," writes Sharon Heijin Lee, the research professor whose work focuses on Korean plastic surgery. The cosmetic surgery industry, she says, doesn't have to advertise because "Hallyu is their global advertising."[7]

The year before COVID-19, 40 percent of all foreign cosmetic surgery patients visiting Korea were Chinese, with Japanese patients comprising the second largest group at 26 percent. The United States, Thailand, and Vietnam rounded out the top five countries from which surgery tourists visited.[8] The growing popularity of Korean aesthetics has fueled Oracle's advancements into those countries themselves. The franchise has expanded to more than sixty branches throughout Asia, with locations in China, Japan, the Philippines, and elsewhere.

Even as Korean franchises like Oracle set up operations in other countries, Korea's Improvement Quarter still remains the regional destination for the newest, most advanced beautification procedures and some of the most skilled cosmetic surgeons in the world. Many of the private surgery clinics include in-house pharmacies, stem cell laboratories, and proprietary diagnostic machines offering 3D modeling of anticipated results. "Seoul, specifically Gangnam, is maybe the most mature plastic surgery market in the world," Los Angeles–based plastic surgeon Dr. Charles Hsu told me. "Definitely a much more mature market than Beverly Hills, in everything. In hypercompetitiveness. In specialization."

The abundance of surgeons and services drives prices to at cost or below; at Oracle in Seoul, an entire region of Botox treatment (for instance, the forehead area, or the frown line) is offered at as low as $30. It's available even cheaper at giant plastic surgery hospitals. In Beverly Hills, where Dr. Hsu ran

his practice for a decade before moving to Los Angeles' Koreatown, clinics easily charge $200 per region. A double eyelid
surgery in Seoul to achieve the shallow crease many East
Asians lack naturally is so common that discounted prices
for it can be as low as $300. U.S. providers can price the pro-
cedure, an upper eyelid blepharoplasty, ten times higher.

The largest hospitals and clinics exhaust enormous advertising budgets to keep patients flowing in. As a result, images of pretty faces are unavoidable in Gangnam—they seem
to glare at you from every direction. For years, inside the
subway stations serving the highest concentration of clinics,
the escalators were lined with floor-to-ceiling ads showing
one Korean woman's flawless face after another, after another.[9] They're accompanied by taglines like: "All the pretty
girls know." "Harmony of eyes, nose, and facial line." "Touch-up
surgeries are our specialty." In recent years, in response to
thousands of complaints from overwhelmed Seoulites writing in to say these irritating ads were promoting unrealistic
images of women, the Seoul Metropolitan Government came
up with regulations to reduce the cosmetic surgery ad blitz.
It banned before-and-after ads inside subway stations, for
example.

Which isn't to say the reminders to fix your face have
somehow disappeared. Aboveground, as soon as cars coast
off the bridge into the plastic surgery belt of Gangnam, it's
easy to spot signs in the windows: Before-and-after images
of women's faces. Close-ups of their noses, foreheads, chins.
I'll never forget one of my early trips to the ritzy Apgujeong
ward; as I emerged from the subway station escalator onto
the street, I looked up and spotted the only English words

emblazoned across the top of a chrome five-story building: *Cosmetic Vaginal Surgery Center.* That center specializes in laser sculpting ladies' inner labia in a way that "considers aesthetic sensibility," according to its literature.

The sheer volume of plastic surgery that takes place in the Improvement Quarter is nothing short of astounding. South Korea leads the world in cosmetic procedures relative to its population, based on the most recent numbers it provided to the International Society of Aesthetic Plastic Surgery.[10] It can also boast the most cosmetic surgeons per capita on Earth, according to a 2018 ISAPS survey. South Korea has twice as many plastic surgeons for its population as the United States, and 150 percent more surgeons than Brazil, the distant runner-up for surgeons per capita.[11]

Cosmetic surgery became a lucrative and competitive business for Korea around the turn of the twenty-first century, when the healthcare insurance system and regulatory climate changed such that the most lucrative practices for doctors focused on "surgical specialization, diagnostic tests, and the prescription of pharmaceuticals."[12] The state even supported the logic of bodily change as good citizenship by providing temporary tax breaks that could go toward cosmetic surgery.

By 2010, boosted by government support of the Hallyu wave and medical tourism, plastic surgery became normalized in everyday discussions and online forums and overwhelmingly accepted by the public. It's commonplace to see the bandaged, post-op faces of patients moving about Seoul. A 2020 Gallup Korea survey found that since the early 2000s, 70 percent of Koreans don't view cosmetic surgery as taboo.

There is nothing to hide about cosmetic surgery in Seoul, even for the body parts we usually hide.

Some numbers:

- One in four Korean mothers with daughters between the ages of twelve and sixteen have suggested plastic surgery to their daughters.[13]

- One in three women surveyed in a 2020 Gallup Korea poll, all between the ages of nineteen and thirty-nine, had undergone cosmetic surgery.[14] A 2019 study showed that the average age when Koreans got their first work done was twenty-three.[15]

- 59 percent of men in the same poll said they would get plastic surgery to improve their chances on the job market, a number that's shot up 30 percent since 1994.[16]

- 66 percent of women said they would undergo surgery if it improved their chances on the marriage market.[17]

Decades of advertising and a preponderance of pop culture—sometimes sponsored by plastic surgery clinics—reinforce the same narratives. Bodies are sites of surveillance and alteration—relentlessly observed and corrected. And superficial work on the body through medical interventions is rather routine. *Let Me In* is a reality game show like *The Biggest Loser*, but for plastic surgery makeover journeys. It ran for several seasons and was among the most widely viewed programs in South Korea. Each contestant on the show got a nickname—for example, Girl Who Looks Like Frankenstein, Woman Who Cannot Laugh, Flat-Chested Mother, or Monkey (a recurring slur against those perceived as lacking in beauty)—and they pressed their case before a panel on why their appearances required a total surgical makeover.[18] While the contestants were pitied, the show made stars of the surgeons who appeared as arbiters of beauty and godlike in their capacities to upgrade women's appearances. The show cut from the "ugly ducklings" getting a doctor's consult to the glamorous reveal by the end of each episode, leaving out the side effects and the long, painful recovery times, and skipping any of the patients' self-questioning throughout the process. A more recent fictional series depicts a girl who undergoes several surgeries before college so she can get a fresh start. It's available on Netflix under the name *My ID Is Gangnam Beauty.*

The flip side of normalizing all this alteration, of course, is that certain physical features, such as a wider forehead, a chest that hasn't been surgically enhanced, a boxier waist, or a small nose, are now medicalized as "deformities" in need of correction.

～

Under the bright recessed lights at Oracle Clinic, Joyce and I were led past other treatment areas into a cramped room with two beds covered with sheets and a soft blanket. Our aestheticians wheeled in a pair of white plastic machines with square bases that looked like humidifiers with vacuum hose attachments. We lay down on heated beds and tucked ourselves under cozy pink blankets. After we got comfy, aestheticians used the machines' wand attachment with a spinning suction at the end on our faces, moving back and forth, sucking out oils, sebum, and other gunk from our pores (accompanied by little vacuum sounds, naturally) while simultaneously leaving hydrating nutrients on the skin.

After the sucking portion of this procedure, I sat under a face helmet that blasted me with UVA light before being covered up by a sky-blue finishing mask, a goop that solidified into a shiny rubbery substance and made me feel like I was being buried alive. As I lay there impatiently, eager to rip that mask off my face, I felt the fluttering of the fetus who'd become my third daughter. I wonder if she sensed my claustrophobia.

When we finished with our facials, Joyce and I stepped out of our treatment room, glowing and sleepy. I felt closer to her. There is something about seeing the grime from your friend's pores sloshing around in a machine that's instantly bonding.

As we were led out into the lobby, I saw more faces covered in numbing cream and topped with plastic wrap. In the States, privacy surrounds cosmetic procedures. At Oracle and others just like it, clients regard revealing what goes into beauty work with a blithe nonchalance. And the work is almost all facial. According to a 2021 survey of Korean women, "petit plastic surgery" (injectables like Botox and filler) was the most common work respondents had gotten done, followed by double eyelid surgery and nose jobs. Liposuction came in fourth. In the second and third largest markets for cosmetic surgery, Brazil and the United States, body surgery had been more common, at least until very recently. Asia is face-first.[19]

Which Face?

There is a Chinese soap opera star from the 1980s named Liu Xue Hua, and her name is seared into my memory. Her *name,* not her face. I can't recall what she looked like. When I was a child, my parents' friends remarked on two things when they came over for dinner parties or mahjong. One, my eyelids, and two, my resemblance to the Liu woman. They'd say in Chinese: "Look at those *shuang yian pi* [which translates literally to double eyelid]. You look like a miniature Liu Xue Hua."

I internalized at a young age that these things—my resemblance to an actress I'd never seen, including her double eyelids—were desirable, even though the reason why these things were worth praising remained mysterious to me. They were advantages I couldn't understand except that they held value for grown-ups. I was in third grade when I first learned that the white folk determined to call out my differences saw Asians as people with "slanty" eyes. The boys in the back of the bus—who never missed a target to torment—taunted me by singing, "Chinese, Japanese, dirty knees, look at these," and pulled their faces taut into slits.

I don't have slanty eyes, I'd think to myself, mystified. They're like yours, round and lidded. Half of all East Asian women are born with double eyelids.[20] That means, of course, the estimated other half are born with monolids. Monolids describe the creaseless "single" eyelids that get maligned as squinty, slanty, or droopy. They can be altered with upper eye blepharoplasty, a procedure meant to lift loose or sagging skin above the eye folds, and when used in a cosmetic way, to create a crease in the monolid, creating *ssangapul,* in Korean—double lids. It is the most popular and common cosmetic surgery performed in Korea,[21] part of the three-pack of discounted procedures offered as high school graduation specials for parents to buy for their daughters and sons.[22]

The next most popular surgery in Korea is rhinoplasty, aka a nose job[23] (also part of the three-pack discounts). As plastic surgery became so widely pursued and accepted in South Korea, the consistent prevalence of these two procedures— especially the double eyelid operation—led to uneasy questions about whether South Koreans are seeking to surgically "westernize" their appearance with white skin, larger eyes, and longer, raised noses. The quick answer is no, they weren't. And the longer answer involves the complexity of how medicine gets tangled with history.

While Korea's cosmetic surgery industry was still fledgling, pre-2000, some researchers connected the eyelid and nose procedures with Western beauty standards.[24] But in the twenty-first century, South Korean doctors and patients dismiss the premise that a "white-looking face" is even a notion. Of the hundreds of people I talked to for this book, not a single one said the motivation for plastic surgery in Korea is to look more Caucasian. "Shifting beauty ideals cannot be reduced to simplistic desires to be 'white'—a racial category that is, in itself, extremely fluid," writes Australian researcher Jo Elfving-Hwang.[25] Anthropologists and scholars like Elfving-

Hwang have considered local histories, cultures, and, crucially, class-based dynamics as the most influential factors in popularizing particular local surgical procedures. Uniformly, they found that the importance of *local* cultural dynamics trumps outside influences when it comes to health and beauty norms. Indeed, many have gone on to point out, it's colonialist to emphasize race as a determining factor in the beauty decisions of Asians in the first place.

On the matter of favoring porcelain-white skin, it predates Western colonial influences by centuries. As early as the first Korean dynasty, Goryeo, founded in the year 918 B C, children washed their faces with peach flower water to make their skin look clean and white.[26] In agricultural Korea, white skin stood as a class marker, a status symbol. The "privileged classes did not toil under the sun," said Korean makeup artist Kim Chung Kyung, "and, as a result, had whiter skin."[27] Today, so-called whitening therapies, procedures, and products abound, sparking controversy in places where they're heavily marketed, like Southeast Asia, where skin shades are naturally darker. As mentioned earlier, the products' so-called whitening ingredients don't lighten so much as brighten, but given the history of conquest and colonization in Southeast Asia by European nations, flooding Indonesian or Vietnamese or Thai populations with messages to lighten their skin isn't a great look.

When it comes to the most popular cosmetic surgical procedure, the recorded history of eyelid surgery dates to the late nineteenth century. In 1896, after performing a procedure he claims he invented at that time, Japanese ophthalmologist and surgeon Kotaro Mikamo wrote the first known article about his surgical technique, which created a double eyelid from a monolid.[28] In the Japanese medical journal *Chugai Iji Shimpo*, he details his method, showing before-and-after drawings and even introducing an improvement on his original work. Mikamo had figured out how to create the double eyelid without an incision above the eye, but with sutures instead, presaging the knifeless "innovation" that doctors started to use when performing eyelid surgeries more than a century after him.

After hundreds of years of isolationism, Japan had opened up to Western influence following the 1854 Treaty of Kanagawa. A wave of westernization moved from food to fashion. For his part, Mikamo did not allude to racial dynamics in his work on Japanese faces. He described the single eyelid as a "defect" and a "condition" that ophthalmologists tended to overlook. "Japanese ukiyo-e artists and novelists, however," he wrote, "paid close attention to . . . a double eyelid, which they regard as a symbol of gentle cuteness. Monolids sometimes make women look unamiable."[29]

Correspondents from the United States were the ones to attach racial meanings to this then-newfangled surgery. In February 1895, an unnamed special correspondent for the *Los Angeles Times* wrote about the Japanese surgery without citing the pioneering doctor, but ostensibly he's referring to the "small blepharoplasty technique" that Mikamo by that time had performed on dozens of patients: "In their efforts to acquire recognition in the civilized world, the Japanese have found their greatest barrier in the unmistakable mark of their Mongolian origin." The writer went on to write that, because "prejudice against Mongolians is undeniable," the Japanese had adopted the surgery to hide the "evidence" and "curse" of their Mongolian heritage.[30]

The procedure didn't really catch on until fifty years and two global conflicts later when, in the aftermath of the Korean War, an American surgeon stationed in Korea invented his version. To be sure, much of plastic surgery's rise is tied to war: it originated as a way to fix disfigurements from combat. The American and European militarization of Asian countries, during and after World War II, was the biggest factor in making cosmetic surgery more common in those areas.[31] (It was also on the rise in the United States and Europe in that period.)[32] "More critical than the surgery itself," writes John DiMoia in his book *Reconstructing Bodies*, "was the postwar context in which it took place, with medical relief frequently mobilized as evidence of benevolent intentions."[33] Surgical trends then expanded from reconstructive to cosmetic, which dominates the plastic surgery field today.

In his 2013 text, DiMoia maintains that South Korea's world-leading plastic surgery industry has roots in reconstructive medicine from the aftermath of bloody mid-twentieth-century conflicts that shaped the country. The United States occupied the formerly unified Korea in the immediate years following World War II, after Japan's long occupation of Korea ended. America then aligned with the South in the Korean War, which lasted from 1950 to 1953, and an alliance continues to this day.

The double eyelid surgery was popularized beginning in 1954, when David Ralph Millard, the U.S. Marines' chief plastic surgeon in South Korea, conceived of his version of the double eyelid surgery and tried it on Korean sex workers, though they weren't his main patients.[34] His work focused on U.S. soldiers and war victims, and he declared postwar Korea "a plastic surgeon's paradise" due to the diversity of postwar injuries and the abundant opportunities for him to practice his craft.[35]

Millard left a checkered legacy. For starters, he considered natural monolids a defect to be fixed, layering his writings with notions of ethnic identity and white superiority.[36] In a 1964 paper, Millard distinguishes between the "occidental eye" and the "oriental eye," acknowledging the surgery is an erasure of this East Asian feature that half of us are born with.[37] Millard's context can't be ignored—his Korean sex worker patients wanted to appeal to their American GI clients. As Nadia Y. Kim writes, "the U.S. military and [Millard] were crystallizing Koreans' sense of inferiority to their White racial bodies," an outgrowth of the power differences embedded within the U.S.-South Korea relationship.[38] Millard popularized a method to change Korean faces for American preferences, and in doing so, positioned the postwar Western male gaze as one arbiter of what was desirable in Korea.

The Korean Society of Plastic and Reconstructive Surgeons was established in 1966.[39] Those early surgeons drew on training and medical exchanges with the United States. In the late twentieth century, when Korea was rapidly developing, beauty ideals were influenced in part by cultural exchange with America and Europe, often disseminated through Hollywood.[40] Early surgical practices were also heavily driven by the U.S., as Korean practitioners learned techniques and surgeries from Western textbooks.[41]

Those techniques may have nodded toward "Caucasian" features in the 1970s and 1980s, but "while the early surgical practices were heavily driven by Western techniques," writes the Korean aesthetics scholar Joanna Elfving-Hwang, "drawing conclusions about a nation's perceived desire to 'deracialize' their bodies in the contemporary context is less straightforward." Which is to say, any period of creating "Western" features lasted for a limited time only. Saying that it continues today is akin to saying everyone who gets a short haircut these days is doing it because Dorothy Hamill had one in the 1970s. Doctors and patients themselves say they have not heard or made "Western" referencing requests, especially not in this century.

Even so, the colonialist notion that Koreans were "westernizing" their eyes stuck.

The idea that mono-lidded East Asians may have simply sought something far more local—the facial features of *other East Asians*—wasn't what we were taught across the Pacific. When the Korean plastic surgery industry's growth caught the attention of American outlets like *The Wall Street Journal* and the *Los Angeles Times* in the 1990s, reporters again fed colonial assumptions and ran stories about Koreans' decisions to "go Anglo"—the common slang at the time.[42]

In truth, the appeal of double eyelids that drove plastic surgery industry expansion in the 1990s came from nearby influences, such as the Chinese actress Liu Xue Hua I kept hearing about, for the Mandarin-speaking diaspora. Or in

Korea, the movie star Hwang Shin-hye, whom Korean media dubbed in the 1980s as the ideal Korean beauty.[43] In East Asia, the double-eyelidded Hwang, not Meg Ryan, had the most sought-after face.

Since the 2000s, when South Korea became a full-fledged "wealthy" nation, what's considered beautiful and how to attain it have been remixed and reclaimed by Koreans many times over.[44] In challenging my own Western-media-saturated assumptions, I returned to the writings of the Japanese surgeon who seems to have performed the first aesthetic blepharoplasties in the late 1800s. Remember what he wrote? "Japanese ukiyo-e artists and novelists . . . paid close attention to this [eye] condition." In my years of reporting, everyday Koreans never said they were trying to look white, but instead younger, more *aegyo*, "cute." And the "cute" standard frankly looked a lot more like anime characters or the enhancements from digital filters on their social apps. In that sense, the Japanese doctor who first invented the double eyelid surgery wasn't just ahead of his time in creating his procedure, but he offered an early, non-racialized reason for its popularity: that surgery to expand the size of our eyes makes it possible for our faces to look more like art. And though the idea of life imitating art is not new, we have much better tools to accomplish it now.

Researcher Joanna Elfving-Hwang points out that conversation around this topic outside Asia "conveniently ignores leaps in biomedical and surgical technologies." Such leaps, she writes, "have meant that cosmetic surgeries in Korea are now designed with enhancing the specific facial and body aesthetic of the Asian body to create a natural-looking Korean beauty (*ssaengʼŏl*)."[45]

~

The jawline is the place on the face where Asian-originated aesthetics are most clearly visible. At the turn of the century, Korean doctors and media began driving a trend in plastic surgery that is so particular to Korean values that it precludes any notion that Koreans might be trying to "go Anglo."

Starting in the late 1990s, Korean doctors started to consider the shape and proportion of the whole face over the size and shape of individual features like the eyes and the nose.[46] Desires for the prettiest or most "balanced" face led to an increased focus on the jaw as the major area for improvement. The facial symmetry preference requires that the upper part of the face (forehead, eyes, nose) appear bigger than the lower half. An ideal face for a younger person typically has large eyes (but not necessarily with double eyelids), a pointy (but not upturned) nose with a slightly raised nasal bridge, and a pointy jawline that meets at a V—a V-line. These ideals are similar for both men and women, with the focus on creating a soft, youthful appearance. An aegyo look.

As with other aspects of K-beauty, the focus on facial proportions has roots in old and new—the old coming from traditional East Asian beliefs about *insang*, or first impressions, and the new in pseudoscience on the exact proportions that make up an attractive face. Insang is historically important in East Asian cultures. It draws on physiognomy, a notion that self-presentation, much of it in your face, is a window to your entire character and can even foretell your fate. Seeking the guidance of fortune-tellers has long been popular in South Korea but grew in prominence after the 1997 Asian financial crisis, when competition for jobs became fierce. The market research firm TrendMonitor found that more than 80 percent of respondents in a 2020 survey said they have used a fortune-telling service, and 29 percent have their fortunes read more than once.[47]

In traditional face reading, which originated in China, the bottom third of the face—the jaw—is used to read the latter part of your life, which could explain some of the interest in jaw shape. So I asked a face fortune-teller, Tao Sok, if the face-reading business, including his own work, was affected by the preponderance of cosmetically altered mugs. "I see more and more surgically altered faces now," he told me. Because of it, he and others in his line of work take surgical changes into consideration when reading fortunes, crediting some patients as proactive for changing their insang and thereby altering their fate. They've arguably taken control of their lives to boost their careers or partner prospects. "If you change your face, the people who are attracted to you may change, so your fate will change as a result," Tao says.

Doctors began popularizing jawline surgery—a procedure that was previously only for reconstructive purposes—as a commercialized cosmetic procedure in the early aughts.[48] Also called V-line surgery, the procedure is aimed at reshaping the bottom half of the face and involves shaving and occasionally cutting, disassembling, and rearranging both lower and upper jaws (maxilla and mandible bones) to achieve a delicate-looking jaw.[49] When you change the size and shape of the jaw, you transform the entire face. Jawline surgery stands out from eyelid surgery or rhinoplasty because it was normalized and popularized in Korea and by Korean doctors. There's some local pride in that: in 2014, a clinic exhibited more than two thousand jaw fragments in two giant glass vessels, each bone labeled with the name of the patient from whom it was carved.[50] Despite its popularity in Korea for more than a decade, it is still considered "foreign" by U.S. and European doctors.

For people who aren't motivated by insang, there's pop science. Clinics use biostatistics to describe the "perfect ratios" of a face, invoking the golden mean or the golden ratio of 1.618. This apocryphal idea is supposed to represent the mathematical proportions that the human eye seems to find most pleasing, be it in nature, architecture, or our own bodies. Whether it's the number of petals on a flower or a seashell's concentric rings, 1.618 is said to be found on its own, without manufacturing, all around us in the natural world. When this ratio is applied to a human face, you divide the length by the width and the ideal result, according to many plastic surgeons, is 1.6—the faces we find most attractive are roughly 1.6 times longer than they are wide. "There is perhaps some academic/intellectual basis to it," said Dr. Hsu, the Beverly Hills surgeon. "A lot of biological developmental processes may be related to fractal geometry, which can be mathematically related to the golden ratio. In terms of actual practice, for me personally, it's not something where we specifically measure . . . After a while you get good at just looking at a face and having a good idea of what is a good aesthetic goal and what is surgically achievable."

So Yeon Leem, a Korean biologist turned social scientist, embedded herself as part of her research for three years inside one of the largest plastic surgery clinics in Seoul, inputting intake forms and guiding patients through the operation and recovery processes. Her years inside the hospital illuminated an even more specific ratio that doctors promote as sought after: 1:1:>1. Instead of considering just the length and width, doctors divide the face into three segments, the same setup you'd get when folding a letter. The forehead, then the brow to nose area, then nose to chin. Balanced proportions are one in which those three parts are equal: 1:1:1. "That's to be average," Leem says. "Being pretty is beyond average, so ideally the nose to chin area should be a little less—0.7."

While she goes on to say this is "totally socially constructed," the doctors make a case for the golden ratio by finding evidence of beauty in nature and in analyzing "beautiful" faces to find what they had in common. "They measure everything," she says of the doctors. "The length between your eyes. Every part of your face."

Crucially, the measuring isn't happening on the three-dimensional surface of the face but, rather, on the photos the hospitals take when patients come in for a consultation. "If I look at your face in person, it's very hard to tell the proportions," Leem says. "But once you take a picture of your face and you see from the computer screen, the monitor, that two-dimensional surface, then proportions are pretty obvious." But, I asked, doesn't this suggest we are privileging how we look in two dimensions over the three-dimensional in-person experience? "Oh yeah," Leem says. "It's different. That's why patients are sometimes disappointed with surgical results."

These proportions are self-reinforcing, creating a feedback loop for desirable faces. Research shows that from 2010 to 2019, Korean plastic surgeons, wanpan celebrities, and reality television each reinforced a narrative that a slimmer, delicate jawline was desirable. Plastic surgeons promised this outcome through a jawline shaving procedure. Celebrities started doing it, creating trends real people wanted to follow. Ostensible "real" people who appeared on "reality" makeover shows celebrated their thinner jaws, thereby advertising the procedure for the surgeons, and so on. A market like this prevents itself from accepting a broad normative beauty. If everyone is beautiful, then no one is beautiful. So the standard becomes narrow, but achievable, if you have the money to do the work.

In her book *Perfect Me,* British philosopher Heather Widdows writes about the conflation of beauty and morality. She argues that beauty has come to function as an ethical ideal and lays out three conditions that must be true for appearance to stand in for a person's goodness: (1) that the body can be changed (body malleability is a relatively new phenomenon); (2) that "body work" or labor is required; and (3) that power is internalized. All these dynamics are happening in a supercharged way in modern-day South Korea.[51]

What makes "self-transformation" technology so compelling is that these fixes are sold and internalized as a means to overcome poor self-esteem or as a way to empower the individual.[52] But, self-empowerment and self-esteem aren't the same. Studies indicate cosmetic surgery can improve one's body image,[53] but the effect on overall "psychological well-being" is "rather small."[54] Psychological outcomes are mixed depending on the types of surgery and the individual's motivations for such procedures.[55] Cosmetic surgery patients who suffer from body dysmorphic disorder can feel the dopamine hit of a tune-up, but the pleasure wears off, potentially leading them to return again and again for perpetual nips and tucks.[56] Ultimately, research shows the quest for perfection can be both addictive *and* self-destructive—setting people on the path to depression, anxiety, and life paralysis when they become afraid to put anything out in the world that could be seen as imperfect.[57] "If the metric is trying to be like a K-pop idol, it's never-ending," Sharon Heijin Lee says. "It's limitless. There is not enough time and labor that can be put into looking like the perfect Korean woman."[58]

Over time, as beauty becomes ever more conflated with morality, and the images of a "good person" and an economically rational individual intertwine, the meaning of *self-esteem* starts to change. Self-esteem in modern capitalist societies (America, South Korea) can come to mean positive self-assessment according to various external metrics.[59] That doesn't necessarily mean self-respect or compassion. Since we must constantly measure, judge, and discipline ourselves to be "successful" in a competitive marriage and job market, we are deriving personal "empowerment" from meeting societal, aesthetic yardsticks. Those metrics don't consider what's going on in our souls.

CHAPTER 8

~

The New Modern

To spend some time with a plastic surgeon, I met an interpreter, So Jeong, a deep-voiced, even-keeled Korean woman in her early thirties who accompanied me to see Dr. Seo Gwang-seok. His practice is found on the twelfth floor of a building that's mostly occupied by a franchise English-test prep company. (Think Kaplan classes for SATs, but for high-stakes English testing.) When we stepped off the elevator, So Jeong chuckled, noticing that the plastic surgery clinic was right next door to a psychology office that specializes in treating anxiety and depression. "Yeah, that tracks," I quipped.

We were led through a lobby of expensive lighting and giant white floor tiles to chat with Dr. Seo in his office. Dressed in purple scrubs, Dr. Seo, who appeared to be in his mid-forties, took a seat across from me next to his two 30-inch monitors and in front of his windowsill, where he displayed a replica of a rainbow-colored human skull, a box of Pepero (chocolate-covered pretzel sticks), and a small Iron-man poster. Everything he said came out matter-of-factly, like we were all supposed to know this stuff already. Sitting there, I felt calm but self-conscious at the same time, aware that all he did all day was judge—and correct—other people's faces.

Seo first opened his practice in 2004 and had performed all the hits—jawline surgery, breast augmentation, rhinoplasty, liposuctions—before making a strategic decision about a decade ago to specialize in what he does best—lifting sagging skin on the face. He estimates 60 percent of his work is the lower lid blepharoplasty, which removes eye bags. The rest of his work is thread lifting of the cheeks and thread lifts of the forehead. Thread lifts are pretty impressive procedures—non-face-lift face-lifts—in which surgeons take a taut, wirelike "thread" with grooves on it and slide it under your skin such that the grooves catch on the inside of your cheeks or forehead. Once that wirelike thread catches, they can pull it up, lifting sagging skin from underneath the dermis.

He chose to specialize in these procedures because in this crowded cosmetic market, he had to claim turf to survive. To be a successful plastic surgeon in South Korea, he also has to work at a pace and a volume that makes American surgeons' heads spin. Dr. Charles Hsu is a cosmetic surgeon I consulted with throughout my reporting. He and I used to sing karaoke together into the wee hours in Taipei, when he was twenty-six and I was nineteen. Back then, he was in Taiwan's capital completing an internship at National Taiwan University Hospital as part of his Harvard Medical School program and I was studying abroad for a semester. After graduating, he continued on to a residency at Stanford and opened a private cosmetic surgery practice in Beverly Hills, because as he put it, "that's where the clients were." In our conversations, Hsu told me that he operates three days a week, which is considered a full schedule for U.S. surgeons.

When I asked Seo how many procedures he performed each week, he said, "How many in a week? How about in one day?" He went on to say he operates every day except Sunday, with as few as two and as many as ten procedures a day. He estimates an average of four surgeries a day, six days a week, and like most of his plastic surgeon peers, he has been working at this pace since he started.

With so much repetition and practice, these doctors become excellent. By the time we reconnected during my research for this book, Dr. Hsu had taken over a Koreatown practice in Los Angeles, which catered to a lot of Korean American clients, allowing him to hear about and eventually study the work of the innovative Korean surgeons. He has visited surgery clinics in Seoul to observe and learn from the doctors there. The clinics allow a steady clip of international doctors in to watch in exchange for small fees. "I visited four or five [Gangnam clinics], I picked up a few techniques," he told me. "Some surgeons there are amazing. Truly excellent skill. Some are scary, because they're so focused on speed that it's like, whoa, shit, I can't believe you're doing that."

Owing to the glutted market and the intense competition, Korean surgeons are constantly coming up with diagnostic innovations and inventing new surgeries. One of them involves surgically pinning the corners of your mouth slightly upward to correct "resting bitch face," giving patients the appearance of constant smiling. Another innovation adds fillers under the eye for a "cuter" appearance, which Dr. Seo showed me as an example of something he and other Korean doctors came up with to address what he didn't learn from medical textbooks during his school days—the needs of Asian clients and their faces. Eyes on East Asian faces tend to have less fat in the lower eyelids than Caucasian or Black faces do, so adding a little pouch of fat under the eyelid works aesthetically in a way it might not for the subjects in his textbooks. "Medicine is a field of study from the West, and I went through a lot of troubles because of this," he told me. "In our country, we can't go by the book."

In his office, Seo futzed around with little folder icons on his twin computer monitors before pulling up a pair of images on the side-by-side screens. On the left, he opened up a tight shot of Angelina Jolie's face. On the right, a similarly cropped image of the actress Song Hye-kyo, one of the "big three" triumvirate of Korean stars, their wattage comparable to Julia Roberts/Meg Ryan/Sandra Bullock in the 1990s.

"Which one is more beautiful?" he asked.

I replied, "It depends on what you consider beautiful."

He casually rejected this. With his rainbow-colored skull mold off to one side, he held up each woman as a token— Jolie as an American beauty, Song as an Asian one. With a long, thin stylus, he began to repeatedly circle certain parts of these celebrity faces to highlight their inherent differences. "See her jawline," he said, jabbing the pointer at Angelina's well-defined jaw. "Here we would think that looks too much like a man. Eh? See?"

Moving his stylus over to the image of the Asian actress projected on the right monitor, he traced her under-eye area, showing how Asian eyes tend to protrude from the face rather than sink in. So, he said, the procedure—called *aegyo sal*, meaning eye smiles or cute skin—adds filler under the eyes to make the face look more like a child's. "So the direction that we do surgery is different. There's a little fat under the eyes, and we actually prefer that trait, so for that, I do a restorative surgery [to add it], but Westerners do not prefer that and tend to get rid of it." For most of his career, he says, patients brought in photos of Korean celebrities they wanted to look like. But increasingly, patients are showing him photos of internet influencers or even non-famous people—their attractive friends—to try and emulate.

Toward a Pan-Asian, Korean-Inspired Face

In December 2021, megawatt American entertainer Ariana Grande posted a photo of herself wearing dark winged eyeliner, a foundation lighter than her skin tone, and a bright red lip often associated with Korean makeup. Online commenters dragged her so fast for "Asian-fishing," appropriating Asian features, that she quickly deleted the post. But some defenders who identified as Asian weighed in to say that associating Grande's look as "Asian" in the first place only confirmed biases about what Asians looked like: pale skin; smaller, slanted eyes. Earlier in the same year, Oli London, a white British K-pop fanboy, underwent several cosmetic surgeries to look like the BTS member Jimin. London then described themself as "transracial," and found themself at the center of controversy as a result. Setting aside the power imbalances of appropriating culture, these examples illustrate on one level that the West as a leader in setting global aesthetic norms is fading much like America's role as a geopolitical standard-bearer.

Ever on the bleeding edge, Korean doctors have already been taking globalism into account. So Yeon Leem, the K-surgery researcher, says clinics are designing and constantly tweaking their computer algorithms for analyzing aesthetically appealing faces so they can recommend optimal procedures to their clients. These algorithms measure the proportions of pretty people of all different ethnicities and analyze the aggregate data to discover "global proportions . . . what the common beauty ideal is in all races." This is part of the technological gaze at work, feeding and creating demand at the same time. Machines learn which faces and traits conform to science-glazed "magic" ratios and present us with the latest aesthetic standards to reach. Inevitably they require costly interventions or more aesthetic labor.

Sociologists had already noted a regional trend, in the 2010s, of the flattening of many desirable traits into a single "Pan-Asian face": a blend of European and Asian features with the focus and favor lying in what sociologist Kimberly Kay Hoang calls "a specific East Asian ideal—round face, thinness and even, untanned skin tone." In her fieldwork, Hoang has studied the beauty practices of Vietnamese sex workers. She found they engage in surgery and alteration to achieve a blend of looks, but one that favors Asianness: "Now the new modern is Asian," her informants said.

The modern Asian face is increasingly defined by a Korean beauty standard, with Southeast Asian women especially looking toward Korea for the latest and most advanced beauty products and procedures. Michael Hurt, the Korea-based sociologist who calls Korea "hypermodern," photographs Seoul Fashion Week every year and has chronicled Korean looks with his street photography for more than a decade. When he visited Vietnam to photograph fashion models in 2019, he thought one in particular resembled a Korean woman. "I noticed when she turned her head in the direction of me, I was like, 'Wow, you really look Korean.' And she said, 'Oh my god, thank you. That's the biggest compliment I've ever had.'"

This transfer of appearance ideals is not linear or one-directional. It's more a mixing and mashing toward what academics call *neoliberal multiculturalism*. Coined by Jodi Melamed, the term is used to mean an ideology of global racial formation that devalues a country's native culture, favoring the blending of multiple cultures. It emerged after the U.S. civil rights movement and alongside the globalization of capital. It's a strain of neoliberalism that *incorporates* multiculturalism, giving extra shine to the profit-first, consume-and-be-consumed ethos of capitalism.[1] Korean cultural researchers like Emily Raymundo see it happening in the melding of globally "beautiful" ideals—large lips from the Global South, bigger butts from Africa and Latin America, prominent noses from Northern Europe. "The consolidation of 'the face' is about a cosmopolitan mélange of beauty standards (K-beauty, Bollywood, Hollywood, Instagram influencers globally, etc.)," she wrote me in an email.

It may not be long before these cross-Pacific differences

are further flattened into a transracial look entirely. Korean beauty standards are today remixed into broader beauty norms as the reigning look in beauty becomes more of an internet-driven global uniformity. In home design, for instance, internet platforms for rentals like Airbnb have led to a sterile, recognizably similar aesthetic across living spaces.[2] When it comes to aesthetic ideals for people, the global pageant on Instagram plays out similarly, landing us on a largely homogeneous set of beauty standards that get further embedded the more they circulate on the marketplace of ideal faces and our desires.

This phenomenon has come to be known as Instagram Face, a term which first showed up in *New York* magazine's The Cut blog in 2016. The term describes a cyborgian blend of Instagram algorithm-approved facial features: unblemished skin, tapered nose and chin, wide forehead, big eyes, high cheekbones, and equally thick top and bottom lips. Eve Peyser, in a *New York Times* op-ed, hilariously described it as "a sexy baby meets Jessica Rabbit," an artificial, filtered, flattened look derived from real people in a feedback loop with available filters and the Instagram algorithm.[3]

Innovation and Malleability

Whatever the "ideal," it's not a fixed one. The traditional Confucian-inspired beliefs that your body is a gift from your parents and not even your hair should be shorn are replaced with the understanding that ideal faces are malleable and changeable, with technology. The "natural" Korean face, which is more circular, with smaller eyes, round cheeks, and wider noses, is associated with a North Korean look now.[4] In fact, cosmetic surgeons offer free or heavily discounted surgeries to refugees from North Korea in order to help them better fit in and adapt to the demanding appearance regimes of South Korea.[5] "This is a transformation in Korean society," says scholar Stephen Epstein, whose work has focused on modern Korean society. "People have gone from bodies you maintain to bodies that should be modified to maintain competitive standards. What's gone on in the last decade is a growing . . . self-commodification."

As dermatology and cosmetic surgery clinics are framed more like hair salons—that is to say, places you return to at regular intervals—surgery patients are regarded as repeat customers. Technology allows for constant transformation, after all—of the surgical technology, but also of the patient. You don't like your brows? Change them. You want a skinnier jaw? Shave it down. Instead of a fixed standard of beauty, changeability feeds the plastic surgery industry and keeps it churning. The points on the continuum of appearance labor—from skincare to cosmetics to cosmetic surgery—simply become habituated and routinized.

Kim Jimin, who is now a Seoul elementary school teacher, recalls her realization of this during her college job working at a clothing shop. "They considered appearances a lot, so the manager made comments like, if you changed this part or that part, you'd be perfect," Kim said. "Three to four times a year my coworkers would get injection procedures or plastic surgery, constantly spending money to be beautiful. They received it again and again, because there is a certain trend to follow for your face. You have to constantly adapt to have a 'more trendy' face. Most people do that with makeup, but more people do that with their procedures—changing the shape of their features."

Dr. Seo has taken to YouTube, where he boasts a modest subscriber base of about 30,000, to call out plastic surgery as an "addiction." But not just on the patient side—on the practitioner side, too. One of his videos points to an example of a double eyelid job that was followed up by eleven touch-up operations to perfect it. He says the profit motive of clinics is driving surgeries that many clients flat out don't need. He name-checks a well-known surgery center in Gangnam that advertises everywhere. It's a hospital with ten surgeons and anesthesiologists, some of whom have appeared on reality shows. These hospitals offer every surgery under the sun, and partner with brokers and government agencies—the national tourism ministry and local tourism boards—to keep foreign patients coming in for services. I tried to get a consultation and interview at the very clinic Seo mentioned, and was repeatedly turned down. I probably would have fared better if I'd just gone in as a potential client.

During our meeting, Dr. Seo told me he worries these hospitals are akin to mills, too driven by the bottom line. And he was critical of the Korean government, which tries to address plastic surgery proliferation at the margins, with more regulation against before-and-after ads, while promoting Hallyu and medical tourism at the same time. "Korean plastic surgery is kind of paired with Hallyu. It gets attention. And the government keeps supporting it," he said.

Doctors pay commissions to brokers who help foreign

patients match with their clinics, something that is considered illegal for domestic patients. The patients don't pay the brokers at all, not even for concierge services like having a caretaker with you throughout your surgery process, serving as the first person you see when you come out of anesthesia. This is all paid for by the hospitals, which rely on a constant influx of patients. As the saying goes, if you're not paying for the product, you are the product.

~

South Korea's plastic surgery industry has been called many things by the international media: an "obsession," "mayhem," an "epidemic." One of the common criticisms is the sameness it encourages. As cosmetic surgery's popularity grew, both domestic and international observers noticed that many Korean women were beginning to have an eerie resemblance to one another.[6] This phenomenon made the rounds in the English-language media in 2013 with a "Miss Korea GIF" that went viral within forty-eight hours.[7] It appeared first on a Japanese blog, then on Reddit, and then in national and international newspapers. The GIF compresses several still images of the faces of beauty contestants into a digital "flip book" that moves from one to another to another, such that the beauty contestants' faces morph one into the next at rapid speed. It was hard to look away—a few seconds in and the women's faces were indistinguishable. The American blog Jezebel captured it with the headline "Plastic Surgery Means Many Beauty Queens, But Only One Kind of Face."[8]

But there was a lie at the center of the story. It turns out the individual pageant queen images had been Photoshopped before the GIF was put together to make the women look more alike. "What was issued as objective visual evidence of Korean women's fanatic obsession with plastic surgery instead reveals a fanatic obsession on the part of Americans for producing and consuming Korean women as such," Sharon Heijin Lee wrote in 2016.

Another prevailing knock on the plastic surgery craze is that the desired results favor "a mindless 'manga' aesthetic with large, wide eyes; a white translucent skin tone; and a pointy chin simply because individuals are unable to resist beauty ideals," as researcher Joanna Elfving-Hwang puts it.[9] But Korean women who have undergone surgeries are not mindless; they are usually choosing the aesthetics to allow them to fit in.

Gawkers overlook the class dynamics of Korean society, where meeting a minimum bar of appearance is considered polite. A Korean woman who gets plastic surgery to fit in in this way is not looking good just for herself. She is showing respect to others in the community. She is also signifying where she fits—or might fit—in the class hierarchy, such that beauty work or body modification can help a lower-class woman "pass" as a middle- or even upper-class person. The democratizing aspects of K-beauty skincare simply extend to K-surgery, allowing women who choose plastic surgery to leapfrog the rigid class hierarchies in the same way that the Factory Girl and the Modern Girl used makeup.

Socioeconomic utility, identity construction, and the alteration of interpersonal relationships can all be gained from fixing your face. It's almost all social upside, so it makes sense that women would spend money on it. It's also not priced so extravagantly that ordinary people can't afford it.

In fact, the "relative affordability of cosmetic surgery means that a discerning individual can potentially present all the signifiers of wealth and middle-class economic status without necessarily having to achieve any other markers of status," Elfving-Hwang found. An "appearance that signifies upper-class status" can even come *before* "other markers of success—such as consumer goods, cars, and perhaps an expensive apartment." Viewed in this way, cosmetic surgery is a democratizing practice within the context of South Korean society. It helps individuals succeed socially and economically. You could read a kind of feminist determination in women choosing plastic surgery. It can keep women visible and valuable in job and marriage markets, to the extent that those matter, and in modern Korea they matter very much.

Beauty work is, at its essence, body work. It stands out from a spectrum of issues surrounding women's claim to bodily and spiritual integrity. Is plastic surgery a kind of violence that a woman inflicts upon herself? I certainly see how aesthetic surgery can be viewed as systemic violence that we've individually come to ask for and pay for. But in hypercompetitive places, being "ugly" can lead to emotional, institutional, and spiritual trauma, especially in cultures where appearance standards are specific and lookism runs rampant. Surgeons make the case they're alleviating psychological pain by making patients look like they belong. In that way, it makes logical sense to exert energy to prevent emotional pain. Every woman I spoke to who explained why they perform beauty work or underwent surgery said they wanted to look better, whatever that meant to them. It is "practical to dream of simply looking all the time the way we do when we're rested, fed, watered, well-sexed, and nicely groomed," beauty journalist Autumn Whitefield-Madrano argues. "In other words, the reason we perform beauty work is because we are engaged in chronic hope."[10]

⁓

The second time I visited Oracle was five years after the first. I was a year away from turning forty, ready to try something besides a pore vacuum, and thrice-vaccinated against the coronavirus that had upended all our lives.

So much had changed by late 2021. A mobile app from the Korean Health Ministry monitored my movements because we remained in a seemingly never-ending pandemic. Each morning, I awoke alone in a cramped, generic Seoul hotel room, instead of my old Seoul apartment with the floors heated to a perfect temperature and our loud and boisterous girls. My solitude felt liberating and lonely at once—Matt was back in Los Angeles caring for our children, but in the intervening years since we had moved home and I had returned to Seoul for this mid-pandemic visit, he and I had split up, ending our sixteen-year relationship during the crucible of the early coronavirus lockdown and uncertainty. On my fifty-minute cab ride from the airport into town, the re-release of Taylor Swift's saddest breakup song played through my AirPods, sending tears flowing down my cheeks as I absorbed for the first time the fragility of being on the other side of the planet without my husband expecting me to call home.

With reporting this book in mind, I wanted to return to Oracle to check out what was new and next for aesthetic improvement. The lobby still buzzed with patients sitting across from intake staffers at tiny round tables, the bottom halves of their faces now hidden behind masks, still huddled over intake forms. A promotional video featuring Korean celebrities endorsing Oracle treatments played soundlessly on a TV in the wall. Underneath, pamphlets were displayed in three long rows, presented like the sightseeing brochures found in low-budget hotel lobbies. They introduced procedures I'd never heard of before: Aladdin Peeling. 10THERA. V-beam. Ultra-Pulse Encore. Blue Peel. Cog thread lift. CO_2. A few brochures detailed the now-common injectables: Botox and fillers under various brand names.

Injectables in Korea have advanced so much in the few years between my visits to Oracle that they can now achieve the results of invasive rhinoplasties, cheek fat removal, and liposuction. Since arriving, I'd heard a few people mention the Chanel Facial, an injectable treatment named after the fashion house but with no association to it and unavailable in the States. I asked my intake officer about them, and she replied that Chanel Facials were already out of fashion. The trendy cocktail to get shot into your face now was Rejuran. Rejuran is a "healer"—an entire class of injectables that's also not available in the U.S. Healers are not fillers in that they don't add volume to face parts in the way Restylane or Juvéderm do. Rejuran uses components of salmon DNA (which is said to be remarkably similar to human DNA) to improve skin elasticity and repair damaged skin. It's shot straight into skin tissue rather than into facial muscles the way Botox is.

"Do you use it?" I asked the dermatologist, an Oracle veteran named Dr. Shin Heawon.

"Oh yeah, of course, every three or four months I get it," she said.

"I hear it's the one that hurts the most," I replied.

"Yes, it's the worst. It's very painful." But, she told me, she chooses it "because of the results."

I considered this as I gazed back at her, her skin as white as chalk, her face so smooth, perhaps from Rejuran, that the best way I can describe it is to say she looked nearly embalmed. Because I refused to try the "really painful" salmon DNA stuff, the Oracle coordinator and the dermatologist consulted and decided that for the frown lines that had begun to show up between my brows and the creases detectable on my forehead, they would shoot me up with "very little" traditional Botox, which weakens the muscles that frown and move your forehead up and down. But then for everything below the brows, they sold me the off-label use of Botox called "skin Botox," which is microdoses of the same ingredients in Botox, but shot shallow, not deep. They send the dermatoxin into your skin tissue, not into your facial muscles, so it can tighten your pores. On top of that, they would shoot me with a hydroinjection called "pink injection," a cocktail of moisturizers, vitamins, and the trendy humectant called hyaluronic acid that would help my skin look both fresh and nourished. Hydroinjections are essentially just shooting your skin with moisturizer instead of your having to bother rubbing it in. The goal is always to look "younger," in line with what philosopher Widdows says is the direction of all beauty projects across the world: thinness, firmness, smoothness, and youth.[11]

After I had walked down a familiar hallway packed with patients wearing full faces of numbing cream, I got déjà vu as I was led to the small treatment room similar to the one where I'd received a pore vacuuming five years prior. I climbed up on the table and laid myself flat.

"You ready?" Dr. Shin said, picking up the first skinny syringe in her gloved hands.

I said "okay" through a wince.

She asked me to frown to see where my lines were before injecting my face methodically across my forehead, then moving to the area below my eyes, before eventually stabbing all over my face except my nose, pausing only to pat with a tissue the bleeds that sprang up. The syringes clanked against a metal pan when she finished with each one. She started with the pink injection (somewhat bearable) and moved on to the dermatoxin, aka skin Botox, along my jawline. It felt like she was stabbing me with little fiery daggers, and I almost called it quits after the left side of my face. "The ingredients change the amount of pain," she explained. "This is most similar to the Rejuran."

Dr. Shin jabbed my face 274 times in total, leaving lines of little raised dots from under my eyes all the way down to my jawline. In total, these injections cost me $625, a fraction of what they'd cost in the UK or Australia (they aren't legal in the United States). The results, Dr. Shin said, would last at most two months, which is why people come and get it done before special events, like anything for which they'd get a blowout or a professional makeup job. The final hundred jabs felt almost unbearable despite all the numbing cream applied to my face beforehand. "How is this worth it?" I whined toward the end. "For beauty, a little bit?" Dr. Shin said with a nonchalant shrug.

I checked my face on my phone as soon as we walked out of the clinic, and lines of raised bumps appeared in rows, tiny red dots at the center. It grossed me out. Then as soon as I returned to my hotel room, I looked in the mirror and started laughing uproariously at how injured I appeared. I looked embossed. How soon would the bumps go away? What if they left marks? How was I supposed to go out in public? *Good thing we're all wearing masks all the time,* my interpreter So Jeong replied when I texted her in panic. Still marveling at how scary I looked, I captured a few seconds of video of myself through my laughter and sarcastically captioned it "fast results," before sharing it with friends.

In South Korea's plastic surgery scene, injectables proliferate like new gadgets, where it's not unusual to anticipate the next thing to shoot in your face just as customers relish getting their hands on the latest phone models. In certain social subsets, everyone will have tried one. Just as K-beauty's cosmetic companies race to be the first, South Korean injectable use is often pioneering—vanguards in the art of shooting chemical cocktails under the skin. The race to be first moved beyond skincare to under-skin care. For those of us who reject elective surgery because it doesn't seem worth the pain, the risk, or the cost, there are more and more cosmetic "technologies" like Botox injections, fillers, and laser treatments that are more affordable and ostensibly less risky. South Korea is deciding the future of laser therapies and injectables in its many plastic surgery and dermatology clinics like Oracle. If invasiveness is the point at which we draw the line on improving our appearance, technological progress will obliterate it.

Injections are so mundane that plastic surgery clinics offer them only as loss leaders, as ways to get you into the door at prices even lower than cost. The giant surgery centers advertise an entire Botox region for as low as $10. Korea can experiment with injections and/or lasers that are impossible to try in the U.S. because the approval process the Food and Drug Administration, which has oversight in this area, follows is so long and bureaucratic many medicine makers choose to skip it.

These days, South Korea has thousands of different kinds of Botox, fillers, and injectable skin cocktails called "boosters" and "healers" for clients to choose from, like pink injection and Rejuran, the salmon stuff. By comparison, Dr. Hsu noted that as of 2021 in the United States, doctors can offer only four brands of Botox, and one of those brands is Jeauveau, from a Korean pharmaceutical company. The microdoses of "skin Botox" I received constitute an off-label use that most doctors in the United States won't do, or at least won't cop to.

~

Side effects or physical harm from these procedures is not completely avoidable, but data on how frequently people are injured is difficult to pin down. The Korea Consumer Agency keeps no official records of accidents or botched surgeries. "These days, there are so many accidents, and nearly every hospital has had a serious incident, so it doesn't matter so much," a medical malpractice lawyer told *The New Yorker* in 2015. "People who are having plastic surgery accept that it's a risk they take."[12]

With Korean surgeons undertaking as many as 10 procedures a day, the potential for error increases. The number of complaints about botched procedures reported to the Korea Consumer Agency in 2020 stands at 172,[13] up from 71 complaints in 2010.[14] There is no accounting of the actual number of procedures conducted each year, but even without a denominator, 170 sounds rather low, and widely eclipsed by the rate of growth of medical tourism to the country alone. In general, we know this: Plastic surgery procedures like liposuction and butt lifts carry a far higher risk than ones that require only outpatient surgery. On the other hand, globally, breast augmentation has gotten safer over time. Figures from the international open access journal of the American Society of Plastic Surgeons show the risk of dying from liposuction procedures is 2.6 deaths per 100,000 patients, about ten times higher than the roughly .25 deaths per 100,000 rate for general outpatient surgery, such as a tonsillectomy or a hernia repair.[15] The same source has no mortality numbers on breast augmentations or facial surgeries. While accurate data on cosmetic surgery complications is tricky to find, it's even harder to pinpoint data for the avalanche of nonsurgical procedures available in Korea. We do know that Botox, specifically, boasts a remarkably safe history when used for cosmetic purposes. Of the hundreds of millions of

Botox treatments given, only 36 serious adverse effects were reported to the FDA between 1989 and 2003.[16]

~

Where do we draw the line on appearance work when the work gets less and less invasive and previously impossible changes become possible? So Yeon Leem, the researcher who embedded for years inside a plastic surgery clinic, said it's ultimately not up to us. Even if we wanted to take modification to extremes, our bodies will draw the line. Nature has the final word. "The only thing that stops the growth [of the industry] would be the body itself. You know, it's hard to stop human desires to be more beautiful. But what I learned from my experience inside the clinic is that you can't change the body just as you want. Because the body has its own force, its own way and will."

A week after my skin injections, back in L.A., I posed for a few photos with a friend before a night out. When I gazed at the snapshots on my phone, I noticed that my smile wasn't as wide—my lower cheeks looked fuller, but in an artificial way. This caused me an immediate moment of distress, seeing the plumped bottom half of my face in such a tight smile. How did getting injected with "skin Botox" (which was not supposed to act as a filler or weaken muscles) constrict the full range of my smile? What happened? The injection had changed my face, and a prized part of it, the part where I radiate joy. No one warned it would turn out this way. For days after, I would twist my jaw, alternating directions, to try and stretch my face out and return it to normal.

In an effort to smooth out my skin and make it look shinier, I felt I'd come back from Seoul as me, but slightly not. Sitting in my car at streetlights, I would peer at myself in my rearview mirror and question how easily I had submitted to this. I had bought into the prevailing notion that injections are "nothing" and "routine" and people indulge in them all the time. Sure, people do, but should I? Had I done it because I'd wanted to or because I'd been told to? I felt pleased with the smoother skin but guilty, too. The results were slightly off, though I don't know what I expected. I wouldn't even have known how to explain to Dr. Shin what I didn't like, because the changes were so minuscule to the outside observer even as they were giant to my own eyes.

I suppose that's the weight of cosmetic work. The individual who chooses to undergo it must bear the brunt of its effects. Don't like the alterations? You chose the treatment in the first place. But when beauty is considered a kind of duty, doing the spiritual and physical aftercare alone is awfully alienating. The imperative to stay on trend is shared. The risks, responsibilities, and blame are not.

Plastic surgeons, in reshaping body parts, plausibly make the case they fix their patients' self-image, making those they treat feel individually more empowered by looking better. And it's true, you are individually rewarded if the aesthetic work looks "good" enough to others, despite being left to fend with the complexities of a change in your appearance and in your identity on your own. I ask myself, what does all this surgery mean for the rest of us if we don't keep up appearances? Even being able to try and keep up is the provenance of the global rich. Leem, who revealed she, too, had succumbed to the lure of jawline surgery about ten years earlier, said she regretted her decision but didn't think she really had a choice.

I asked her whether she considered cosmetic surgery "gendered violence," as some academics call it.

She considered for a beat. "Yes," she finally responded, without elaborating.

"Why?" I followed.

"It's like marriage," she said. "Some people consider marriage very natural. You know, not all married women are miserable or unhappy. So . . . it doesn't mean women who take cosmetic surgery are victims or anything like that."

Of course not, I said. You choose it.

"Maybe this is just wordplay," she said, "but I don't think having choices is free will. Maybe all choices we make are related to, are affected by, the system. So I don't really like [the binary] free choice vs. structure. I think our choices are all structural. I would say . . . I mean, even when I choose my cell phone, like Samsung over iPhone, I don't think that's my free choice." She still had to have a phone in the first place.

All this consumption of plastic surgery ultimately illuminates how market-driven priorities of self-care and managing our bodies are coded to us as necessities even as they're described as "choice." Doctors might turn down patients who they believe suffer from body dysmorphia because such patients would likely never be satisfied. But few doctors question the ethics of their work in a larger way. They're not asking, "Is this necessary?" or "What responsibility might we have in reinforcing impossible beauty standards?" Rather, the surgical industry poses a different question: "How can we advance our work in the name of technological progress and profit?"

~

The possibilities of bodily improvement and change are refracted through the social internet, where injections or surgery are sold among the many upgrades available to us in the name of "progress." As cultural critic Haley Nahman observes,[17] a tentpole of modern life is the belief that more technology is always better than less. It leads to some benign-seeming examples of "progress" that actually make things worse, while the companies behind them make more money. She cites TurboTax, Face ID, or self-checkout and writes: "It's easy to name examples of pseudo-progress and harder to imagine our trajectory not barreling toward an increasingly 'optimized,' frictionless, smooth-brained world. One where the conditions this pursuit has thus far created—alienation, hypernormalization, mass inequality—only grow starker." Botox fits into this framework as something sold to us that relieves our individual stress about forehead creases—aka, aging—but not good for the collective. It is an investment in a worldview that we *should* be creaseless at midlife or even older. And it feeds anxieties for those who aren't.

Normalizing the injections and transplants of increasingly lab-made parts (silicone, threads, salmon DNA, or whatever is en vogue) creates a cosmetic underclass—people who can't afford the surgeries, lasers, or shots—while ever improving the chances for the haves to look the part of the dominant culture. (This is to say nothing of the actual underclass, which has been excluded from these transactions from the start.) As this happens—as more people do what it takes to fit the norm—the technological gaze can further narrow beauty standards and inch them further out of reach, all the way down to perfectly sized pores.

The technological gaze "invites you to examine the flaws in your skin minutely as if under a microscope. This way of looking at the skin is only possible with technology . . . Once we recognize the flaws in ourselves, we can then fix them by buying the right products or undergoing the correct procedures. The technological imperative should not be underestimated as a driver in the race towards perfection (at the top end of the scale) and as influential in the raising of minimal standards and in the narrowing of normal (at the bottom end)," philosopher Heather Widdows writes in her 2018 book.[18] "While fixing individuals reduces prejudice directed towards particular individuals," she adds in the following chapter, "it increases prejudice in general."[19] I think they call this the tragedy of the commons.

One of the biggest concerns about the social internet is that it's just too big—we weren't meant to all be in a community of this scale, in which everyone has become our neighbor. It forces us onto the same handful of platforms to present ourselves, platforms that remove distinctions by forcing us to fit into their predetermined forms and profile options. And we come to the internet pre-wired for our visual encounters to shape what we desire. Under the theory of French philosopher René Girard, humans are extremely good at mimicking one another, and we learn what we desire, and what to desire, based on what our neighbors do.[20]

"We assume that desire is objective or subjective, but in reality it rests on a third party who gives value to objects," he wrote. "This third party is usually the one who is closest, the neighbor."[21]

When the entire internet population is your neighbor, this is a recipe for conflict. Scholars who study mimetic theory argue that the sameness it produces leads to escalating competition and rivalry. The platforms, writes Geoff Shullenberger, "convert all users into each other's potential models, doubles, and rivals, locked in a perpetual game of competition for the intangible objects of desire of the attention economy."[22] With advances in cosmetic surgery, that competition and the imitative nature of humans means these competitions can play out in real life, in physical space, where fixed-up faces and bodies are signaling to others in order to determine who's in and who's out.

Incidentally, the knock on the stereotypical Gangnam Beauty (*gangnam-miin*), the name for a young South Korean woman who has undergone multiple plastic surgeries and achieved an "artificial" face, is that these women have overdone it in the eyes of the public. Their critics believe these women have achieved a bland interchangeability among themselves, similar to the effect of using digital photo filters, which offer the same suite of choices for our appearance as the most popular cosmetic procedures in Seoul: smoothness, larger eyes, thinner jaws.

The faces of Gangnam Beauties do often appear pleasing, but in a two-dimensional way. These patients aren't soulless, but their faces are devoid of texture, asymmetry, and surprise, making them seem slightly inhuman. As So Yeon

Leem observed, that's kind of by design. While some clinics have moved to 3D modeling, recall that many plastic surgery centers deduce ideal proportions from a flattened image. This is yet another way the virtual representation of a thing gets privileged over the actual thing.

In Gangnam, as he shifts in his desk chair in his purple scrubs, Dr. Seo sounds rather resigned to the world-leading Korean plastic surgery industry remaining on a quest for sustained growth. He finds creating the desire for more surgeries and looking for the next trendy thing to sell both distasteful and potentially dangerous. Finding new areas of the body to fix has led to Korean expertise in surgeries like skull resculpting, which smooths or reshapes the natural grooves in the back of your head, buried under your hair. Seoul doctors also specialize in morally questionable surgeries like "revirginization" or penis enhancement, which involves implanting silicone or the patient's own fat around the shaft of the penis.

Seo holds himself up throughout my visit as an example of prudence, noting that when patients come to him for a second opinion, he often advises them not to change a thing, to the patients' surprise. He resists making his service function like a salon, where clients return regularly, lured back for repeat touch-ups. "I'd like patients to come in, get the work, and be done," he says.

As he gets up to leave, he stops and addresses my interpreter, So Jeong. He's standing over her in a conversation clearly not meant for me. His tone is amiable, and he gestures vaguely. Her mouth drops open and her hands instinctively touch her cheeks. "What, really?" she says in Korean, words I can understand. He says something else and then strides out of the office, bound for his afternoon of surgeries, leaving the two of us alone.

My eyes fix on hers, eyebrows raised questioningly. "He said I could use a lift for the bags under my eyes," So Jeong tells me. "He said he would just cut small incisions and I'd look much less angry." She's unnerved by this for the rest of our time together. Maybe even still.

~

CHAPTER 9

Free Size Isn't Free

A youthful look, poreless skin, and manicured nails all matter, but perhaps nothing counts as much as having an acceptable body size. What constitutes slim in Korea is a skinniness without comparison. Korea has nearly the lowest obesity rate in the developed world, with only about 6 percent of its population considered clinically obese. (For America, the most obese country in the twenty-seven developed countries that make up the OECD, it's more than 40 percent.)[1]

The appearance discrimination, or lookism, that runs rampant across Korean society is most noticeable if you're thick enough such that you literally cannot fit. Clothing at most boutiques comes in only one size, a size they call "free." Free size is the equivalent of a U.S. size 2 or a UK size 8. When you go shopping at any of the local boutiques that line the popular Garosugil shopping streets, you'll find they offer the same pants or tops in numerous colors and cuts, but not in numerous sizes. For *kun saiji* (big sizes), we giants were relegated to the "foreign" neighborhood, Itaewon, near the longtime U.S. military base. There, even at my usual non-pregnant proportions, shopkeepers would take note of my five-nine U.S. size 8 frame and yell, "Big size, big size!" to me from their storefronts.

My measurements came off as gargantuan because a U.S. size 8 is the equivalent of a Korea 66—the starting point for plus-size, or extra-large.[2] Department stores rarely sell Western designers' off-the-rack dresses in anything larger than a U.S. size 4. Clothes shopping persistently filled me with irritation about the exclusivity of all this and with envy of everyone who could fit. After a shopping outing, I would find myself especially conscious of my lumps, admiring women on the subway whose already small clothing seemed to hang off them.

If "free size" wasn't enough of a constraint, Korean mass media and advertising reduce women's body parts to letters of the alphabet. Not unlike the science-y language around the V-line jaw of the face, the S line describes the way a woman's body should appear when viewed in profile: her breasts forming the top curve of an S, her butt the bottom curve, going in the opposite direction. The X line correlates with the hourglass proportion that women should have when gazed at head-on—a skinny waist with ample boobs and hips. Women's breasts are deconstructed into the letter W. The letter Y is also used for the décolletage. Ys are also mapped onto a woman's crotch, lower back, and butt. It's "easy to lose sight of the utilitarian, utterly reductionist view of women that this alphabetization process relies on," writes Korea-based writer James Turnbull, who runs the Korean feminist blog The Grand Narrative.[3] Women are conceptually dismembered. And then that pile of "perfect" body parts is taken to market, or marketed, for consumption.

On the Matter of Legs

In Korean beauty culture, the body parts that matter most are legs. The attention that breasts get in the West is given to legs in the East. The visual language of K-pop girl groups, for example, is most identified with bare legs, the prominent way by which female Korean idols distinguish themselves from global celebs around the world. Camera angles shoot upward at legs, lengthening them visually, and stars accentuate the ways they move in expertly choreographed, perfectly executed dance moves. Skirts are worn so short that they barely cover the butt. Just as the face has a "magic ratio," so do the legs: 5:3:2.[4] The numbers refer to the thickest part of the thigh, the thickest part of the calf, and the ankles. In Korea, legs are the third most popular place to use Botox, in order to slim down the calves by weakening the muscle.[5] The second most popular region for Botox, after the face, is the base of the neck—neurotoxins are injected into trapezius muscles to make them smaller and give the illusion of a longer neck.

Bare legs are expected, while bare arms are unacceptable, as I learned on the subway my first summer in Seoul. Why was this? Bare legs, I discovered, have come to hold a particular cultural power. As the Korean Wave and its magnetic idols pushed into new countries, "women's legs became a showpiece item for the propagation of a triumphant discourse of Korean physical beauty and commercial power," write Korean studies scholars Stephen Epstein and Rachael Joo.[6] Image makers weaponized bare female legs in South Korea's soft power battle for cultural dominance.

In this way, legs function as a marketing tool and a "branding technique for an enticingly toned and 'impeccably executed'" Korea, as Epstein and Joo note,[7] and historically it's led to some amusing and unfortunate outcomes. In 2012, the Thai government and media expressed concern after the incidence of dengue fever among Thai women shot up after girls and women adopted Korean-style hot pants, which exposed more of their bare legs to mosquitoes.[8] No publicity was bad publicity, however. Epstein and Joo note that when Korean media picked up on stories like this, it only further corroborated that Korean soft power was on the rise.

As living emblems of soft power, K-pop performers are expected to toil to maintain their magnetism. Promotional videos put out by their management companies offer glossy glimpses of the life of idol trainees. Documentaries and news features show trainees living in dorm-like settings to bond, studying foreign languages to appeal to fans around the globe, sweating through intense dance practices, and then goofing off during downtime. Kong Youjin, who became the lead singer of a now-defunct girl group called BONUSBaby, is one of the few former idols who has spoken out about the toll of her trainee days now that she's out from under the management contract she signed at age fifteen. In a video call, the now dressed-down, makeup-free, bespectacled teen looks like an easygoing college student. But nothing was easy about what she went through as a trainee.

The six members of BONUSBaby were brought together by a small management company called Maroo Entertainment, which also manages Park Ji-hoon, Teen Teen, and Ghost9. Kong told me that Maroo insisted on a uniform weight limit of 46 kilograms (101 pounds) for BONUSBaby members. She further explained that because the girls all fell between five-four and five-six, the company could conveniently set one single weight that no one was to exceed, without adjustments for height differences. "If we weighed even a little bit over 46 kilos, a few grams or a few hundred grams, they would say something to us. So if we wanted to eat or drink water comfortably, we had to be under 46 kilograms," she said, which led some members to drop more weight than required.

Kong's agency is not unique. Numerous accounts over the years from other K-pop artists have revealed weight mandates are as common as K-pop's cotton candy–colored music videos. Online amateur-made video montages abound of K-pop idols fainting during performances, presumably from dehydration and overexertion.

To track the young performers' weight, managers subjected them to a bewildering ten weigh-ins a day, which Kong listed for me as she described a typical day: "When we woke up in the morning in the dorm, we would weigh ourselves once. Then after arriving at the company, we would weigh ourselves again. We practiced freely from ten to eleven. Before eating our first meal, we would weigh ourselves. And then after eating our first meal, we would weigh ourselves once again. After that, we would usually have two hours of vocal practice or two hours of dance practice in the

afternoon. On days we went to a vocal academy, before going, we would weigh ourselves at the company and then go
to the vocal academy for lessons. And then after we came
back, we would weigh ourselves again. And then before eating dinner at the company, we would weigh ourselves again,
and then weigh ourselves after eating dinner. And then at
night, we would have dance practice and vocal practice and
then weigh ourselves before going to the dorms. And then
we would weigh ourselves once more after getting to the
dorms. And that's the end of our daily schedule."

Kong shed several kilograms by subsisting on a handful
of almonds, a juice-box-sized serving of soy milk, and "as
many cherry tomatoes as we wanted" each day. She dropped
weight until she hit 42 kilograms (92 pounds). Still, for her, it
wasn't enough. "Faces look different on screen, so . . . even
after losing that weight, my face was not that much slimmer," she said. "That's why I decided to voluntarily lose more
weight."

As we talked, I noticed I sat completely frozen, stunned
by how little Kong would eat while somehow managing to
dance and sing for hours every day. Then an embarrassed
flush zoomed through me. Despite my decades-old, hard-
won body satisfaction, somewhere in me a competitiveness
cropped up. I thought, I never ate as little as she did when I
starved myself. And why not? At my most restrictive, I allowed myself a meal of four ounces of frozen yogurt for
lunch and the same for dinner.

BONUSBaby debuted to a tepid response. That they didn't
take off made it easier for Kong to leave the group when she
found her mind and body were breaking down. Her family

had the means to help buy her out of her contract and she walked away from the surprisingly long seven-year deal she'd signed onto, allowing her to share these details publicly. "If I say it was enjoyable, that would be a lie," Kong said. "I wanted to just play, like my peers. They took away our cell phones and any electronics, and we also lived in the dorms with a manager . . . it was like a prison."

Just as today's Gen-Z Americans are naming "social media influencer" as a career aspiration, many Korean youth say they want to be "idols" one day. But even if they don't seek that particular dream, millions want to *look* like K-pop entertainers, with eternally childlike faces, baby-soft skin, wide eyes, and tiny waists.

It makes sense, then, that everyone I spoke to pins the blame on mass media, both traditional and social, for the ongoing objectification of women and perpetuation of skinny standards. In physical spaces, K-pop culture is all around—in the background music in the streets, in the life-size cutout advertisements (where celebrity endorsements make up more than half of all ads[9]), and etched on the faces of regular Koreans, parroting the K-pop aesthetic. "Where K-pop stars excel is in sheer physical beauty," *The New Yorker* declared.[10] "I think a lot of young, female entertainers are being consumed by men in this country as 'ideal' female figures—physically attractive, pleasant and docile," Ahn Sang-soo, a researcher at the Korean Women's Development Institute, noted in 2018.[11]

The kind of thin-spiration, or thinspo, promoted by "breakable" thin legs reaches not just the pro-anorexia (pro-ana) online enclaves but all mainstream platforms—TikTok, YouTube, Instagram—anywhere K-pop is celebrated. Global K-pop idols are held up as "thinspo" so commonly on TikTok that just by being a Korean pop culture fan, you'll easily encounter fan videos or posts about how to get that look, which is conflated with crash diets, training until you faint, and all-out starvation. "It seems like the beauty standard is becoming narrower and harsher," said therapist Yuna Kim, whose childhood eating disorder inspired her work specializing in treating patients with disordered eating. "It's because of the widespread use of social media. If I watch one thing, related things keep showing up. Pro-ana starts appearing, and if I see that, I'm going more extreme, doing severe diets."

It is another example of how technology feeds demand but also creates it. Tech platforms serve children and teens a lot of content, and individuals interested in K-pop or K-pop idols are then treated to an endless scroll of videos about food restriction. The environment around us shapes our perceptions, a notion especially true for young people while their brains are still developing. A psychological process called perceptual narrowing works in two ways: improving a developing human's ability to perceive stimuli it encounters a lot—say, their own family's language or race—but also diminishing the child's ability to perceive what they are not exposed to—say, the sounds of a language their family doesn't speak, or people of a race they don't often encounter.[12] I worry that all the thinspo images and tips served up to children and amplified by social algorithms distort young people's idea of what constitutes normal weight, making an effort to be rail-thin seem like the only reasonable path.

K-pop management companies aren't the only ones setting goal weights. So do the purveyors of love: Korea's abundant dating and marriage matchmaking companies, which number above a thousand, make no secret ideal weight ranges for their women clients.[13] Matchmaking services have long been trusted by middle-class Korean singles, with advertisements appearing all over subway cars. One of the oldest and most established matchmaking companies, Sunoo, creates a spouse index that quantifies a client's value with three main subcategories: the social capability index (education, occupation, salary), the family environment index (the education, occupations, and assets of parents and siblings), and the body index, which is based on height, weight, and "attractiveness" as assigned by the agency. Women should be between 163 and 168 centimeters tall (five-three to five-six) and weigh between 45 and 50 kilograms (99–110 pounds), just like the K-pop trainees, to receive the highest score. Points are deducted for deviating from this range.[14] Sunoo is not alone—most all matchmaking services develop similar indexes, differing mainly in how the subcategories are weighted.

The Korean pro-anorexic community coalesces around its own arbitrary (and more extreme) metrics in the discipline of their bodies. To find their "ideal" weight in kilograms, they take their height in centimeters and subtract 120.[15] For example, I am 175 centimeters tall (five-nine). In the pro-ana formula, I should weigh 55 kilograms (121 pounds). But the goalposts keep moving—more recently, pro-anas encourage one another to subtract 125 from their height. That would mean I should weigh an alarming 50 kilograms (110 pounds) on my five-nine frame. When I entered this height and weight combo in a body mass index calculator (a flawed but widely used indicator of healthy weight), the BMI it returned was 16.3. That's far under the "normal weight" range of 18.5 to 25 and meets a criterion for an official anorexia diagnosis.

These formulas are shared online, tagged with aspirational keywords, images, and videos of chopstick-skinny legs and skin-and-bone bodies, similar to what you might see on pro-ana sites in the U.S. One popular Korean hashtag? *Deuthan pal dari*—"arms and legs that look like they could break."[16]

Extreme Measures

Extreme measures to reach those goal weights include but are not limited to: Gobbling up pills. Surreptitiously spitting out food and/or purging after eating. Mummification by pressure-wrapping oneself with bandages. But most commonly, women and girls do as the trainees do and consume so little food that clinicians would label the practices as actively anorexic.

Park Boram first came to minor fame as a "chubby" teenager with a voice well beyond her years. In 2010, when she was fifteen, Park finished among the top eight in Mnet's *Superstar K2*, one of many reality talent competitions on Korean television. Nearly five years later, after her agency put her through training in dancing, singing, and acting, she debuted (the term used for K-pop idols who are introduced as branded personas). By the time of her debut, Park had dropped an alarming 32 kilograms (70 pounds), and producers named the lead track on her EP "Beautiful."[17] In the video for "Beautiful," which translates more directly as "I Became

Pretty," Park, wearing a fitted pastel-colored dress that flares out at the waist, emerges from a magenta music box with her hands clasped at her midsection. She's personifying a literal doll inside the box, spinning slowly. After a few quick edits, the video cuts to a scene of Park sitting in her kitchen, weighing her food on a scale and singing the lyrics "One banana, two eggs, it's so hard to become pretty like the others."[18]

The boldface names of Korean pop culture openly share their height and weight stats, and the regimens they follow to shrink down to size. Park worked the narrative of her drastic weight loss into her debut single, crooning of the work she put in to achieve Korean beauty ideals:

Short skirts, skinny jeans, doesn't matter,
I can wear them now (I'm good)
(I want to be bold and not care about what others think)
All day, I'm only looking in the mirror

Another line says overdoing it was worth it. "I think a lot of people, after listening to this song, were motivated to exercise more, lose weight, and diet," Park told me in an interview. "I think a big reason is because I put my story into it. Like, one banana, two eggs—eating just that, and you see the results in me, and that was motivating for people." These lyrics aren't exaggerated for a song. Park said she really did follow that diet, eating a single banana and an egg for most of her meals.

The message is plain: becoming "pretty" delivers the goods for the good life, and she is a walking advertisement that it can happen. "I Became Pretty" climbed up the Korean charts, finishing among the Top 20 singles in 2015.[19] The same year, Park became a spokesmodel for a diet drink called Fat Down.[20] In objectifying herself all the way to the bank, Park endorses a framework for a self that exists to be looked at and projects the message that disciplining her body with a starvation diet earned her love and success. The vast majority of K-pop audiences receiving this message are women and girls.

During that interview with Park, I wanted to find out to what extent producers are mandating how their idols should look. Unable to make it to the interview in time, I slouched over the speaker phone of my home office while my assistant and interpreter Haeryun met the singer and her team in a café near her Hongdae recording studio. "What guidance did you get to change your appearance, from your managers?" I asked. Haeryun paused for a moment, knowing this might be touchy, but forged ahead with asking the question in her native tongue.

We were immediately met with silence. Park, who had been distant but politely forthcoming throughout the conversation, suddenly managed only a slight headshake to indicate no. Her management rep, who flanked her throughout this interview, communicated with Park wordlessly. For what felt like an eternity, Haeryun and I waited, not rushing to fill the void. Park's minder's very presence had already shut down the question. Park continued to say nothing at all. I eventually moved on.

It's not worked into a catchy song lyric, but diet pills are often aiding the weight loss. Korea's consumption of diet drugs ranks near the top of the world.[21] A 2017 Korean Health

Ministry survey of middle and high school girls found nearly one in four had attempted to lose weight with "improper" methods, including vomiting after eating or taking laxatives, diuretics, or controlled diet drugs known as nabiyak, butterfly-shaped appetite suppressants.[22] These drugs are officially available by prescription only and are recommended for use only by the clinically obese. The active ingredient is most commonly phentermine, Korea's most frequently prescribed narcotic appetite suppressant, according to data from Korean lawmaker Nam In-soon, who brought up the abuse of these drugs in a 2021 parliamentary audit.[23] Phentermine production in Korea was about $17 million USD in 2010 but had doubled to $34 million by 2015.[24] The amphetamine is used in the United States as well, to treat obesity. It's the "phen" in the controversial weight-loss drug combination fenfluramine/phentermine, or fen-phen for short. Fen-phen was pulled from American pharmacy shelves in 1997 after makers of the "fen" part withdrew it from the market after research showed it did damage to heart valves.[25]

In total, four prescription appetite-suppressing substances for obesity treatment are available for sale in Korea.[26]* The European Union prohibits all of them for safety reasons. Numerous studies have shown these amphetamine-based appetite suppressants, when used off-label, can induce psychotic disorder and dependence, as well as suicidal thoughts.[27] "Users don't know of these dangerous side effects and think they'll just try it once or because their friends are doing it or because their parents are making them diet," Seoul-based

---

* These are phentermine, phendimetrazine, diethylpropion, and mazindol.

therapist Yuna Kim said. "Especially if they are experiencing eating disorders, it's very harmful to their body."

Critics, such as lawmaker Nam, say these drugs are too easy to procure from unregulated online sellers, which is how many Koreans score the drugs without prescriptions. In 2021, when the Korean Ministry of Food and Drug Safety monitored the web for illegal resale of appetite suppressants, their online investigators turned up 147 offers inside five days.[28] Lawmaker Jung Choun-sook proposed legislation to tackle this problem,[29] noting psychotropic appetite suppressants are commonly bought in large quantities with fraudulent prescriptions and resold illegally.[30] So far, that proposed legislation has gone nowhere, and the drugs remain easily available to those motivated enough to buy them illegally.

Plus-Size

All the size limitations give off the impression everyone in Korea is rail-thin, but that's not the case. Korean companies, responsive to a largely but not completely homogeneous population, don't make larger-sized clothes because they assume there aren't enough people to buy them. For those who don't fit, like a 90-kilogram (198-pound) social media manager turned plus-size model Bae Gyo-hyun, shopping happens exclusively online, and with way fewer options. "I wish free size meant more than small," Bae laments. She suspects business logic drives these limitations.

But there are Koreans of different shapes and sizes, a fact I pressed in an exchange with fashion industry vet Kyungho Lee, who worked for Decathlon and Nike in Korea. He acknowledged there is a market beyond one size and characterized the one-size-should-fit-all system as an unfortunate cultural holdover. "The minority isn't regarded because they assume everyone can still adjust to this one idea for the country," Lee said. The clothes don't adjust to fit the people; the people are expected to adjust to fit the clothes.

As a foreign woman in Korea, I felt insubstantial as a matter of course. But my extra-largeness by Korean standards made me even more unaccounted for. I could not participate in the market for most clothes. In my nearly four years as a resident of Korea, I bought a total of three "free-size" clothing items: a navy blue button-front linen dress and two camisoles with straps that dug into my shoulders.

Factors in Asian Eating Disorders

Researchers have found that fatphobia and the pressure to be thin are more pronounced in Korea than in the West even though Korean women as a whole are objectively thinner to begin with.

The rise of eating disorders across East Asia closely tracks globalization, urbanization, industrialization,[31] and the overall expansion of capitalistic pursuits across the region.[32] "In sum," Kathleen Pike and Patricia Dunne write in the *Journal of Eating Disorders*, "as these countries have grown more industrialized and globalized, eating disorders have followed."[33] The spread of eating disorders across the region closely tracked the countries whose economies transformed Asia.[34] Japan led the pack, followed by the economies of Hong Kong, Singapore, Taiwan, and South Korea; then a second wave happened, made up of the remaining Southeast Asian countries—the Philippines, Malaysia, Indonesia, and Thailand; and lastly, China and Vietnam.[35]

But Korea really stands apart. It seems factors unique to living in Korea drive the trend toward extreme thinness.[36] Native Korean women are significantly slimmer and have more disordered eating patterns than Koreans living abroad or Korean Americans, for instance. And in a study comparing college women from China, Korea, and the United States, Korean college women had the greatest degree of body dissatisfaction and disordered eating behaviors, followed by Chinese women, and lastly, U.S. women.[37] Korean women are also by far the skinniest. As the rest of the world— including Korean men—grow heavier in the aggregate, Korean women ages twenty to thirty-nine are going in the opposite direction—more and more of them have become underweight. During the early 2000s in Korea, when parents began pushing appearance as a vehicle to attain the "good life," researchers noted a statistically significant rise in underweight rates among Korean women between the ages of twenty and thirty-nine.[38] The percentage of underweight Korean women rose 60 percent between 1998 and 2007.[39]

One explanation for the rise of eating disorders after modernization is that female societal empowerment led to backlash—a media-led doubling down on heteronormative gender ideals.[40] Seventy-four percent of South Korean women attend college, far more than Korean men, at about 66 percent, and women also make up an ever-larger share of law school students.[41] In the past, panic over gender roles and masculinity has often come about during times of economic crisis. "It happened in the 1980s under [Ronald] Reagan and [Margaret] Thatcher," feminist writer Laurie Penny notes. "It happened in the 1930s in Europe and America. It happened in the mid-1800s, as revolutions rolled and tumbled across the Global North. It's happening now."[42]

Further, Sandra Lee Bartky and others have argued that when societies make strides toward gender equality, media portrayals of unrealistic gender norms tend to accompany them.[43] There's evidence to back this up. As Europe industrialized in the 1870s, for instance, a women's movement grew.[44] And that's when accounts of anorexia nervosa first sprang up. The thinnest women were showcased in American fashion magazines just as momentum built for women's rights in the 1920s and then again in the 1970s. Korea's case is particularly striking not just because of modern life but due to the restrictive, patriarchal nature of the country's traditions, baked in as they were with interpretations of Confucian ideals.

Another explanation for the rise in body dissatisfaction and ever-shrinking women is Korean society's we-ness—the focus on looking good for others, not yourself. Those in collectivist cultures such as Korea may be more vulnerable to eating disorders because the pressure to be like everyone else makes it hard to differentiate "internal states from external expectations," which contributes to eating disorders.[45] A 2000 study by Woo Mee Park found that despite the smaller body size of Korean women, they were more negative about many of their physical characteristics than U.S. women were, since people with a high sensitivity in social situations (read: the ability to read a room, which is valued in collective societies) are also more likely to feel worse about social criticism.[46]

A systematic review by Jon Arcelus and colleagues published in the *Clinical Psychology Review* found the same: women who have difficulty expressing their own emotions and who prioritize other people's feelings are more likely to exhibit restrictive eating behaviors.[47] That suggests that a defining trait of Korean society—heightened social awareness and sensitivity—is also fertile ground for starvation diets. In this case, the Korean notion of *nunchi*, or being good at reading the room, proves not a superpower but a curse. Women are shrinking themselves to make everyone else more comfortable.

When losing or maintaining weight isn't for yourself but for everybody else, external cues—not your own body—tell you how much you should weigh. It can foster a real sense of alienation from your own body. Countless talk shows, advertisements, digital messaging, and social platforms perpetuate the idea that being underweight—the arbitrary 48-kilogram (106 pounds) standard—is an appropriate ideal. Husbands and boyfriends enforce this standard on their female partners in heterosexual relationships.

For bodies that don't, or won't, shrink to fit into "free" size or to achieve the right alphabet soup of body lines, the overriding belief is not that your existing physical form cannot achieve it, but that it's a failure of work and will. Korean research subjects who failed to drop pounds experienced deep frustration, anger, and self-hatred that resulted in low self-esteem and low confidence in their ability to exercise self-control. Painful emotions stemmed from anxiety about being judged for not being thin and attractive, as we might expect.

The critics can go beyond noxious and become downright dangerous. I asked dozens of Korean women their first memories of being judged for their appearance. The vast majority bring up classmates fat-shaming them in elementary and middle school. "By the time I was ten years old, the boys came up to me and started saying, 'Look at your thighs,'" college student Jeon Hye-min told me. "I started thinking about my weight and dieting from that point on."

The "plus-sized" in South Korea (most of whom would be regular-sized anywhere else) describe overt discrimination and its effects.[48] When Bae, the successful plus-size model, was a child, she recalls random people on the street openly calling her "elephant legs." Other Koreans who don't fit are denied seating at restaurants, face questions from hiring managers such as "Can you work quickly with that body?" and avoid sitting down on buses or subways for fear of taking up too much space. Online, they are the target of fat-shaming onomatopoeia: "*paohu,*" to poke fun at the sound fat people supposedly make when breathing, and "*kumcheok kumcheok,*" the sound people who are overweight supposedly make when eating food.[49]

The policing of other people's bodies can be particularly devastating for those in public life. Undesirable traits like muscles (egad!) can bring on a tsunami of shaming. An especially tragic cautionary tale is that of Sulli—real name Choi Jin-ri—of the K-pop group f(x). When Sulli was sixteen, national broadcaster Arirang TV described her as "the ideal lady of all Korean men," but picked on her "fatal fault!" of "thick ankles and calf muscles."[50] The idea that healthily developed muscles detract from a woman's attractiveness was met with perhaps surprisingly fierce resistance at the time, suggesting—refreshingly—the highly prescriptive standards for the body don't meet with universal approval in South Korea. Others, however, weren't so forgiving.

Arirang made the clip private on its YouTube channel after complaints, but it never apologized.[51] In the public eye since she was a fifth grader, Sulli was the most googled person in South Korea in 2017, ahead of then president Moon Jae-in.[52] By 2019, she faced a nonstop barrage of cyberbullying from vicious anonymous commenters for a slew of supposed transgressions—exercising her agency both bodily (like going braless or appearing drunk on social media) and relationally (calling older male actors by their first names instead of the deferential full name and honorifics).[53] As one of the world's first fully wired societies, Korea is really good at cyberbullying. Maybe the best. They had cyberbullying and doxing before much of the rest of the world knew about them. In October 2019, Sulli's manager found her dead in her apartment, following an apparent suicide.[54] In the days that followed, her death was described as a "social homicide," and petitions were posted at the president's office, arguing that targeted hate content contributed to her death, and that the nation needed to reckon with its culture of rampant cyberbullying.[55]

~

What emerges from my research and conversations with Korean women is that plastic surgery and body modification through disordered eating—both practices where Korea stands out—share similar motivations and expressions. On one hand, the fear of being a social outcast, and on the other, a genuine desire for empowerment in a system of aspirational capitalistic individualism. In Korea, after the Asian financial crisis, everyone is expected to be a hardworking entrepreneur. Appearances matter as much as, if not more than, abilities. The endurance of extreme dieting culture can't be written off as girlish superficiality. Rather, it's viewed by many of its adherents as empowerment in a highly visual, consumption-heavy system where our bodies are laboring and competing in the market. K-pop starlet Park Boram said it: *You see the results in me, and that was motivating for people.*

South Korea's modernity created major shifts in the practice of Korean womanhood. Women went from primarily identifying as mothers, then primarily as wives, and now in the current era of consumer culture, they can compete as sexy enterprises of their own. As such, as sociologist Cho Joo-hyun argues, body enhancement and modification are a means of enhancing human capital that does not depend on "the womanly virtues of traditional ethics," such as motherhood, but instead "on measurable and quantifiable factors such as height, weight, and BMI index."[56] Or a 1:1>1 face. Korea's factors are both unique to its history and culture but also share American thinking—unquestioned faith in markets and belief in individual responsibility. It reminded me that Korea's local pressures and influences don't happen in a vacuum. The Korean Dream, as Sharon Heijin Lee has described it, is a combination of collectivist values and neoliberal ideas—a souped-up version of the American Dream, in which what the market needs, and what we can privately gain, take precedence over everything else. There's nothing hard work and money can't get you.

Modern culture urges women to become "neoliberal entrepreneurs," prioritizing managing ourselves by managing our bodies. For Koreans, those of us influenced by K-culture, and anyone who's internalized the logic of maximizing our appearance to be competitive, K-beauty, K-surgery, and restrictive eating are means to that end. If you're trying to wring the most out of an asset—in this case, a human—you can get didactic about how to do it. Haein Shim, for example, fell into an eating disorder after her parents began restricting her food when she hit puberty. Once she dropped to a sub-50-kilogram (110 pounds) weight and appeared as a smaller, slighter, and quieter version of herself, "Everybody around me told me that I'm so wonderful at self-care," she said. "I'd been starving and working out. I was far away from self-care. However, in Korean society, the term *self-care* refers to women who regulate their weight and follow the grooming standard." Self-care is circumscribed with values of achievement and conformity.

Empowerment, in this framework, is not internal. It is attaining our imagined selves on the outside, and more often than not, our imaginations are limited by what everyone else is striving for. It introduces artificial scarcity. Diet culture and fatphobia have reduced our understanding of "beauty" and "health" into ever more exclusionary boxes.

Some K-pop writers have noted that women in K-pop in the 2020s claim far more agency than the early days of K-pop idols.[57] In the early 2000s, the management "factories" for manufactured performers made headlines. Now girl group BLACKPINK is one of the most famous K-pop groups globally, bested in sales only by BTS. The group's four women are lithe, probably plastic-surgery-perfected paragons of the global beauty norms of firmness, thinness, smoothness, and youth, but as observers note, they are not demure—they evoke a decidedly determined, empowered vibe. Another group, the chart-topping women of Red Velvet, are unafraid to shy away from feminist signifiers, which invites controversy and backlash in deeply patriarchal Korea. Plenty of their young women fans say they admire these performers because they are "empowering, strong" women, not for their sex appeal. But on the road to empowerment, the monumental work it takes to look the way they do, to keep their bodies as small as they are, goes without mentioning. It is . . . incidental. The way these models of "empowered" femininity look—their unattainable beauty—is so expected and internalized that somehow it's just the bare minimum! Sexualization (for men) is tangled up with self-commodification (for the market) in a knot that feels impossible to tease apart. Despite the kind of sacrifice and self-denial it takes to look that way, the expectation of thinness is taken so for granted that it isn't questioned.

~

North Korea conducted its fourth ballistic missile test of 2017 in early April. I went on the American airwaves with this news in my pajama pants from my windowless home office in Seoul on a Wednesday night, my Comrex broadcast device safely resting on my returned pregnant belly shelf. The very next night, in the same pants, I hoofed my 39-week-pregnant body into a familiar place—the birthing center south of the Han River. After I labored for four hours, a breeze compared to the previous two kids, our third daughter was born. We named her Luna.

When she was eight weeks old, I brought Luna to a video shoot and lingered in a day spa lobby, holding the swaddled infant in one arm, like a football, chatting mindlessly with the photographer, Jun. The diminutive spa owner hollered something at him in Korean from across the lobby. I stood there like a dummy, my default posture when Korean flies back and forth around me. "She says you can come back for postpartum body fat treatment," he interpreted. The owner then strode toward a poster picturing a woman wrapped in some sort of shrink wrap swaddle for adults. The photographer hesitated a moment, then translated sheepishly: "She says you can get this service for your thighs and lower belly." The two of them shot glances at those parts of my body. I let out a half chortle and responded with *Algeshimn-ida*, meaning, "I see," followed by a "Thanks."

Never did I try the slim wraps. During each pregnancy I let my body expand and contract without "wellness" service intervention. But I still felt a pang of anxiety at every pregnancy weigh-in at the doctor's office. The numbers would tick up in kilograms, which were (conveniently) all in the double digits and unfamiliar. I stayed blissfully unaware of what those kilograms meant in pounds until the very end of my final pregnancy, when my inner thighs ached from carrying all that extra weight. The last day I was pregnant, I entered "81 kg to lbs" into a Google search, driven by a morbid curiosity to know just how much I'd grown.

Having already survived a year of near starvation as a teen, I know overvaluing appearance, and size especially, doesn't lead to flourishing. "Well-being is derived from valuing, and placing value in, a range of capacities and capabilities," philosopher Heather Widdows writes in *Perfect Me*.[58] But just as you don't need to put your hand in a blender to know not to put your hand in a blender, it shouldn't take psychologically bottoming out to find self-awareness. Diet culture is bad for our bodies and our souls. British health psychologist Nichola Rumsey puts it this way: Imagine a healthy sense of self as a pie, with different-sized pieces contributing to overall well-being. If appearance makes up too much of that pie, this means failure in that area would be destructive in a way it wouldn't be if it was just one smaller component of your sense of self.[59]

But as I saw in contemporary Korea, beauty is so often the conduit for contentment and possibility. The thin girl is the hot girl, the hot girl is the happy girl, and by some transitive rule, to be thin is to be happy. The formula lures countless young people to dedicate their time and energy to it.

I cannot emphasize enough how distracting it is, how psychologically taxing, to fixate on exercise and weight. I cannot quantify how much time I've lost lingering in front of mirrors focused on "problem" areas, silently calculating calories in my mind, journaling what I ate each day, or thumbing through *Shape* and *Self* magazines from the early 2000s to memorize the most calorie-burning workouts. My seventeen-year-old self could have spent that time building stronger relationships, absorbing ideas, taking personal risks, or trying new experiences. Instead, she whirred with obsession and ached with hunger. Thoughts of food, when to eat food, what to do to burn off the food occupied the mental space equivalent of the Pacific Ocean.

The pressure on Korean women for thinness and certain body lines stands out as particularly staggering. But the project of unlearning body dissatisfaction and fatphobic ideas is universal. We cannot do it if we don't interrogate how we learned and normalized the ideas in the first place that certain bodies are worthy and others are not. "We can't stop the cycle of passing them down to future generations . . . And we can't unravel these ideologies without acknowledging the deep, often unrecognized trauma they have inflicted," American culture writer Anne Helen Petersen wrote, of noxious fatphobia writ large.[60]

~

I wonder how these forces will show up for my girls, girls of a new generation, as they approach adolescence. The other day my now nine-year-old, Eva, who is a long-limbed and limber young dancer, stood gazing at herself in front of a full-length mirror in my bedroom. She reached her arms high overhead, her eyes fixed on her reflection, and declared, "I love my body." I paused and looked up from the laptop I'd been lost in. Her language sounded so dissonant to my ears. I don't have a single memory of reveling in such appreciation of my body, especially as a nine-year-old. More aware these days of my own (abundant) internalized shame as I research and write this book about body image, I wondered, at what point will Eva stop loving her body and become critical of it? Next year? The year after? Or am I projecting my own childhood hang-ups onto someone who's nothing like me, growing up in a totally different milieu and part of an entirely new generation?

I sure hope today's teens find the pressure to be less and the times to be more accepting, but researchers have found body dissatisfaction and shame remain so chronic and widespread among young women that some have called for it to be recognized as a public health problem. Myriad devastating consequences are attached to it—lower self-confidence, diminished well-being, disordered eating, lower activity, risky behavior, mental and physical health issues.[61]

Beyond the time and energy suck and the mental toll, these practices, based on arbitrary ideals, make us more likely to be heavier in the long term and are so dangerous that they can kill us.[62] No one knows where 5:3:2 legs or S lines or X lines come from, but I can hazard a guess that these metrics are maintained by whoever wants to sell us something to correct our lines and ratios. "Those who earn money through this have the biggest responsibility," therapist and eating disorder survivor Yuna Kim says. "Diet companies or entertainment companies or those who make money off of this? These people create the beauty standard."

The global weight-loss industry was valued at $255 billion in 2021, and it's expected to reach $377 billion by 2026.[63] "Mass media promoting [impossible] ideals of women's body shapes distorts how men view women's bodies, and in turn this encourages women to fight against their own bodies. The real winners in this war are not men, nor women, but rather the beauty, cosmetic surgery, advertising, and mass media industries," Korean writer Bae Guk-nam writes of her fatphobic country.[64] Though the same could be said of mine.

~

CHAPTER 10

Escape the Corset

By 2018, South Korean women were so over it. Fed up with a slew of inequities and fueled by a global #MeToo movement, a group of them pushed back—a big group. Off-line, tens of thousands poured into the streets for the largest women's rallies in the nation's history.[1] Online, they launched a sustained campaign against appearance standards, known in English as #EscapeTheCorset. Women rallied against a knot of outrages: sexual violence, secret camera surveillance, and modern-day "corsets"—constraining norms on how to look and act. Though I was still living in South Korea at the time, I didn't make it to a single one of their rallies. I blame Kim Jong Un.

The North Korean despot opened that year with his annual New Year's Day address in Pyongyang. Standing before a neat row of black microphones in a light gray suit and matching tie, Kim announced in his deep baritone that his country had completed "the great, historic cause" of "perfecting" its nuclear forces.[2] He had even gotten a nuclear button installed at his desk, he claimed. Then Kim pivoted, signaling openness to entering talks with his country's longtime foe, the South. Relations on the peninsula had hit such a nadir at that point that the two Koreas hadn't engaged in diplomacy in two years. To say that Kim surprised the world with this turn is an understatement. Especially when he went further to say he'd be open to sending a North Korean delegation to the Winter Olympics that South Korea would host the following month.

Both Matt and I rushed to file spot news reports for our respective outlets while our children stayed up late and unsupervised.

The Tilt-A-Whirl of North Korea news dominated the first half of that year, as new developments continued to unfold at a dizzying speed. History-making inter-Korean talks happened within ten days of that New Year's speech.[3] The two Koreas agreed to field a first-ever joint team at the Winter Games.[4] By February, a North Korean delegation crossed the border to participate in said games,[5] where one night at a hockey match I found myself among a bunch of North Korean cheerleaders, a few rows behind Kim Yo-jong, the North Korean leader's petite freckle-faced sister who served as Pyongyang's propaganda chief. In March, for the first time since he'd taken the helm of the reclusive state in 2011, Kim Jong Un ventured out of the country to meet with another head of state—Chinese President Xi Jinping.[6]

My days were rushed and frenetic. Hunched over my laptop, I worked from overheated buses that dried out my skin, from taxis that crept along Seoul's clogged arteries, and from KTX bullet trains as we sped so fast past the Korean countryside on my way to the eastern coast that it appeared to me only as a fuzzy green apparition.

I worked such long and random hours away from home that both Luna and I gave up on my intention to breastfeed her until she turned a year old. She weaned in February, at ten months, after I returned from three weeks of living in a newly built but exceedingly isolating media apartment in Pyeongchang, from where I was covering the coldest Winter Olympics since 1992.

"There are people from all over the world here," I texted a friend. "And yet I feel so lonely."

"I imagine it's like being adrift at sea and dying of thirst," he replied.

By late April, Kim Jong Un and South Korean president Moon Jae-in were holding hands and giving joint remarks at the highly symbolic 38th parallel that has divided the Korean Peninsula since 1945.[7] My brain felt like a bowl of soggy oatmeal and my hair was falling out in clumps—postpartum hair loss is real. "One day the relentlessness of the North Korea beat will end," I wrote in my journal at the time. "But not before it ends me first." Kim Jong Un was appearing in my dreams.

~

While I was otherwise occupied, long-simmering gender tensions boiled over into a women's rights reckoning in South Korea. Women were in "total rebellion" against Korea's deeply patriarchal structures that had found "cruel new forms" in the digital era.[8] I paid only passing attention to this, as by that spring, my reporting focused on previewing and preparing to fly to Singapore for a hastily announced summit between Kim Jong Un and Donald Trump, the first-ever meeting of the sitting U.S. and North Korean heads of state. In the quiet moments between filing posts and radio dispatches, I was nagged by a feeling of missing out. Around me, South Korean women were organizing a series of mass demonstrations against sexual violence that would be the largest women's rallies the country had ever known.[9]

The catalyst for this historic moment had come two years before. In May of 2016, at a noraebang, or karaoke bar, near the bustling Gangnam subway station, a thirty-four-year-old man stabbed to death a twenty-three-year-old woman in a public restroom.[10] His victim was a stranger. Security footage showed the man passed over six men who entered the bathroom before singling out his female victim.[11] His explanation? He told police that women had "belittled" him.[12]

A woman preyed on in the course of going about her day. A perpetrator who despised women and was willing to inflict violence on them. For many South Korean women, there was something all too familiar in the death of the woman, whose name has never been publicized.[13] It sparked grief and outrage, and in the days that followed, Korean women swarmed near the scene to pay tribute to the victim, covering the glass-domed Gangnam subway station entrance with a rainbow wall of multicolored Post-it Notes carrying messages of sympathy and recognition: "It was misogyny that killed her."[14] "I survived, only by coincidence."[15] "What happened to you happened to me."[16] The collage became a makeshift memorial, filled with sobering messages and stories of sexual violence and fear. Safer behind screens, even more women spoke up online about their experiences.

By 2018, a flood of sexual misconduct accusations forced

a prominent theater director,[17] a famous poet,[18] and a liberal provincial governor, Ahn Hee-jung, out of public life.[19] Korean women channeled their collective discontent into organizing like never before, in numbers previously unheard of. On the two-year anniversary of the Gangnam murder, in May 2018, an internet-organized rally for more accountability on sex crimes drew an estimated 20,000 people.[20] Participants wore red but donned hats, face masks, and sunglasses to obscure their identities.[21] "It's difficult in the movement. You can't be visible," says Kim Jimin, whose introduction to feminism began that year. "Since you have concerns about violence, you feel helpless."

The women also used their anonymity to make a point. Just like women around the world, South Korean women live under the threat of domestic abuse, sexual harassment, and rape. But Korea's technological modernity saddles its women with sex crimes of a specific type: *molka*. Women live under persistent digital surveillance of their most private selves, thanks to a network of molka, or hidden cameras secretly installed by bad actors in clothing store dressing rooms,[22] in public bathrooms,[23] at school,[24] in hospitals,[25] and on buses.[26] Everyday middle-class perpetrators—who run the gamut from schoolteachers[27] to doctors[28] to civil servants[29]—secretly install molka to capture content from private homes and public spaces, taking video of victims doing mundane private activities, and anyone with an internet connection can upload, sell, and circulate the footage. It is a national epidemic of spycam pornography.

The overwhelming majority of the content—more than 80 percent—is of women's bodies, filmed without their knowledge.[30] It's almost always captured by men.[31] These hidden cameras also film revenge porn, which can find an eager audience. "Spycam porn" is its own genre on the South Korean porn hubs.[32] At the May 2018 rally, the masked women held up matching signs reading MY LIFE IS NOT YOUR PORN.

Human Rights Watch calls molka a form of sexual violence,[33] and crimes of this type jumped sixfold inside a decade.[34] But molka crimes are so rarely prosecuted that they are functionally legal. In the United States, a jury awarded sportscaster Erin Andrews more than $50 million for emotional distress in her case against a man who videotaped her naked.[35] Untold numbers of similar situations are believed to be happening to Korean women each day, and under South Korean law, digital exploitation carries at most a maximum of five years in prison. That's on the rare chance the case is even pursued. Korean authorities often say these crimes are too difficult to prosecute. Except for the time, in the spring of 2018, when police did manage to arrest a *woman* perpetrator of a digital sex crime.[36] They nabbed a female art school model who secretly filmed a male model in the nude, even though this type of woman-films-man instance is dwarfed—in the estimated tens of thousands—by molka that victimizes women. In the streets, women chanted as they pumped their fists: "Innocent if you have a dick, guilty if you don't . . . Men aren't the only human beings!"[37]

The May rally was repeated in early July, with a bigger turnout—roughly 60,000 people attended—and other protests followed, nicknamed *bulpyunhan yonggi*, or "uncomfortable courage."[38]

The off-line protests against sexual violence coincided with a fast-spreading online campaign in which women took aim at the prescribed ways they're supposed to look. Dubbed Corset-Free or Escape the Corset, the movement had spread from a handful of hashtags in 2016 to thousands of participants by 2018. An estimated 300,000 Korean women, mostly in their teens and twenties, visibly rejected appearance ideals by cutting their hair, crushing their makeup compacts, and daring to go out in public with no makeup at all.[39] The women anonymously posted defiant pictures of clumps of hair they'd hacked off and cosmetics they'd smashed, and accompanied them with a Korean hashtag: "Proof of discarded corset."[40] When posting their makeup dumps, the women expressed feelings of deep relief and relaxation. Presenting as a socially acceptable woman doesn't come with off days, and finally, these women were giving themselves an overdue break—joining a general strike against aesthetic labor.

This was my final year in Seoul, and reactions to two strains of technology where South Korea distinguishes itself—technologies of surveillance and self-improvement—had collided and ignited the biggest women's rights rallies ever, fanning the flames of a modern liberation movement and a bitter battle of the sexes.

Fearful for their safety, feminist women operated without visible leaders and spokespeople. But many who "escaped the corset" could be spotted on college campuses or in workplaces. These women wore their protests in the form of their short hair and bare faces.

To appear without preening is a tougher stand to take in South Korea than other places, precisely because the pervasive beauty culture makes nonparticipants stick out so much. These women are subject to unsolicited taunting and public humiliation. "Instead of calling by my name, my coworkers just call me 'boy,'" said Heo Jooyeon, a movement member, a podcaster, and an editor at a publishing house. "'Why are you like that?' they'll ask me. And my family tells me they think [appearing with short hair and makeup-free] is unsafe for me. Everyone comments about their own discomfort. At first I tried to explain my thoughts and values, but that's not what they wanted to hear, so now I'm just ignored."

A few beauty YouTubers joined the cause. Lina Bae is one of them. She had previously grown her subscriber base by spending hours a week before ring lights and a digital camera, giving makeup tutorials. But in a mesmerizing video called "I am not pretty," Bae meticulously puts on layer after layer of heavy makeup while in the same frame, a scroll of online comments appears alongside her.[41] Commenters pelt her with insults about her appearance throughout this process, even as she is putting in all the effort to perform femininity to the standards dictated by society. Then she reverses course, wiping off all those makeup layers, revealing only her bare face. Bae then smiles for the first time in the video before it cuts to black. A final message appears on screen: "I am not pretty. But it's ok not to be pretty."

This video went viral, and CNN and the BBC both featured clips of it.[42] In the span of her short video, which has since been removed from the internet, Bae expertly called attention to the double bind for Korean women. When they reject beauty norms, they are considered outcasts, chided for poor manners and not "trying." But when they do put in effort, they're criticized, too, for not doing it right or overdoing it, earning nicknames like *doenjangnyo*—Soybean Paste Girl—the derisive term for women considered superficial for spending too much on appearances. Women are ridiculed for attempting to capitalize on appearance, the singular attribute society encourages them to cultivate, and even more ridiculed when they don't. Maybe today's twist on the Modern Girl of the 1920s and the Factory Girl of the 1970s, both of whom used their makeup as a form of protest, are the "girls" who refuse to participate in beauty culture at all.

Another Corset-Free movement member is twenty-six-year-old Choi Yujin, whom the boys nicknamed Darkie and Godzilla when she was ten years old, for her "darker" skin tone (which in Korea is medium beige, or approximately the color of light sand). Today, as she hunts for a job in information design, she wears her dark hair in a short bob with long bangs. She is neither tan nor chubby. But she recalls that even her childhood best friend, a girl, "playfully" called her an ape. "Failing at beauty made me feel like I was a failure all my life," she says. "I never thought they made these comments to hurt me, but instead that they were for my own good." Choi said people whose looks didn't pass muster could choose one of two responses: disappear and drop out of the social sphere, or assimilate, which requires sidelining your dignity and putting yourself through enormous labor. "I stayed visible in order to belong, but then they made fun of me and my weight." It wasn't until the Escape the Corset movement that it dawned upon her she was worthy and could contribute to her communities, regardless of her appearance.

Yun-Kim Ji-Yeong, a professor at the Institute of Body

and Culture at Konkuk University in Seoul, has followed the Escape the Corset movement since its beginnings. She said Choi is not alone in failing to realize the power of appearance culture until after "escaping" it. Women had been taught their whole lives that it was their own fault for not being smooth, thin, firm, or youthful enough. "The constant feeling of obsession, self-hatred, and fatigue in this competitive society robs us of the energy to address its fundamental structural inequality," Yun-Kim said.

At first, hearing that they were worthy on their own, regardless of appearance, sounded utterly alien to these young women, who had never heard anything of the sort. Choi, the girl dubbed Darkie, said the first feminist meetups she attended really did "raise her consciousness," as American second-wave feminists called it. They challenged every message she'd received growing up. For instance, when she was in high school, her dad would say to her, "If you don't improve your looks, you won't get a husband." But other women in the movement exposed her to an eye-opening notion: Why should that be a threat? Why does a woman even need a husband? What is looking "beautiful" for?

Korean women were taught traditionally that beauty was their biggest asset because it leads to finding a marriage partner. By getting married, they could exchange their most valuable bargaining chip—their bodies—for social and economic status. Those views affect women's options and choices related not only to marriage but also to careers and motherhood. Today, thanks to a more open society, younger Korean women are finding another kind of transaction available. Under a kind of feminist capitalism, a woman might be her *own* enterprise. She can achieve social and economic status by getting a leg up with her looks and presentation. And yet in neither path do women get to transcend an economic machine and the neoliberal logic that we individually must take full responsibility for ourselves in an endless competition in a market. In both types of transactions, the Korean woman is taught that if her beauty isn't acceptable enough, she has no worth.

Young women who learned feminism only within this movement liken the Escape the Corset campaign to a "red pill" moment from *The Matrix*, when they realized they were meant to be more than interchangeable commodities. This epiphany led them to discover the truth of gender oppression and the myriad forms it takes. A number of them recount the way they passively followed their peers, making themselves up to look how they thought they were supposed to by mimicking the celebrity-led beauty trends of the day. Along the way, it became difficult to discern what they would want to look like if they were freed from expectations and allowed to choose for themselves.

The recent burst of women's rights work helped Korean women acknowledge the power of prescribed gender roles and limit that power by naming the rot. Writer Lee Min-kyung, who is a leader of the movement and has documented it over the years, said so many women found that once they realized there was no "there there" in the quest for idealized beauty, they felt liberated and found healing. "And especially because mental health issues are stigmatized here and there's not much help for it, activism has been a form of therapy for us," Lee said.

Against an Entire Structure

Occasionally, the protests have been characterized as a movement to bring down the beauty industry. But what's happening reaches much deeper. In the 2018 demonstrations, women rejected both the fact that they're surveilled and the psychological tax of that surveillance—the enduring notion that appearances matter above all else. When viewed through this lens, the protests against molka digital sex crimes and the protests against beauty norms are struggles against the same thing. As Yun-Kim told NPR in 2019, "Their aim is to subvert the huge male-centered matrix called the patriarchy."[43]

Women want their full selfhoods. They want to be out from under all the surveillance and to be released from the expectations that come with their gender. That's how Escape the Corset extends to a critique of the androcentric framework in which the "ideal" or typical citizen was the male worker, the breadwinner and head of household. Under this framework, the male worker's wage should support his family, and his wife's wages, if any, were merely supplemental. This deeply gendered, outdated "family wage" construct has been around since the dynasty days, but replays in modern life in the Korean neoliberal (and the American) social ideal. A family with a dad who works and a mom who stays at home is a signifier of tradition and upward mobility, and that family structure is still the basis of state policy in employment, welfare, and development. "When dating, even among the younger generations, when the boyfriend introduces his girlfriend to people, she needs to help him look good in front of them. In marriage, to be a good mother and wife, you have to be there for your husband and child," said Yun-Kim, the professor at Konkuk University in Seoul.

Rejecting appearance standards has led a growing number of young women in Korea to reject the behavioral standards at the root. Many are boycotting marriage and motherhood as *bihon yeosung*, "no-marriage women."[44] In choosing to be single and child-free, they are defying the expectation that women play their parts as self-sacrificing caregivers. Many of the twentysomething feminists I spoke to count themselves among this camp. While this boycott is now more explicit, women in Korea were already refusing to be pressured into making babies and taking on unpaid domestic work, before #MeToo. South Korea's fertility rate fell to a record low the year after Escape the Corset went mainstream, and has continued to drop.[45] By 2020, its rate was the lowest in the world.[46] At this rate, Koreans will be extinct around the year 2736.[47]

The Future They Want to See

When you meet the women of the movement today, years after they first gave up their old routines, they are similar to Choi Yujin. Many wear boy cuts, gender-neutral loose-fitting clothing such that you can't make out their silhouettes, glasses (a no-no in Korea), and only sunscreen or BB cream on their faces, if that. But every single one I met was able to pull up a before snapshot of themselves in which they very much looked the socially prescribed part: hair reaching down to the waist, lips cherry red or peachy coral, brown eye makeup perfected, and milky white skin flawless. They looked like K-pop ingenues. They posed looking coy, hands at their waists, their eyes turned downward and away from the camera or aimed straight into the lens, with their lips in practiced pouts. When these ladies hand over their phones to show me the before photos, a lot of them look amused and aghast at their former selves. "I look like I was in drag," said one of them, gazing at the picture of her teenage self.

They tallied the hundreds of dollars a month—$500 to $700 each—that they used to spend on skincare and services. Some of them have kept the handwritten lists of the amount of time they spent each day grooming and readying themselves to appear in public. These lists serve as a reminder that the fantasy of fitting into the "feminist capitalist" dream of achieving power by commodifying yourself works only for those with the money, able bodies, and baseline good looks to pursue it. Now they spend neither the money nor the time.

These women stand out in Korea precisely because their numbers are relatively few compared to the millions of women who adhere to the norms. They've paid a high price for escaping the corset—they've been fired from jobs and reportedly assaulted,[48] and prospective bosses have told them they "don't look feminine enough." But they still wear their protest on their bodies, each and every day.

$$\sim$$

As I thought about the short hair of these feminists, it struck me how often in Korea people wear their politics on their heads. Perhaps because in Confucian times, individuals didn't cut their hair at all as a tribute to their elders, hair has been an ongoing site of protest in South Korea, a way to demonstrate commitment to a cause. During the 1960s and '70s, when South Korea was under military dictatorship, dissidents would often shave their heads as a sign of resistance.[49] I learned this in my first month in the country when I myself saw citizens shave their heads as protest. One collective head-shaving happened around the one-year anniversary of the Sewol ferry disaster. (The ferry sank en route to Jeju Island in 2014, drowning more than 300 Korean students who were on a high school trip.).[50] I covered an anniversary demonstration in Seoul's Gwanghwamun Square, where grieving mothers, unable to bury their children because the ship had yet to be lifted up from the bottom of the sea, pleaded for a thorough investigation into what went wrong. My assistant Haeryun and I crouched under dozens of television cameras filming as these moms and dads shaved each other's heads and donned yellow capes in protest of the ongoing lack of investigation, tears flowing down their faces and some of them wailing in grief over the sound of the buzzers. By the end of the event, a dozen moms and dads in their forties and fifties looked like Buddhist monks.

Hair matters so much that wearing it short-cropped means too much. People read into it in reductive ways. An San, Korea's three-time gold medalist in the 2021 Tokyo Olympics, was relentlessly cyberbullied because she wears her hair short, which led critics to question her gender politics and label her with what is still the kiss of death in South Korea— a "feminist."[51]

Emergence of Body Positivity

But expressions of resistance can vary. It's a symbolic corset these women are escaping, after all. Bae Gyo-hyun, the twenty-nine-year-old plus-size model I mentioned in the last chapter, was among the first in modern Korea's fledgling body positivity movement. She calls herself fat, proudly, and is as visible as possible with her body, which doesn't fit the expected norms.[52] While she doesn't eschew makeup or hair styling, she along with other plus-size people are establishing an alternative model of beauty, one that's become increasingly accepted, albeit in small increments. Before her, the category of "plus-size model" didn't exist in Korea.

Bae models exclusively for the online clothing brand JStyle. She is confident in the way she moves, shaking her hips on TikTok and Instagram and sauntering down Seoul's sidewalks in tight-fitting clothing and crop tops on her heavier frame. At five-three (160 centimeters) and 90 kilograms (198 pounds), she wears her black hair long and curled at the ends. Her face is primed with foundation each day. She is matter-of-fact about it, but dressing in body-hugging clothing in a place where she's endlessly trolled online and body-shamed on the street is a radical act.

"I don't reject all beauty norms," she said. "I think you can use standards as a reference. Figure out what looks good on you and what you like. I think if you are able to focus on yourself, reference what you see, and find yourself, you are able to find your own beauty." Bae emphasizes that there is no single way to be a woman.

That is true especially for Korea's transgender women, who are not officially tallied, as the country has yet to affirm LGBTQ+ rights or pass any antidiscrimination measures to protect sexual minorities.[53] "We are invisible," says transgender lawyer and activist Park Hanhee. Her communities celebrate traditional femme ideas of beauty, often accessorizing and wearing makeup as a powerful and joyful way of either coming out or feeling like they are wearing on the outside what they feel on the inside. From a queer lens, makeup and high heels can carry power and affirmation of an identity they had to seek.

The cisgendered Escape the Corset women described feeling as if they were in discomforting disguise when made up to fit the prevailing beauty norms. For transgender women still considered unacceptable by large swaths of Korean society, appearing femme can serve as their armor. This tension has fed debate and disagreement within Korea's feminist communities.

Transgender artist Lee Shieun grew her hair long so she could pass in society as a woman, but says she then faced criticism from other feminists (some of them TERFs—transexclusionary radical feminists) for trying to pass in the first place. She found this cruel and perplexing, given she agrees beauty culture feeds unrealistic ideals. "I also feel decoration is a burden and the pressure to look good is too much," said Lee. "But it's different for trans women because cis women don't get called 'not a woman at all' if they don't wear makeup. Passing is related to survival," she said. The existential threats for transgender people are staggering. One study found transgender people are four times as likely to be victims of violent crime than cisgendered people.[54] One in two transgender individuals are sexually abused or assaulted at some point in their lives.

Just walking around on the streets can feel scary. "People yell stuff at you if you don't look feminine enough," Park Hanhee, the transgender activist and attorney, said. She explains that for some trans women, getting facial plastic surgery is more urgent than gender affirmation surgery because "there's a lot of stress from not passing as a woman, so plastic surgery [to feminize facial traits] can be essential."

To those who claim trans women are solidifying gender stereotypes by relying on a lot of beauty work to try and pass, Park points out there is plenty of diversity among the trans community in how women choose to look. Some may embrace an ultrafeminine look. Others won't. Park, for one, doesn't wear makeup at all, got no surgeries, and doesn't feel like she has to. "The ones you see may affirm certain stereotypes," Park says, but the community isn't monolithic.

What all of us who identify as women share, she says, are gendered standards for how to look and act. "There's added pressure for trans women to pass so we aren't denied as human beings. So when you raise questions [about our looks], it shouldn't be against trans women but against the gendered social structure that allows for this kind of discrimination in the first place." Of Korean society, she says, "we don't have much experience treating others as just human to human, regardless of their gender."

Park and Bae, a lawyer and a model, are two women who want to see far more choices in self-presentation and to broaden the definitions of prettiness beyond the narrow, market-defined norms smacking all of us in the face. Ideally, they say, women and girls should escape from social comparison and reliance on external validation for self-worth.

As someone who doesn't fit the exact societal expectations, Bae never received external validation to begin with—and so it never came to matter much to her. "We have to live in this society," Bae said. "And we know it's hard to change the standards. But we are giving people different options to see."

In the years since 2018, when a broader awareness of women's rights came on the scene in Korea, Bae points out that there have been a few noticeable shifts. Her social media comments are no longer dominated by nastiness, though a recent scan shows messages like "I'm surprised they didn't break the floor" when Bae and other heavier girls danced together. When people do throw shade, she says, defenders often rush in. She says her employer, JStyle, has seen at least a tenfold increase in submissions from plus-size girls wanting to model for the brand. "I feel beautiful. And that is not restricted to certain types of women," Bae said. "And more and more young people are seeing this, when they see me."

~

Some consumption data shows a decline in beauty-related spending among Korean women in their twenties. Numbers from the Ministry of Economy and Finance indicate that between 2015 and 2018, sales of cosmetics, hair products, and other beauty-related goods dropped 53.5 billion KRW (approximately $44.8 million) among women in their twenties. Plastic surgery—another common playground for young South Koreans—saw a 64.4 billion won ($53.9 million) dip among consumers in that same demographic.[55]

Women acting collectively can count other hard-won gains within the past few years. Many powerful figures, including film directors and actors, priests, teachers, and coaches, not to mention that popular presidential contender, have been held accountable for sexual misconduct after survivors spoke up. In 2016, feminists successfully campaigned to shut down the website sora.net, which hosted an avalanche of molka videos, images and instructions on how to buy date rape pills.[56] The molka protests also ushered in several new laws against spycam surveillance. In 2019, Korea's highest court ended the country's decades-long ban on abortion.[57]

There are other signs of change. It was once considered daring for a K-pop singer to appear on TV with a *ssaengul* ("bare face," without makeup). That now happens more frequently as stars support the Escape the Corset movement. The girl group Mamamoo wore baggy sweatshirts at a recent concert. When Hwasa, the group's youngest member, was asked by a fan for advice on losing weight, she said, "Just eat!"[58]

And over the past decade, books and movies that give public voice to the plight of South Korean women have become cultural touchstones. A slim novel called *Kim Jiyoung, Born 1982*, which clinically describes the life of an everywoman in modern-day Korea, debuted in 2016 to meteoric success, selling more than a million copies its first year. It's the bestselling piece of Korean literature outside of Korea in the past five years, selling more than 300,000 copies in overseas markets. Translation rights sold in roughly twenty countries—maybe more by now—and the bulk of overseas sales have come from neighboring China and Japan.[59] "If we women all go through these experiences, then they should be discussed together, in a public way," author Cho Nam-Joo told me.[60]

The Backlash

The most meaningful way to upend social imperatives is to listen to the women caught up in them, and for them to lead reforms. Many are finding their voices. But they're all too often drowned out by the aggrieved young men of Korea, who feel they, too, are being left behind by the economy and scapegoat women for it.

Korea's feminist gains have come against a backdrop of scarcity. In a tale familiar across the developed world, wealth inequality is deepening and youth unemployment had hovered around 10 percent in 2016 and 2017, which was nearly three times the national average.[61] Young men and women, who might cooperate (or couple up) in more abundant times, instead find themselves in fierce competition for what jobs are available. Insecurity, entitlement, and mob misogyny on the internet fan a bitter gender war.

In a country with one of the worst women's rights records in the industrialized world, where women earn 68 cents to a man's dollar[62] and occupy only 5 percent of corporate board seats,[63] where women's representation in the legislature is almost as low as in North Korea[64] and nearly 90 percent of victims of violent crimes are women,[65] some 79 percent of South Korean men in their twenties feel they are the victims of discriminatory policies.[66]

Women's suicide rates spiked during the COVID-19 pandemic.[67] But a suicide-prevention website that was set up to deal with this crisis temporarily went off-line amid a wave of cyberattacks by internet mobs that claimed it disregarded men's lives. And in 2021, distressed Korean men waged a bizarre campaign against images of pinching fingers (really, just that—any images where fingers were pinching), claiming they were meant to mock the size of men's genitalia.[68] Major companies and state agencies removed these images from their promotional materials and issued apologies.

As men maintain a white-knuckle grip on the status quo, women's political power remains elusive. As we've seen throughout the world, the right bets on anti-feminism as a winning strategy. In South Korea's 2022 presidential election, the conservative party candidate openly courted men's rights activists by vowing to get rid of the Ministry of Gender Equality and Family, which supports, among other things, programs for single mothers, babies, and immigrants.[69] Abolishing the ministry is a goal of anti-feminists, on the grounds that supporting single mothers encourages divorce. The candidate also slammed a post-2018 law meant to curb the trading of digital sex crime footage, decrying it as a form of censorship.[70]

Buoyed by a resounding majority of male voters in their twenties and thirties, that candidate, Yoon Suk-yeol, won the South Korean presidency in 2022 by the slimmest of margins. Alarmingly, not a single presidential candidate among major parties in the election—even among liberals—included women's rights as a key part of their platforms.[71] Feminism in South Korea is considered such a taboo term that a majority of men in their twenties say they would break up with their partners if they described themselves as feminist.[72]

~

Women aren't immobilized. All the backlash and the gender strife can be interpreted as an indicator of their gains. Famed Korean poet Choi Young-mi, who gave Korea's early days #MeToo movement momentum with her own survivor story, described her country's women's rights struggle as a battle between the past and the future. Countless Koreans who support gender equality may exist in the shadows, since the pitched vitriol of Korean misogynists is both exhausting and potentially violent.[73] Feminist organizers are trying to lure into the open supporters of gender equality. "More and more individuals have to engage in this kind of activism and be visible," organizer Kim Juhee says. "Because nowadays it feels impossible to say something that's wrong is just wrong. So I want society to be changed such that if something is unjust we have to say, 'This is unjust.'"

In neither assimilating with nor exiting their beauty-obsessed society, women who don't comply with appearance standards live amongst their fellow Koreans in a permanent state of refusal. I don't know whether these person-by-person resistances can effectively upend prevailing gender norms and expectations. But the women have certainly changed their relationships with themselves, and that holds potential for changing society, or at least modeling another way. During our time together, I asked these women variations of the same question. However you define beauty, when do you feel most beautiful? Some said it's when they feel most connected with family or friends. Others said the answer was irrelevant. "Not all women are beautiful. But women don't need to be beautiful," Choi Yujin, the twenty-six-year-old activist, said. "I'm like this, and I'm going to live my life like this. My values are not my hair and makeup, but myself. Now that I'm speaking about myself this way, I feel beautiful. And if I feel this way, I can help other women."

These women behave as if their lives matter and their happiness counts. They embody that with a devil-may-care attitude about what other people think. I wish I had the self-possession of twenty-three-year-old college student Lee Daheun. As a child, her mother tried to incentivize her to look more girlish by offering her money to wear a skirt or to style her hair. She refused. Today she exudes an inner calm, giving her the appearance of a maturity beyond her years.

"When do you feel most beautiful?" I asked.

"Always," she said, and a smile exploded across her face. The easy conviction of someone who just told the truth.

CHAPTER 11

Child's Play

My eight-week-old was late for her facial. I swerved into an underground lot in our white Hyundai and slid into a spot four floors underground, beneath my go-to Seoul spa. Baby Luna's fusses of *Nnnnhn, breh, muhh, arrehh* indicated she might be hungry, so I crammed myself next to her car seat, unbuckled her, hiked up my sweater to my collarbone, and stuffed my right boob in her face while we sat in the parking garage. Milk dribbled down her cheek and onto my tummy roll, which folded over the top of my jeans. After the passage of some minutes (too long for me, too short for baby), I pulled my top back down, tossed a swaddle blanket over my shoulder, one-armed the baby, and headed upstairs to see an aesthetician.

After laying Luna flat on the table, her wide eyes circling the ceiling above her, the aesthetician went to work, massaging the baby's temples gently. When I asked the giggling aesthetician who was the next youngest person she'd ever performed a treatment on, she told us another client comes in regularly for facials to treat gastrointestinal issues, and he's three.

On went the treatment (and giggles), the facialist standing behind the baby, who was swaddled like a large breakfast burrito. Luna's face was treated with a clear oil said to be gentle on new skin. She seemed to like it, never looking distressed. She easily relaxed into her indulgent skincare service. When we wrapped up, a hungry Luna kept rearranging her mouth into different shapes and licking her lips.

This was summer 2017, more than two years into my life in Seoul. By then, I no longer found it unusual for anyone—including an infant—to go for a facial. I was curious whether a spa would even take a baby client and whether such an experience would feel bonding for me and Baby Luna. To be honest, I was surprised when we called my spa and they said sure, a baby facial could be arranged. Babies don't need facials, of course. But Korean skincare expectations had successfully wormed their way into my thinking. I saw an Instagram post of a Korean toddler getting a spa treatment, which was all the inspiration I needed.

Around the same time, Luna's sisters, both under five, were increasingly exposed to appearance expectations. They were figuring out how much their looks mattered before they learned their ABCs. As little girls growing up in Korea, they faced a pervasive lookist culture, with specific notions about what looking like a "girl" means. I remember catching my own daughters admiring themselves in the elevator mirror after strangers who stepped on or off called them "beautiful" or "cute" in Korean, which is the only Korean vocabulary they learned, outside of "Hello" and "Thank you," because the only comments they heard from adult strangers were about their appearance.

For girls, the formula is fragile. Sweet. Pink. "Everything is pink from top to toe," says Minyeong Park, a mom who's raising a chatty, spunky eight-year-old daughter named Ahin. "Just everything is pink. All the toys. The clothes. Girls very young are sort of taught they have more limited choices," she said. At "kid cafés," moms can sit around drinking coffee while their children tumble around and play pretend in elaborate indoor playrooms decked out with ball pits, tunnels, and toy kitchens. For little girls, cafés offer dress-up racks with princess costumes of Cinderella, Elsa, Snow White, Rapunzel, Belle, and child-sized mirror vanities with an array of play makeup—lipstick, powder, brushes of different sizes.

In toys and children's merchandise, girlhood in Korea is filled with endless options to play dress-up, play makeup, and more. My daughters received birthday presents of plastic hair dryers and attachments, beauty tools, and sparkly nail sets so they could pretend they were going to the spa. But actual appearance services, even for young kids, are considered possible and normal. I realized this when one afternoon, at a kid cafe with two mom friends, as our preschoolers chased each other while riding various farm animals on wheels. They asked me if Eva's long eyelashes were extensions. She was just shy of four.

Were we to have stayed, the girls might have been wearing real makeup by the early years of elementary school. In 2016, Sungshin Women's University surveyed 288 elementary-aged girls and found that two in five of them wore makeup.[1] And that number has likely increased since. "The age in which children do makeup is continuously decreasing," said Kim Ju-duck, a professor of beauty studies at Sungshin, who conducted the research.[2] Another study bears this out.[3] It found 43 percent of South Korean students surveyed said they started putting on makeup in elementary school, compared to a far smaller percentage—7 percent—of kids a few years ahead of them, the twelfth graders. Kim adds that not only are kids wearing makeup younger, they're wearing more of it. "In the past, people just did lipstick and manicures, but now kids will put on mascara and eyeliner and do makeup on their entire face," he said.

Minyeong Park is raising Ahin in an education-obsessed ward of Gangnam, where the streets are lined with cram schools called *hagwons* and dance and singing academies for young K-pop trainees. Park said among her daughter's friends, she has observed makeup on their faces at special events, like elementary school graduations, or as part of costumes, but felt like she hadn't seen everyday wear on first and second graders yet. As she was saying this, Ahin, seated at her mother's side, piped up to point out she has seven-year-old friends who at least wear bright lipstick to school every day. Her mom thought for a moment. "Oh, right," Minyeong said.

"Nowadays, if a child doesn't do makeup, then they could get bullied by their peers. Because of this, they do at least lipstick and light foundation," researcher Kim Ju-duck said. He says the main culprit is the hyperdeveloped internet culture, which feeds kids an onslaught of visual media and makeup tutorials from an early age. Most important, he says, in digital or physical space, children are influenced by other children. And makeup is embedded in how girls play.

After school, South Korean children are sent to more school—hours and hours of hagwons, where they're hunched over tiny desks sometimes until as late as eleven at night. It doesn't leave room for good old-fashioned outdoor play. Instead there's a lot of screen time during breaks. Kim says face filters and designing Bitmoji-like avatars that approximate or upgrade how you look, and decorating your own image or images are part of games—and the central point of many apps—that kids are using.

On YouTube or other social platforms, kids watch other kids make themselves up. The popularity of cosmetics for minors is reflected in the sheer number of makeup video tutorials in Korean for children, often starring children themselves. "This is a kind of play culture, and it concerns me," Kim said. "If children get interested in their appearance from a young age, when they grow up, this can lead to them to becoming obsessed with it."

Kid beauty, such as it is, gives the beauty industry an in with the next generation. It could potentially mean long-term loyalty, and it's a business move with immediate gains. In my reporting, I kept hearing insiders call the existing personal care market a "red ocean," bloody and shark-infested with vicious competition. Capitalism's central conceit is growth, so they search for "blue oceans," places where there's little or no competition, instead. "Brands try to expand to new territory," observed Mintel's Korean beauty industry analyst Lee Hwajung. "Kid makeup is one of them."

So far, the push into a younger customer base is led by

start-ups and not cosmetic conglomerates. "Kid makeup is still very niche," analyst Lee said. "It's a vague [area] between play makeup for babies, and teenagers" (who wear adult makeup). The leading company to fill that age gap is ShuShu & Sassy, a once-stand-alone brand recently acquired by a kids clothing line. The current CEO counts twelve children's cosmetic boutiques across Seoul, and two of them include complete kid spas, where children between the ages of four and ten can go to get skin, hair, or nail treatments designed specifically for their age group. The cosmetics are kid-safe and free of alcohol-heavy ingredients, and their bestselling product line, nail polish, is all water-based, such that it can be removed without using acetone.[4] Inside the spas, everything "is pink and white," their young client Ahin Yun recalls. "The ceiling, the walls. The sofa, more pink. And they have bunny robes, pink bunny robes. We get a little headband. We have a little headband that has some bunny eyes bunny ears on top." The line is represented by mascot bunny characters of ShuShu and her younger sister, Sassy. The bunnies appear on branded nail art stickers and as the animals on top of nail polish bottles.

Children can snuggle into those bunny robes and enjoy ShuShu & Sassy spa services at prices between $25 to $35. The most common treatments last 30 minutes and offer the clients a choice of a foot spa or a face mask and hand massage, or a face massage and a lip-related service. Longer services include a foot and calf massage and a mani-pedi. You can pay more for additional services such as hair styling, braiding, or sparkles in your hair. "I liked to get my nails done because it made them pretty," Ahin told me. Now eight, she first enjoyed a ShuShu & Sassy spa treatment at age four.

To keep their top spot in kid beauty, the brand pays careful attention to design and that specific elementary-aged cohort they target. They must hit a sweet spot of products that don't seem too babyish but aren't for teens, either. "At that age, children need cosmetics and want to use products that are as stylish as the products that their mothers or adults use. Because of this, I want to satisfy children's desires in a safe way," ShuShu & Sassy CEO Lee Chiyeon told me.

Going forward, she says she's expecting healthy growth and more competition. Her spas are pushing into China, Singapore, and Southeast Asia, where five-star hotels are beginning to offer kid-spa services under the ShuShu & Sassy brand. She said she expects to see as much as 300 percent growth annually over the next five years.

Moms Co-Opted into Marketing

Children are master mimics. Eva loved to mimic cooking and climbed up on the step stool to try and scramble eggs at age two. Isa would drag brooms across the floor, copying our helper when she cleaned the floors. If left to her own devices, baby Luna would scribble her entire face with red lipstick. When little girls copy their mothers, it's developmentally vital, often delightful—and a behavior that marketers and corporations can seize upon. Commercial messages that have long positioned beauty work as women's work now build on that idea for the kids' market, framing body labor as bonding experiences for mothers and daughters to share. "I watch my mom and I follow her. I am growing up," a digital advertisement selling makeup kits for six-year-olds proclaims, with a photo of a young girl in school uniform applying lipstick.[5] A YouTube video of a seven-year-old putting on lipstick, titled "I want to wear makeup like mom," has attracted 4.7 million views,[6] while similar videos show young girls sharing their "elementary school makeup routine" and "unboxing my Hello Kitty makeup kit." These brands are selling appearance labor "as imperatives masked as pleasure and bonding," Sharon Heijin Lee points out.[7] "Mothers model, mold, and shape their children toward market demands." Viewed that way, my bringing baby Luna in for a facial was a realization of that kind of exchange before she was old enough to roll over. As a treat to bond with my baby (maybe?), we shared in a beauty ritual that costs at least $100 USD. And as children grow into adolescence and young adulthood, regular facials are normal.

Teenagers

The majority of affordable Korean cosmetic brands like Tonymoly, Banila Co, and Etude House already make and market adorable fruit-packaged lip balms, sparkly eye shadows, and animal-face sheet masks anyway, but for the teen and adult market. That makeup is both affordable and designed as playful is savvy strategy—it gives an implicit permission to girls to start using these products when they're quite young. Researcher Kim Ju-duck says he watched it happen. "Children started to use makeup around the year 2000, when cheap cosmetic brands like Missha or The Face Shop started to appear," he says. "The products were easily accessible to middle school and high school students, the products were cheap, and the way that the stores themselves were designed was appealing to these students."

By the time these kids are full-fledged teenagers, major cosmetic brands are clamoring for them. The market for teen cosmetics is reportedly growing at a rate of 20 percent a year. A study by the consumer-advocacy group Green Health Solidarity found that roughly 74 percent of middle schoolers had used products like lipstick and eyeshadow.[8] That's because by middle school, makeup is expected, and the result is, girls are seen as objects—or self-objectify—rather young. School uniforms marketed for girls include "lip tint pockets" on the inside lining of their blazers, designed to fit lipstick and lip tints perfectly.[9] In 2018, when teen girls took part in the Escape the Corset movement, they targeted these lip tint pockets and the fitted skirts they have to wear as restrictive and an obstacle to learning. "I think, in general, school uniforms for girls are often too small. We are often told that this is the 'right' size for girls, and that wearing clothes too loose is not ideal for students," Kang Eun-ji, a high school student, told *The Korea Herald*.[10]

When the Gender Minister at the time, Chung Hyun-back, met with high school girls to discuss this issue, an unnamed student spoke up to recount trying to buy a uniform blouse one size bigger. "I told the salesperson that the 'right-size' blouse was too tight on me and I was very uncomfortable in it," the student said. "But she said that if I got a size bigger, then I wouldn't look pretty and I wouldn't look right.

At my school, if a girl wants to wear pants instead of a skirt, then you have to have 'special reasons,' such as having a visible scar on your leg."[11]

The only way to get out of wearing a skirt at school was if her leg was too unsightly.

Who is creating this image of girlhood? Culture-makers, industry, schools who make rules for tiny uniforms, or the children who show preferences early on? Whether it's lip tint pockets for uniforms or spa experiences for kids, beauty industry leaders say they're simply downstream from existing demand. "We are following the data, the statistics," ShuShu & Sassy CEO Lee Chiyeon said. The data show, for example, girls gravitate toward pink, and she cited something like 80 percent of girls in her target customer base show a preference for the shade. And market surveys also indicate they enjoy getting mani-pedis and other prettifying services. "I'm strictly about the data," Lee said.

The view sidesteps the part where the industry can *create* demand, and how the unfeeling algorithms of social media's attention economy fan it for their own profits, exerting the beauty ideal's influence on children before they're old enough to read. I've seen it in my own home, when my kindergartner secretly brushes blush all over her face in the mornings before school "to look spiffy." Or when my eldest came in over the weekend to request facial moisturizer because she wanted to start a skincare routine. That I wound up with daughters so interested in skincare and makeup as I've gone bleary-eyed over a laptop a few feet away, questioning beauty culture in these pages, is some sort of cosmic joke. And it shows the power of cultural influences.

Younger and younger the next generation is learning to shift, change, and mold their bodies to fit market demands. The perfection shown to us by advertising, social media, and the commoditized self-care culture makes it feel like we're living in an absurd, inescapable fun-house mirror. But we're taught that looking even passably pretty will be worth it. And being exceedingly pretty? Well, that can potentially give us everything, if we keep it up. We also learn to shift, change, and mold ourselves by adhering to what the market wants to sell us. We are simultaneously consuming and consumed. Will future generations crumble under the pressure of not just unattainable, but—thanks to synthetic technology—increasingly unnatural beauty standards? What happens to everyone who doesn't make the cut?

Beauty work is complicated because so much of the care we do for our hard-laboring bodies is also so intimate, so human, so communal. For all the ways it has been commercialized, body-care rituals can also be deeply connective—to one another, and for ourselves. Last year when my dad was staying with us for a week, Luna, then three, went upstairs and brought a purplish nail polish for him. "Where's a hard surface? I want you to paint my nails, Opa." My dad reacted with bemusement and surprise. He immediately agreed, but admitted, "Wow, I have never done this before." Luna was undeterred. She stood there with her hands out, palms down and ready to plop them on a big book so a manicure from Grandpa could commence. She held still as my dad carefully applied shimmery purple polish to her tiny fingers. "Heyyyy, this is so easy, it's just like painting," he observed, his eyes trained on Luna's hand while he slowly proceeded with applying the polish. They shared a sweet moment of connection and touch, and my seventy-seven-year-old dad delighted in learning a new thing.

Dressing up and playing pretend is a lot of fun. It's part of the magic of being a kid. Water-based kid nail polish really does seem harmless for second graders. "I never looked at going to a kids' spa as, 'Oh, I'm teaching you to try to make yourself look like something that you're not.' It was more like you're getting lotion on your face and your toenails painted in colors, and you like the paint," said Seoul mom Hallie Bailey, about bringing her Korean daughter to kid spas.

And so we dance, carefully twirling between care and consumerism, trying to balance the freeing, nurturing, and developmentally supportive aspects of pampering children against the insidious commercial elements that creep in as they get older. Against the cultural forces that say women don't look good enough as they are and should buy more to look better. Those forces are already in the air. All I have to do is lift my head and I catch their scent. Admittedly, they sometimes smell enticing.

~

Kim Ju-duck, the researcher who studied the ever-younger age at which children start wearing makeup, supports regulations to bar advertising makeup to youth, in the same way marketing cigarettes has limits. Short of that, he pushes for education and disclosure. "On products that kids use a lot, I think companies should disclose the fact that certain substances can cause certain side effects," he said. "Because the government cannot stop [kids] from doing makeup, I worked with the Ministry of Food and Drug Safety to develop materials to teach students the right way to use it by educating instructors."

Beyond policy changes, awareness of the flood of for-profit forces at play is important in responding to or resisting them. Because given the narrow band of what "beauty" means in places like South Korea, what passes for choice is highly prescribed. This "should ring alarm bells for those who claim that beauty is just a matter of individual choice," philosopher Heather Widdows writes. Nearly 90 percent of Korean girls and young women, she notes, citing a 2013 study, "believe how they look matters more than what they do and say. While we may still want to tell our daughters that 'it's what's on the inside that counts,' they would not believe us, and, given the evidence, we would not be telling the truth."[12]

I pressed Kim, the kid makeup researcher, for a vision of where this all winds up.

"What is the end point of this?" I asked.

"Unless we abolish the internet, there is no end point," he quipped.

~

CHAPTER 12

Of Marketing
and Men

At the multistory JennyHouse salon in Gangnam, an Alice in Wonderland theme of pink and white walls, luxurious thrones, and warm light from modern fixtures transforms into something different on the fifth floor. After four floors of a feminine Wonderland, it suddenly looks more like the inside of a Texas steakhouse chain. Walls of dark wood and stone, exposed ceiling pipes, and ornate picture frame moldings as decor make clear we've reached the "Men's Salon" part of JennyHouse, where male clients come for cuts, color, eyebrow shaping, and root perms (for volume). Stylists can apply BB creams and offer JennyHouse-branded lip balm as part of their salon packages. As I wind through the space with my JennyHouse tour guide, a long-time manager named Hong Chae-won, I spy male clients reclined in specialty camel-colored leather barber chairs (which cost $10,000 apiece, she says), lazing into head massages or cocooned under futuristic-looking curved wands propelling over their heads. A slender frosted-glass-enclosed booth purrs in the corner; it turns out it steams and freshens clients' clothing while they're being pampered. These hair treatments in the men's salon aren't wholly different from the women's services on the other floors, but the experience is designed for dudes, Hong tells me. The ambience, the privacy, the spirits. "We used to offer whiskey, before COVID."

Forty percent of JennyHouse clients are men. They start coming in their early twenties, just before their big profile photo sessions following college graduation. JennyHouse offers a postgrad head shot primping package for half off the standard 330,000 KRW (roughly $250) price tag. But once they're lured in, at least one in ten become repeat customers. "The goal is for them to experience this and then come back when applying for jobs and before they have interviews. And after they are hired by a company, or when they have blind dates," Hong said. And so on.

As K-beauty has exploded in popularity over the last decade, South Korea's men have led global grooming trends industry-wide. Roughly 13 percent of the world's skincare products for men are consumed by Koreans, making them the largest per capita spenders on male skincare products in the world.[1] Korean men are a testing ground and a springboard for innovation. Men's lip balm in South Korea, for example, has evolved to include anti-aging claims and light tints, with products like The First Geniture for Men Tinted Lip Balm, by the luxury skincare brand, O HUI.[2] Last year, Innisfree rolled out a gift set that includes camouflage cream in the shades of army green, brown, and black for men who are doing their mandatory military service. According to marketing materials, Extreme Power Camo Cream is for men with sensitive skin, comes with SPF 50 and made from "black yeast from Jeju." Someone's buying it. Between 2011 and 2021, the country's market for male skincare grew by 25 percent, according to Euromonitor.[3]

The easiest explanation for the standout statistics is Korea's appearance-obsessed culture, in which men, too, are not exempt from the stringent demands of the Korean beauty imperative. Nearly half of South Korean respondents in a 2021 Mintel survey said they agreed that it's "important for men to use beauty or grooming products daily."[4] Three out of four Korean men said they use skincare products, and more than half said they use makeup products, according to a survey by GlobalData.[5] They are similarly unafraid to seek nips and tucks in Gangnam. A Gangnam clinic told the newspaper *Hankyung* that 37 percent of their customers in 2020 were men, compared to less than 10 percent a decade before. All ten clinics that reporters reached out to said they've seen male clientele expand significantly, most commonly to get work done on their noses and eyes.[6]

For twenty-eight-year-old Kim Minki, makeup is both his business and his pleasure. His daily skincare routine makes him feel confident, he tells me. And he's also steeped in this stuff for a living, as a cosmetic ingredients researcher and a beauty YouTuber. Online, he goes by Groomin'. He describes his morning routine as pretty average for other men his age: cleanser, toner, ampoule, a lotion or a cream, sunscreen, a little BB cream as foundation, a translucent powder, brow filler, maybe a natural-colored eye shadow, a slightly tinted lip balm "to make my lips just a little bit brighter," he says, and then he blow-dries and shapes his hair with product. He also goes in every three months for Botox and other injectable treatments. "I get more procedures than the average Korean male," he explained. "I get my face waxed, and I think more than half of us do that. But I also do laser hair removal, dermatology injections, and lifting lasers."

Isn't this exhausting? I asked.

"Of course it's very tiring," Groomin' says. "But at the same time, because we are sensitive to trends, we feel satisfaction when we see ourselves. This is also the reason why the cosmetic market can grow every year."

Entrepreneur Hellen Choo got into men's grooming more than a decade ago with her Swagger men's beauty brand, a line that includes hair pomades, gels, sprays, body washes, and eyebrow markers. The brand is now so popular it's sold at Olive Young, Korea's one-stop shop that combines the selection of Sephora with the scale of drugstores. When I visit Choo at her company's expansive floor of office space in the Mapo district of Seoul, I find a petite, no-nonsense woman who speaks in long sentences. She wears fitted slacks and wire-rimmed glasses. She apologizes that we can't meet in her product showroom, as investors were on-site closing a deal with her team.

Design explains her early success, she says. "Our product really stood out in the market in those days. I mean, (a) because it was a new category and (b) because it was very well-designed, like, we won like five awards with this product. Global awards as well. So we started getting featured in magazines, but getting to Olive Young is a whole different thing. If you get into Olive Young, you've made it." Her background in brand design is evident all over her office. Pencil sketches of men's hoodies and pants are taped to the white-board behind her desk, next to a line of black-and-white pho-tos of different Korean men's haircuts and a photo of an old CK One cologne bottle cut out of a magazine.

She sneaks back into her sample closet to show me what she's talking about. Much like JennyHouse created an entire "men's salon" experience separate from the ladies, her men's personal care products are designed in a way that signal "manliness," giving permission for male consumers to make forays into beauty.

For Swagger's body washes, she intentionally designed containers that looked like whiskey bottles, in heavy plastic that gives off the look of thick glass. The bourbon-hued shower gel smells like black licorice and has TOBACCO LIQUOR written in English on the front. Another shower gel is clear-colored but emblazoned with DIRTY on the la-bel. Male customers, she tells me, "want products that say, 'For men' written really big and that looks like it's for men . . . So we've actually seen how fragile they can be, to need to have gender pronounced to feel good about 'yeah, taking care of my skin.'" It's not unlike the way men's grooming sec-tions at Target feels in the United States, where the color tones are dark, the products reassuringly include "Dude" in them (read: Hims vitamins or Dude Wipes), and the focus is on distinctively masculine concerns like their beards.

Though men's skincare is expanding in Korea, culturally, the mane is still the main thing. In 2022, one of the lead-ing Korean presidential contenders—the one who lost—promised that if he took office, he'd expand public healthcare to cover hair treatment for male-pattern baldness.[7] "Can you imagine that being a legit campaign promise in any other country?" observed David Yi, the Korean American editor of men's beauty site Very Good Light.

Well aware of broader trends and the cultural importance of hair, Choo has decided to keep her focus on haircare and not skincare. A 2020 Gallup Korea poll showed that among the men who said they care about their appearance, half of them reported hairstyle as their top concern. The next most popular priority, clothes, trailed way behind at 26 percent, body came in at 12 percent, and skin at 10 percent.[8] "I know [skin] beauty creams are a big thing among the young men, Gen-Z," she says. "We just haven't been very successful with it. I—we've tried and spent a lot of money trying to boost our BB cream."

She suspects that Gen-Z's gender fluidity will mean less demand among younger consumers for makeup branded specifically *for men*. Men's makeup is generally concocted with the same formulations anyway, just in different packaging. Choo observes that the younger boys who use makeup—who tend to fall into the camp of ultra-discerning and skincare-educated Korean consumers—don't mind going straight to brands traditionally marketed to ladies. "Men who do wear makeup wear a lot of women's makeup," she says. "Like for foundation. Because [women's makeup] is just so much more advanced. There's not that many choices within men's makeup, right?"

Flowerboys

Korean pop culture gave rise to the *kkotminam*, or flowerboy, an aesthetic that is redefining traditional masculinity. (In

Korean, *kkot* = flower; *minam* = handsome man). Flowerboys subvert the traditional signifiers of masculinity by being sweet-natured and in touch with their feelings. They emanate a gentle wholesomeness that enriches rather than detracts from their masculinity. Flowerboys are facial-hair free, often waxing or lasering off even a hint of stubble. For a visual reference, the flowerboy aesthetic is seen in the K-pop boy band NCT 127's "Touch" video—full of pastels, florals, and "generally being a lil cutie," as the BuzzFeed writer Lauren Strapagiel put it.[9]

The origins of flowerboys can be traced to the emergence of Hallyu in the late 1990s and a cultural collision between South Korea and neighboring Japan.[10] Japanese manga that featured lithe androgynous male protagonists flowed into Korea when South Korea's government loosened restrictions on Japanese goods. On television, softer men in Korean dramas like the classic *Boys Over Flowers* began to appear. In music, the legendary K-pop mogul and SM Entertainment founder Lee Soo Man[11] (who coined the term *cultural technology* and said Korean music should be marketed as cultural commodities[12]) created the first iconic K-pop boy band, H.O.T., making Korean kkotminam a regional sensation. Lee had witnessed the rise of MTV while living in the United States,[13] and he had a keen sense of how a similar model could succeed in Korea. He spent years surveying girls on what kind of pop star would appeal to them, and he emerged with this wholesome, boyish group that offered an antidote to a *namjadaun namja*, manly man, or a warrior-type presentation of Korean masculinity.[14] These prototypical flowerboys wore eye makeup and unnatural hair colors, forebears of K-Pop idols today. H.O.T.'s biggest hit, "Candy" (which I still choose at noraebang joints), is a bubblegum pop song about an innocent crush. Singer and actor Kim Heechul, one of the biggest Korean wave stars and a member of Super Junior, is another early days kkotminam icon. K-pop audiences are "predominantly made up of girls," the Korea scholar Roald Maliangkay observed in 2010, who are "likely to favor artists who they perceive would not treat them as sexual objects of attraction but as equals."[15]

Nowadays the audience is far broader and more diverse than just "girls." But K-pop idols distinguish themselves with their squeaky-clean reputations and their total silence on personal relationships, giving off an availability to a reciprocal relationship with fans.[16] Constant fan stewardship and continuous communication further disrupt the likelihood they're simply seen as superficial sex objects. They have depth, dimension and approachability.

Scholars and culture watchers believe Korea's economically precarious conditions after the 1997 IMF crisis normalized the flowerboy as an idealized type of man. Reverberations from that economic quake dislodged the idea of a financially reliable, traditionally macho male provider. "That aspect of power disintegrated," social scientist Min Joo Lee, who specializes in Asian gender studies, told me. She distinguishes the flowerboy of the 1990s from the metrosexual of the West in that metrosexuals were depicted as men caring about their looks but not assumed to be necessarily feminine or asexual. "People interpreted the iconic metrosexual of the 1990s, David Beckham, as 'refined,' not 'feminine.' Flowerboy is also mainly about aesthetics, but to add on to that, people (especially those from outside of Korea/East Asian cultures) interpret them as feminine and somewhat nonsexual or queer," Lee explains, even though the flowerboy aesthetic doesn't map neatly onto sexual preferences.

Other researchers have found the fondness for "soft masculinity" is an outgrowth of women's growing economic empowerment. "As the socioeconomic status of women rises, their changed view of men appears to promote the feminization of men. Women no longer need macho qualities or patriarchal authority," researchers Jaeil Kim and others wrote.[17] Echoes Lee: "The [heterosexual] woman had to find another aspirational masculinity to desire, and that was the flowerboy. A man who takes care of his aesthetics even though they didn't have money."

Today, the "flowerboy" is "one of the most popular icons in Korean pop culture" and across the world.[18] In Japan they're known as *bishonen* (pretty boys); in China, as *xiǎo xiān ròu*, or "little fresh meat." This modern Asian boy archetype has melded with the West's evolving definition of a "softboy" to become "perhaps the most culturally significant teen trend to emerge" in the late 2010s, as Quartz reported.[19] "The way they (K-pop stars) play with masculinity, what it means to be a beautiful man in a heterosexual or non-heterosexual way, it opens up possibilities for men on the street," longtime Korean cultural researcher Joanna Elfving-Hwang told the BBC.[20]

When BTS first burst into global consciousness while I was living in Korea, skeptical observers, many of them in the

United States and Europe, still held the members' male "prettiness" at a remove. One critic claimed BTS fans had a "twink gay fetish," which reveals more about the homophobic attitudes of the critics than the idols or their audience.[21] And as it turns out, the haters were on the wrong side of history. The softboy trend is now emulated across TikTok with the #softboy hashtag, in the celebrity looks of Timothée Chalamet or Harry Styles, and in streetwear fashion. As more and more men have claimed the softboy label as their own, they have elevated the meaning beyond fashion or style to embodying a different, more delicate type of man entirely: "And young men are obliging—showing emotional vulnerability, publicly crying, going to therapy, and being the little spoon," Quartz has noted.[22]

Asian marketers began leaning into this aesthetic at the turn of the century, and over twenty years later, the rest of the world is still catching up. Korea's beauty companies began actively hiring men and male actors and idols to help sell their product lines to women. Despite all its products targeting women, The Face Shop hired Kwon Sang-woo, a first-generation K-wave actor, as a spokesmodel.[23] Missha signed the mega-heartthrob Won Bin not long after.[24] Be it Innisfree, Nature Republic, or Mamonde, they have all featured male celebs as spokesmodels who are plastered on billboards hawking products like serums and moisturizers as a way to stand out.

The trend spread across the region, moving well beyond Korean borders. "I think Korea is a trailblazer in men's beauty culture, definitely in Asia at the moment, if not the world," Elfving-Hwang said to the BBC.[25] When Korean brands entered China, the marketing strategy explicitly highlighted kkotminam in order to attract female consumers. "Just put the long-legged *oppa* [brother] Lee Minho's full-size billboard at the shop's front door, the Chinese girls would swarm in," reported a Chinese entertainment news outlet, in 2016.[26] Incidentally, Lee Minho, a megawatt star in Asia ever since his time on *Boys Over Flowers*, is enjoying crossover appeal across the Pacific these days, thanks to his leading role on the Apple TV+ series *Pachinko*.

We're used to seeing women celebrities model makeup. This reversal flips the usual scripts of cosmetics ads away from the male gaze on female subjects. Ads now cater to the female gaze, showcasing the male models heterosexual women might want to see. "South Korea, when it comes to pop culture at least, is defined and viewed through a female gaze," David Yi says. Research in the past twenty years, the era when the flowerboys began popping up, indicates that "the emergence of a 'soft' male ideal in CJK [China, Japan, Korea] culture coincides with the increased buying power of women and the young, [sic] groups that use the Internet most effectively."[27]

～

The inversion of traditional gender norms in marketing is happening as the pitched gender battle rages in South Korea, between feminists and an anti-feminist backlash. The softboy trend is notable because it does seem to reflect a different, more equalizing path, given Gen-Z's ease with gender fluidity.[28] Industry analysts are watching gender neutral cosmetics, which would be a boon to brands because they are inclusive of younger male consumers, effectively doubling the potential market size for their products. "Men-specific beauty may not grow," says Mintel analyst Lee Hwajung. "But the future of the overall men's grooming market is expected to be bright thanks to the growth of genderless cosmetics."

But as gender constructs collapse, or at least as they're disrupted, it changes the traditional gender disparity in body work. In the past, women were the ones who had to primp and prune, while men could get away with just slapping some water on their face in the mornings. Body-monitoring pressures on men mount in a social-media-laden, increasingly gender-fluid landscape, where the demands of body work—be it cutting, bleaching, dyeing, or starving—increasingly fall on all of us, men included. Ordinary Korean men are obsessing over working out to keep their tummies flat, trying to achieve "chocolate-bar abs—" six-packs as well defined as a Hershey's bar. A member of BTS said he once ate only chicken breasts for ten straight days.[29] Videos of men (including Groomin') detail elaborate daily skincare regimens and amass hundreds of thousands, if not millions, of views.

It complicates the idea that appearance standards subjugate women under a male gaze, as the bottom-line-driven and internalized technological gaze widens and subjugates men, too. Korea again is a potential leading indicator, as its consumer beauty culture expands and sends male product consumption upward. "They have to look perfect," David Yi says, of everyday Koreans. "And if women have that pressure, now, men have that pressure as well."

It is gender equality, kind of. But not a desirable end point, according to philosopher Heather Widdows. Even if this pressure led to the extinction of gender and gender roles, "it would still be morally problematic," she writes. "The problems with the increasing demands of beauty are not just that they are demanded more of one gender than another but the nature of the demands."[30]

Still Worse for Women

For now, Yi and others caution that so long as a gender binary exists, the pressures will remain much heavier on women. For those of us who identify as such, we innately understand how punishing it is if we fail to meet or fail to put in effort to meet the beauty ideal. Beauty can benefit men, as the good looks of politicians like, say, Justin Trudeau may give him an advantage. But the lack of good looks is not an insurmountable problem for men. (I will spare you examples of unsexy male politicians.) For women, not meeting a minimal bar for attractiveness can be outright disqualifying. As Korean cultural researcher Sharon Heijin Lee put it, "For women, beauty work is compulsory. For men it's a frivolity. It's 'I have enough income and time and energy to do this,' whereas for women, it's more of a 'you must.'"[31]

There also isn't a single emerging global male ideal in the way females face the worldwide ideals of firmness, smoothness, thinness, and youth. Flowerboy may be an increasingly popular aesthetic, but muscular hypermasculine looks are also lusted after. So are hairy, chubbier lumberjack types.

Generally, norms for males are broader and less demanding. K-pop men deviate from conventional gender norms toward the feminine, but the vast majority of women K-pop idols don't have the leeway to deviate in the other direction, toward the masculine. A thought experiment: How would audiences receive a K-pop girl group of cropped-hair women with masculine aesthetics?

Swagger CEO Hellen Choo points out that the mainstreaming of the flowerboy and the adoption of daily wear makeup exists for only a sector of Gen-Z's hippest corners. Generational differences persist, such that older men are still okay with soap and water, and that salarymen in their forties remain more likely to buy their body wash if it comes in containers that look like liquor bottles. The broader lot do participate in grooming, but not in makeup, something she learned after a lot of experimentation. "I see a lot of men and millennials and Gen-Z going crazy over fashion. They would, you know, queue up anywhere to get the new merch and all that. But I've never, ever seen men queue up to buy cosmetics, you know what I mean? So the fervor is very, very different," she says.

I push back, pointing out investors were in her office at that very moment to throw more money at her company.

"Actually," she says, "I've secured recent investment because I've just launched two women's brands and they're doing very well."

~

CHAPTER 13

The Wisdom of Ajummas

A few years ago, a meme circulated about the aging of Asian women. It's divided into six comic panels. The first panel reads "Age 18" above a drawing of a black-haired, thin-waisted woman in a green shirt, with soft features and a wide forehead. The next panel, labeled "Age 20–30," shows the woman looking exactly the same except her shirt is blue. In the third, "Age 30–50," the woman again looks the same except her hair is in a bun and she's flanked by two small children. The fourth panel is just the word "MENOPAUSE" in giant bubble letters drawn on a comic book style orange starburst. The fifth box is the punch line: when she reaches "Age 60–70," the youthful Asian woman who was as skinny and appealing at fifty as she was at eighteen suddenly looks eerily like the former North Korean leader Kim Jong Il. Sporting sunglasses and a perm, her features chubbier, she's in a tracksuit. In the final panel, "Age 120," she has shrunken so much that her head barely peeks above the bottom of the frame.

The meme gets at something we intuitively understand: For as long as an adult woman possibly can, she's supposed to look younger than her numerical age. She might do this through the help of cosmetics—sold helpfully under labels such as *age-defying* or *anti-aging* or with the promise to "smooth fine lines and wrinkles." Or she might do it through physical discipline or surgery.

The meme also traffics in the popular notion that Asians appear slow to age, taking longer than white women to wrinkle—"Asian don't raisin," the saying goes. At least until after menopause, at which, according to the comic, we get to look like we've aged almost overnight. My friends in Korea called it "ajumma-fication," the process by which a woman, released (at long last) from the notion that she should look young, accepts her aging body as it is. The "ajumma-fied" woman is one whose waistband has been liberated, whose hair no longer has to be worn long, and whose face is allowed to carry lines.

In my interactions with ajummas, a term for elderly Korean women or aunties, I noticed that I would instinctively make myself small, like a child. I know the oldest generations in Korea have seen everything. Many were born either before or during World War II, and witnessed their country cleaved in half during their childhood before the devastation brought on by the Korean War. At seventy and beyond, the ajummas seemed freed from sexist expectations that women be gracious, pretty, and polite. Ajummas have a license to tell you what to do. One might wrench your baby out of your arms to shush them or offer care and feeding tips (this happened to me numerous times) or scold you on your behavior (in my case, it was how I didn't wrap the baby in enough layers). Others would squeeze past and cut in line to get onto elevators first or jam their carts into my ankles at the Costco in Seoul, making a trip to the big-box store feel like a harrowing contact sport. Most colorfully, ajummas have the freedom to choose garish perms, get their thinning eyebrows tattooed on, and wear multicolored tracksuits, affecting the "Accidental Asian hipster" look. They transcend to a status in which they behave like total bosses. My friend Patrick jokes he wants to come back in his next life as an ajumma.

The ajumma and the halmeoni (grandma) have a rarefied, reverential status in South Korea for a combination of reasons. In Eastern societies with Confucian roots, the signs of aging confer honor and dignity, rather than shame.[1] And Korea's specific history of "mother power" further buttresses the societal understanding of elderly women as figures of strength. The Goryeo Dynasty (918–1392) was matrilineal, meaning family wealth was passed down by mothers. In the Joseon Dynasty (1392–1910), power shifted to a male-dominated system, but "mother power" remained a cultural currency. In Joseon society, there was an expectation—transcending class lines—that the mother would give her children the moral foundation they needed to become responsible citizens. At a more practical level, women who successfully brought up their sons (to pass the high-stakes national exam) and their daughters (to marry into wealth) would earn status and power as they aged. Their children, having secured an education and/or a husband, would elevate or maintain her status for her.

Contemporary Korean women past seventy have aged into a demographic beyond the realm of the bulk of beauty marketing. The onslaught of messaging about the best "lines" or "ratios" don't target them. I wondered whether it felt liberating to be out of the beauty industry's cross hairs after being locked in its sights for so many decades. Those tracksuits in that aging meme really do look so comfy! Once you've made it past society's sell-by date, does it represent a kind of freedom from factory-issued appearance standards? When I reach my ajumma years, will my new status let me blow past constraining behavioral boundaries, too?

~

A few years after I moved home to America, specifically L.A., home of the largest Korean population outside Korea, I reached out to Korean American retirees to better understand beauty in life's golden years. Every Monday at an Orange County planned community for "active seniors," Alice Hahn is among the hundred or so retirees who form neat rows in a spacious multipurpose room to learn line dancing. Every student in the class looked at least seventy. The graying and energetic instructor wears a headset and teaches the entire class in Korean, demonstrating steps before starting the music. "I know it looks hard," she tells the class, "but it's not too bad." Once the music starts again, the class moves as one harmonious unit.

Alice, now seventy-two, was born in Seoul the year the Korean War broke out. She has no memory of the war, but many memories of her junior and high school years in a Seoul that was transforming radically as it recovered from two back-to-back wars. She remembers drab matching uniforms, the Park Chung-hee government-regulated haircuts that were all the same, and no time for frills. "We didn't think about looks at all," Hahn says. She went to college at the elite all-girls Ewha Womans University and went on to earn a medical degree, which she didn't use after emigrating to the United States in the early 1970s. She wears bright pink tennis shoes to the line dancing class and only sunscreen on her face. She describes her daily skincare routine as "two or three steps" of cleansing and lotion or cream. She admits she dyes her hair after first letting it go gray at age seventy. When she moved into her Orange County community, "everybody was dying their hair and they asked me, 'Are you that old?' So after that I dyed it."

Her friend and line dancing classmate Elizabeth Kwon, seventy-three, a former nurse who was also born and raised in Seoul, wears her hair naturally gray but puts on makeup before she goes to class—light foundation, a plum-colored lipstick, and some eye shadow. "I want to look decent to be etiquette, you know, to present myself, to not be rude," Kwon says.

She explains this motivation as *jibon yewi*, basic social etiquette. "That's to respect other people. Not taking care of myself is very un-respectful to other people. That's how I learned." The women go on to unpack *yewi*: Ever since they were young, they had been taught that maintaining a neat, put-together appearance is part of the social contract. The focus isn't to attain the reigning beauty standard but instead to demonstrate care within the community. It's about reciprocity, not competition. Maintaining an acceptable appearance helps grease social connection, which redounds to both ends of a relationship.

Their sentiments echoed the work of Joanna Elfving-Hwang at the University of Western Australia. She interviewed twenty senior women (above the age of sixty-three) who lived in Seoul. She found that contrary to Koreans at earlier life stages, older women saw cosmetic surgery as more of a choice and less a need.[2] I suspect it's because they're freed from the most competitive arenas of contemporary life, like searching for a job or a mate.

The Korean American women I talked to, most of whom have been marinating in American culture longer than I've been alive, rejected plastic surgery altogether, suggesting one of the differences in perspective and attitudes between Koreans in Korea and Koreans who emigrated to other countries. They criticized their birthplace as way too "materialistic" lately, with people feeling too much "peer pressure" to look alike. "I think these days in Korea, they all want to look like a celebrity. They want to have big eyes and big nose. And I did not see no personality over there anymore," Kwon says. "Since I came over here [to America], I feel so good because nobody bother me. They don't care I have long face and big mouth. I'm here. I feel so good."

Kwon underlines a distinction between the striving for beauty in her native Korea and her own daily rituals: "I wanted to be always natural and clean look. But I wasn't thinking I'm pretty or anything because . . . how can I say? I'm ugly."

To my American ears, this matter-of-fact declaration of

ugliness sounded dissonant and felt uncomfortable. But before reacting, I pause. "Did people say that to you growing up, that you're ugly?" I ask.

"They didn't have to say to me, but I feel it. I know I'm the ugly one, because in Korea, everybody have a small mouth, you know, the round face, or something. But I look different than them a little bit, right? I have a big mouth, long face."

I had a knee-jerk instinct to reassure her that of course she's pretty. But I stopped myself because her friends did not chime in to rebut Elizabeth. I realized my instinct to praise her appearance said more about my discomfort than Elizabeth's—that over time I have regrettably learned to link physical attractiveness with a person's value, and the absence of it, as lack. Elizabeth doesn't. Her self-acceptance makes it easy to say, *Hey, I'm not pretty and it doesn't matter.*

Her friend Alice Hahn shares one more ritual in her otherwise unfussy list of appearance work: a monthly facial. She says she enjoys the feeling of her face being lovingly cared for and covered with soothing serums, and the shoulder massage that comes with it. "I feel very comfortable, relaxed," Alice says. She reminds me that for many, a facial, a foot rub, or a manicure might be the only time they're touched by another human. Toward the end of their lives, women are more likely to be unpartnered. Around the world, they are outliving men by an average of four and a half years.[3] The touch of beauty workers is soothing, affirming, and connective. What feels better than the scalp massage before a haircut, if you can afford such a luxury? Or that communion with a hairstylist who really knows you and has been involved in the stories of your life every time you sit down in the salon chair? Alice ultimately describes her facials in spiritual terms: "I feel blessed when I do it," she said.

The Korean grandmas also distinguish between beauty practices like facials or fillers, which seem rational to them in the quest to enhance beauty, and face-lifts or nose jobs, which can drastically change a person's appearance. In their view, the latter treatments are steps too far. "Botox is like makeup now," Alice said. "But I don't wanna get any surgery," Elizabeth interjects.

Elizabeth rejects surgery out of hand. For Alice, something about the allure of looking slightly better persists. She says she is considering going to Seoul for a nip and tuck for her drooping upper eyelids. Elizabeth quizzes her on whether it's for health or vanity, and Alice answers by saying her vision is not impaired. "I used to have big eyes," she says.

Thinking back to the meme about the aging of Asian women, I asked the postmenopausal grandmas if at some age we can just let go.

"Let go? Nooo. Of course not!" Elizabeth laughs, aghast. "I still care! I put some moisturizer and a little liner to look like I'm awake."

Alice jumps in. "Never." She waits a beat. "Well, I thought it was seventy. But maybe when we're eighty."

They emphasize that they want to maintain their good health as long as possible, because it gives them more time to enjoy life. "If we're laying in a hospital, then we're, you know, burdening our children," their friend, seventy-one-year-old mother of two Cho Young Lim, says through a translator.

"Yeah, we want to be healthy until we die," said Alice.

Elfving-Hwang's research concluded that for old Korean

women, maintaining a positive appearance signified a control over their bodies as they aged so that they could maintain health, longevity, and a full life. Their beauty rituals allowed them to continue to take pleasure in what their bodies were capable of. "The ageing body both as an object of enjoyment, and ritual object to acknowledge the feelings of others, points to an important new way of conceptualizing positive ageing," Elfving-Hwang concludes.[4] Acceptance of aging doesn't mean body care is finished, but rather that care becomes driven by community-building and soul-nourishing priorities.

What I found refreshing about my time with the line dancing ladies was their lack of anxiety about their appearance and the freedom inherent in their self-acceptance. To them, aging is just a part of a full life. "Well, you know, you have to accept it. Everything's kind of going down. Eyes, face, everything," Alice said. Life doesn't end when youth does.

"The Japanese fairy tales tell us," the great Japanese psychologist Hayao Kawai wrote, "that beauty is completed only if we accept the fact of death."[5] The notion that change is constant, that this passing moment is ephemeral, makes these ladies beautiful.

~

American suffragette Elizabeth Cady Stanton, in her famous lecture "Our Girls," described the marketing materials for a beauty cream and observed, "Again, the recipe says, 'The Magnolia will make a lady of thirty look like a girl of sixteen.' Now what sensible woman of thirty, with all the marks of intelligence and cultivation that well spent years must give, would desire to look like an inexperienced girl of sixteen? . . . When it is only through age that one gathers wisdom and experience, why this endless struggle to seem young?"[6]

Youth is novelty, and for proof of how much it is valued, we only have to observe that the highest praise for an older woman is to say she looks young.[7] To see the value of youthfulness in numbers, I point you to the recession-proof cosmetics industry. Thirty-five percent of the cosmetics market consists of skincare products, a category that includes anti-aging and firming products.[8] But the gospel against aging is, crucially, anti-nature. It is a biological fact that our bodies are dynamic. They change each moment—cells die, skin sheds, muscles strengthen or weaken. That's why the whole notion of "getting your body back" after pregnancy makes no sense to me; what body are we trying to get back? Our bodies are never fixed. Nothing in nature is fixed.

Alice recalls that in high school, one of her teachers said, "You'll never look as good as you do now." But who do you want to look like when you look in the mirror today? I ask the women. Myself, each of them says. "The number-one thing I hear from women when I ask about their reasons for performing beauty work is not that they want to change how they look, but that they want to look like their best selves," beauty journalist Autumn Whitefield-Madrano wrote.[9]

The ajummas show us a way to preserve and celebrate our bodies without forcing them into any rigid norms; to reject factory-issued beauty standards but arrive at the best version of our selves at whichever age we're at. Their kind of self-care emphasizes caring for *one another*, the pleasures of bodily movement, and nurturing touch over product purchases. It accepts both getting old and not necessarily being pretty. It considers community and reciprocity. In other words, body care in old age is a way to enjoy it and feel satisfied with it. Theirs is a form of body work that nurtures the soul.

What these women showed me is that to address the paradox of beauty and body work, we should ask ourselves if the labor we're undertaking is ego driven or soul driven. Does it lead to more connection (with ourselves and others) or disconnection? At advanced ages, the balance clearly tips to more connected, soul-driven body work, which takes less money, energy, and time, something to which I aspire. Following a soul-directed standard to make active choices about our bodies and to care for ourselves in the ways that we need honors what makes us each unique.

Watching the women line dance, laugh with each other, playfully slap each other on the backs in agreement or support, I took in how distinct each of these women is from the others. How uncontrived and fully themselves they are. Each was pleasant to be around, but in highly personal, specific ways. They reminded me that the pursuit of perfection is not just tedious but boring. Beauty is subjective and mysterious for a reason. The industry's (often successful) plays to suggest there is a standard, its attempts to codify beauty with formulas and then commodify it, have led younger generations down a path of obsession, anxiety, and exhaustion. Worse, as seventy-three-year-old Elizabeth Kwon put it, "Everyone looks the same. They are not interesting."

What makes us appealing to others isn't meant to be easily found on the surface, nor broken down into ratios and V or S lines to understand and command. True beauty, not the factory kind, springs from the diversity of multitudes. "People are different," Alice Hahn said. "Look different."

To my eyes, these ajummas look joyful. As if they're really enjoying themselves. They look loose, dancing synchronously among dozens of other Korean retirees, born in the 1940s ashes of war, doing the boot-scooting boogie to the 1990s tunes of Billy Ray Cyrus.

Conclusion

~

When the Korean moving men came to begin our transpacific journey home to the United States, they took off their shoes at the door and padded around the apartment in soft white socks, packing up our things into thick white cardboard boxes with tiger logos on them. By then our youngest, Luna, was sixteen months. She could walk but preferred to be picked up and plopped on top of counters. On moving day, Luna giggled as we sat her high on top of stacks of boxes, her legs dangling, knocking her heels against the cardboard. After we watched the men load the final boxes into a shipping container truck, I stood outside the apartment tower and quizzed our three-year-old middle daughter, Isa, who was born in Korea:

"Where are we going?"

"Cal-ee-for-nee-ah," she replied, stretching out her vowels.

"Where?"

"CAL-EE-FOR-NYAH!" squeaking it out twice as fast.

After covering the bone-chilling Winter Olympics, I shared

with the NPR bosses that I was finished with winter entirely, and they approved a move to Southern California before the end of 2018. A harried packing week and a twelve-hour flight later, we emerged bleary-eyed at Los Angeles International Airport.

For the first month after arriving in California, we stayed in temporary housing in the Los Angeles neighborhood of Venice, six blocks from the beach famous for its very L.A. vibes. Green juices. Skateboards dusted with sand. Shirtless men working out. I suffered some serious reverse culture shock: The drink vessels were so large! The people all looked so different from one another! Strangers spoke English! On the day we landed, I took a walk to Eva's new school, where she would start kindergarten within the week, and women of all sizes wore leggings or workout pants openly as they strolled down the sidewalks. Some wore only sports bras as tops, their bare midriffs out for everyone to see. In Seoul you will not find women walking around in tight athleisure. You certainly won't find them walking around in a bra top.

Especially in L.A.'s more well known neighborhoods— West Hollywood, Venice, Santa Monica—so many "pretty people" surround me that my friends and I play games like "Celebrity? Or just rich?" On hikes it sometimes seems more plausible that the hikers, with their Restylane-plumped lips, snatched waists, and curiously creaseless foreheads are actors playing the roles of hikers. The everyday fashion and style distinct to Southern California is more ostentatious than in Korea, far less traditionally feminine (read: no pencil skirts), but certainly requires its own labor. In my pre-Korea home of Washington, D.C., people were performative about their careers, talking about how little they slept or "hard stops" at meetings. In my post-Korea home of Los Angeles, people are performative about their leisure and fitness—monitoring the live beach cameras for the best waves, talking up trendy new workouts they'd tried. But looking good requires untold hours and serious dollars' worth of work. At the first L.A. gym I visited, for a workout involving souped-up Pilates Reformers colloquially referred to as "Megaformers," millennial and Gen-Z ladies spent $50 for a single class and wore eyelash extensions a mile long while they exercised. After class, as we put our shoes back on over our grippy socks, I listened as classmates carried on long, informed conversations on diet and exercise strategies, how to sculpt specific body parts, and the vagaries of hair removal and where to get it done.

My friends will mention they're trying a hair serum "from my Instagram feed," say "I got this swimsuit from sponcon" or acknowledge "the algorithm has me pegged," revealing a savvy about the ways social media marketing shapes our desires, but are willing to internalize the standards all the same. Knowing that beauty imperatives are largely social or cultural phenomena doesn't stop us from trying to chase them. When I came back from Seoul, I saw more surface difference and a lot less homogeneity between people. I love the diversity of L.A. But the same forces from the beauty industry that demonize getting older or having pores are in play here, as we maneuver within the same overarching global definition of beauty—thinness, firmness, smoothness, and youth.

~

A couple of years have passed since our return. My oldest daughters, Eva and Isa, are now nine and six. The other night, after I tucked them into their bunk beds, I tiptoed down the hall to my bedroom and overheard Isa parrot my words. She said to Eva, "Momma says it doesn't matter if you're beautiful, it matters if you're clever."

Her older sister replied, "Momma just says that because she's already pretty."

From my spot down the hall, I stopped in my tracks. Despite my incessant protestations otherwise, my nine-year-old has a sense of the implicit benefits that accrue to people who make the cut. All she had to do to absorb this was to be born and pay attention. Even Luna, a toddler, comes home from school and will mimic the phrase she's hearing from her Mandarin-speaking teachers at her Montessori preschool: "*Ni de yian jing ne meh da!*" (Your eyes, they're SO big!)

Their intuitive understanding is similar to what any woman at any size and color can tell you. Just as believing in "color blindness" doesn't negate the reality that racism exists and discrimination does harm, trying to insist everybody is beautiful or looks don't matter have not tamped down the persistence of narrow, industrialized beauty norms and the harms of lookism. The message that "all women are beautiful, flaws and all!" is "really nice, but it isn't fixing the problem," said Dr. Lindsay Kite, the codirector of Beauty

Redefined, in a talk about her research into beauty standards and self-worth. "That's because girls and women aren't only suffering because of the unattainable ways beauty is being defined—they are suffering because they are being defined by beauty."[1]

We can, and many of us have, individually turned down the scripts that link appearance to worth, an ongoing project of my adult life. But it doesn't change standardized beauty ideals and a profit-centered beauty culture for everyone. "As an individual I cannot—whatever I personally feel—make it suddenly beautiful to be big-waisted, with bingo or bat wings, cankles, and cellulite," beauty philosopher Heather Widdows has argued. "I might even resist appearance norms altogether . . . However . . . this becomes harder as appearance becomes more prominent, as culture becomes increasingly visual and virtual, and as technological fixes become accessible and affordable and as the beauty ideal functions as an ethical ideal. Thus, while some might continue to resist the ideal, in the current context, resistance is harder, becomes political and is increasingly regarded as abnormal."[2]

My nearly four years in Korea proved powerfully instructive and changed me. On my first night there, to apartment-hunt in the makeup mecca of Myeongdong, as overwhelmed as I was by all the neon lights and noise, I was also kind of judgmental: What was with all the flesh-colored post-op face coverings? Why was everyone shamelessly selfie-ing everywhere? By the time I moved home, I saw modern middle-class Korean women in a far more nuanced light, and with compassion—so many of their choices are made within a limited set of options. They function within a structure of the most stringent requirements. As long as particular beauty ideals persist, and as long as class stability and economic and social success are dependent on meeting the standard, it is only logical to put in the work of appearance labor.

Korea is a uniquely fertile territory for appearance-focused industries to thrive. Contemporary Korea combines a vestigial Confucian emphasis on societal harmony, a hypermodernity that fuels technologies of self-improvement, and the aspirational Korean dream of "making it" by getting rich. After the highly visual digital era and our economic system cemented the conflation of the body with the self, the idea of betterment through external beauty—and the desire to keep working to pursue it—has kept the industry growing. But these forces are not limited to Korea. They're just more pronounced there.

It took moving to the other side of the world and living in a wholly unfamiliar culture to see how insidious, industrialized beauty ideals have influenced so many, maybe all, of our lives, and how they ask way too much of us. We reinforce the ideals with our willing—and often passive—participation.

～

Beauty culture is fueled by our relentless labor. Whether it's hair removal that you start and cannot stop, or wrinkle removal that you start and cannot stop, or other rituals requiring never-ending product purchases, I've come to view beauty work as labor that we don't just do for free, but pay to do. Women's bodies are objects and subjects; conduits for consumption and worksites all at once.

Even more draining is the emphasis to look "natural," meaning you're supposed to look like you don't do the work at all—effecting effortlessness out of enormous effort. The Korean term for it is *kku an kku*, which literally translates to "decorated not decorated." We don't measure the time, energy, and effort put into skincare, fillers, dental work, hair straightening or coloring, and so on. But that should not obscure the fact that appearance labor does require money and time: researching and purchasing products, scheduling and attending appointments, regimenting your body—all these add up. What would the hours we've spent trying to fit into the beauty ideal look like on a time sheet? "While many women (and some men) rail against the gender pay gap, too often, we don't consider the gender gap in time and money spent on beauty," Renee Engeln, a professor of psychology, muses in her book *Beauty Sick*. "But time and money matter. They're essential sources of power and influence and also major sources of freedom."[3]

I think back to how many of the women I interviewed expressed variations on the same theme: that their appearance labor was both a choice and not a choice, especially in Korea. Especially because of its ties to the job and marriage markets, body work is necessary to survive the competitive individualistic capitalism of this moment. And our economic system promotes more and more body work. We constantly absorb messages that aesthetic self-improvement will make us feel empowered and good about ourselves. But it's so often a mirage. What an isolating feeling, doing all this unsatisfying, unrecognized labor. We work unlimited hours, with an ever-expanding scope of work. The culture writer Haley Nahman wrote that her own experience obsessing over beauty was like "living paycheck to paycheck, only the labor was self-beautification and the currency was self-worth."[4] Costly products, procedures, and practices are often cloaked as self-care. Where is the care while we exhaust our bodies, time, and wallets?

When we absorb a neoliberal economic system like this, when we believe we're all self-starting individual entrepreneurs who must regulate our bodies to "win," it means we tend to judge ourselves harshly when we need help, and judge others harshly if *they* need help. You "take on a much gloomier view of other people. Anyone else and their needs is kind of a threat to my own kind of rugged individualism and independence. So it keeps us really isolated," psychologist Devon Price told me in an NPR interview. "[It] can kind of create this downward spiral of just workaholism and isolation."[5]

We should not stay isolated in our individual narratives about beauty. I wrote this book because we need a more intimate knowledge of the way it's affected each of us so we can truly focus on widening our gaze and advancing women's power.

So much beauty work is about not falling behind—not losing class status, visibility, or value to society. But there is a difference between beauty as a spiritual concept and aesthetic beauty as expressed by consumerism. The beauty our souls crave is far richer, far more idiosyncratic and varied—not simply the stuff on the surface. Beauty industry critic

Jessica DeFino has suggested to think of it like art: "When you see a beautiful painting, you don't just admire its canvas, right? The beauty isn't in the rectangular shape or sharp edges of its form. The painting is beautiful because of its essence: the way it makes you feel, what it has to say, some unknown *something* about it—and yes, in part, its aesthetic. Beauty is the culmination of all of these things. And that can't be standardized."[6]

In the face of new trends or standards, I have learned to be mindful of the larger forces at play—the predatory practices of the beauty and medical tourism industries, which are predicated on problematizing the way we look. The V-line jaw, for example, is a made-up standard where supply first created demand. "It came about just about fifteen years ago and now it's accepted as the thing to be," Korean feminism writer James Turnbull told me, in illustrating how profit-driven industries can make standards stick.

I by no means eschew body rituals completely, because they can be nurturing and inherently human—an expression of our hope and striving. Beauty products can exist as expressions of joy, portals to soothing care rituals, and a place for experimentation and expression. For those on the margins, such as North Korean women in South Korea, beauty products and communities have meant a path to regaining control over themselves, representing freedom from a harmful state regime. For transgender women, appearing femme, as Korean trans activists have said, can be a matter of survival as well as self-expression and experimentation.[7] But however personally empowering it is to creatively cope with our appearance-obsessed culture, individualized solutions fail to address conditions for everyone. They are at best incomplete, while corporations reap the rewards. All these products and services are expensive to start, and costlier to keep up with. The worldwide medical aesthetic market is projected to be worth more than $21 billion by 2024—a significant leap from $10 billion in 2016.[8]

Can consumers discipline our waistlines or get plastic surgery or injections without perpetuating unrealistic beauty expectations in the first place? I'm not sure we can. Everything I do to make myself look individually "better" affects the expectations within my community for how we should look. I could feel better about my appearance by Botox-ing again, maybe, but it compounds the problem for everyone else. I can individually prevail in society where being "beautiful" affords me privileges like more professional or personal success. But "winning" through self-optimization in a hypercapitalist system is a precarious way of life for those at the top. And it relies on the aspirations of the underprivileged to give it power.

Without the millions who buy into narrowing beauty ideals, the system can't survive. There is revolutionary potential in not linking outward appearance to a woman's value. To begin divesting from beauty culture, we must examine our own attitudes, habits, purchases, and pressingly, where we direct our attention. As author Jenny Odell pointed out, what we pay attention to—or not—becomes how we render reality, and what we feel is possible.[9] We can turn our attention away from "fixing" supposed flaws and toward a more affirmative vision that celebrates *everyone*'s worthiness. We can reclaim our time. We can be freer than we are. The philosopher Martin Hägglund has argued that to "be free" doesn't mean norms will go away, but rather, that we can be free to negotiate, transform, and contest them.[10]

The greatest risk, I think, is to put in the labor of makeup or Botox or food restriction without interrogating it and "letting these costs become an integral part of your life without ever truly deciding what you do or do not want to spend time and money on," as Renee Engeln describes.[11]

I now think about body work on a continuum. I actively take note of the amount of work I'm signing up for every time I start using a new product or when I purchase a procedure that the beauty culture is selling me. I'm mindful of industries whose growth is reliant upon the extraction of our energies and access to our bodies. I am constantly questioning what adhering to a trendy standard could mean for my daughters—Is it work I want *them* to take on? Are we being good ancestors to future generations?

But rather than finding individual enlightenment about bodily obsessions that stymie us, we could act together to reimagine the superstructure entirely. Instead of competition, our norms could be governed by an ethic of consent, community, and connection. It should start with a simple notion: all bodies are worthy of respect, dignity, and care. Those who don't fit "free size," those who aren't able-bodied or who are otherwise excluded from the ruling appearance norms of the day are equally worthy of care. Relying on my lessons from K-beauty as a guide, I am including here some ways we can rethink beauty culture writ large:

Expanding Our Standards, Embracing Difference

We need more media representation of all races, abilities, gender expressions, and sizes, because the narrower our view of "pretty" gets, then the wider our view of "ugly" becomes. Let's widen our perspectives to see beauty refracted in different and more surprising ways than the dominant narrative sold to us by corporations. In the United States, for instance, it feels like there's already so little representation of Asian girls that what we see of Asian women is often represented by K-pop idols that even the South Korean government have now faulted for looking too similar to one another. It reminds me of what feminist writer Laurie Penny wrote: "This is the intimate edge of neoliberal feminism, the meritocratic fantasy that, in this freest of all possible worlds, any woman can be anything she wants to be, as long as she slices her face and dresses her body to look exactly the same as everyone else."[12] The kind of beauty we see in nature, or in art, shows us how beauty emerges from diversity and multitudes rather than sameness.

Our current standards are not just unachievable, they're mostly arbitrary. The plastic surgery clinics keep trying to apply math or science to quantify beauty: to pin it down, put a number on it, and arrive at a perfect ratio or "golden mean." But these standards are too often solutions in search of problems. Even the seemingly conventional wisdom that humans are drawn to symmetrical faces is questionable. It's backed by some studies, while other studies show the opposite.[13] Yet the theory that symmetry signals attractiveness really stuck. It is so universalized that TikTok abounds with this preoccupation. There are over 100 million videos on TikTok with the tag #symmetricalface, and a number of apps, such as Symmetry, further invite this fixation.

TikTok is a reminder of the extent to which today's ideals are increasingly algorithmically determined, further granting omniscience to a fallible, invasive, dangerous technological gaze, driving a reversion to sameness in our social feeds. So far the algorithms seem to chase a bland middle, propagating a basic "Airbnb aesthetic" for apartments and a basic transracial prettiness with "Instagram Face." What we humans celebrate and appreciate in other humans is far richer and vaster than what these algorithms capture.

Challenging the rigid obligations of female appearance ideals is not to deny beauty in the world, but instead motivated by, a desire to see more of it. The antidote for the poison of profit-seekers is to embrace our brownness, blemishes, or belly fat, because it is our uniqueness that propels us as individuals and makes our communities more inclusive. To stand in our own power and not erase our differences is to claim them as our own.

Digital spaces in the metaverse could be places where an infinite number of aesthetic possibilities are suddenly available. Instead of recycling our preferences back to us, the design of metaverses *could* mean an expansion of visual options for our outer shells rather than fewer options. To be clear, that would require a shift from the direction visual culture is currently taking us.

Body Neutrality

What if we didn't use our bodies as barometers for worth? What if beauty wasn't worth pursuing in the first place? An expansion of cultural norms should not be solely focused on aesthetics. We should do more to interrogate and take apart a world where external appearance matters too much. It is weird and messed up that our moral worth is so linked to our physical appearance! Our looks don't have to be the central paradigm for the self.

For all the diversity in the Dove "Real Beauty" campaign, critics have pointed out body positivity campaigns like these can go only so far if they're focused on external "beauty." They risk reinforcing the long-standing norm that women should want to be beautiful in the first place, as writer Kaila Prins has noted.[14]

One of the most egregious parts of Korean hiring culture is that every job is treated like a modeling job—height, weight, and head shots matter. The business world must stop linking looks to competence. Parents and teachers could stop inculcating ideas about beauty and worth at a young age, which is where many Korean women expressed a wish that things could have gone differently for them. "We have to change the notion among the general populace that it's okay to comment on people's appearances," twenty-six-year-old Choi Yujin said. "They have to change the way they talk to young girls because they teach at a very young age that their value is only their appearance. We have to stop using that language." Changing beauty culture requires, at a minimum, changing not just how we talk about looks and our own appearance but where we direct our attention—how we use our time and energy toward chasing industrial beauty standards, or not.

Under the framework of body or skin neutrality, instead of classifying skin as "good skin" or "bad skin," it's just skin. You don't have to particularly love the skin you're in, nor loathe it for letting you down, because being "unpretty" doesn't have to exact a cost, just as Korean American Elizabeth Kwon, one of the Southern California ajummas, exemplified. The lingerie designer behind Hey Mavens!, Annika Benitz Chaloff, put it this way to Fashionista: "Body neutrality says, 'all bodies are bodies.'"[15] It means not worrying whether a body is beautiful or not and accepting it as it is. "Appearance does not have a bearing on your inherent value." I don't think this idea would have clicked for me in my teens. But after moving around in the world as a woman at middle age, I intrinsically get it now.

Body neutrality says we could look around and say, *Hey, maybe I am not particularly beautiful by current standards, and it does not matter.* The message could change—instead of how to best suppress your pimples, it could be how to best support your skin. Less about manipulating its appearance and more about meeting its basic needs.

Opting out from fitting in and resisting the ideal gives others license to opt out as well. The Escape the Corset women also point a way in that they chose to strike from appearance work and boycott beauty buying. For now, it comes at great social cost to them. Progress would look like opting out of appearance labor and not paying a price.

Celebrating Bodily Capacities for Doing and Feeling

The work of Céline Leboeuf at Florida International University makes a case for going from bodily shame to a proper body pride with an approach called sensualism, which celebrates our bodies for what they can do or what pleasures they can feel.[16]

It could mean celebrating the act of whistling. Or, for the able-bodied, walking. Or moving together in a line dancing class. Or how we can use touch to connect and communicate with one another. I came to feel less alienated from my body after pregnancy, birth, and nursing. I also feel a connectedness to my physical self in the satisfaction of a really good stretch.

This framework celebrates athleticism, at any size. Or overcoming certain obstacles at any age or ability. This would mean expanding access to physical activities across a wide range of abilities.

"For many of us, participating in sports or other activities that involve movement (for example, dance or yoga) is a meaningful part of life. Therefore, we should continue creating accommodations for those with physical disabilities to engage in sports and related practices. Moreover, we should honor the achievements of persons who may not fit standard representations of physical accomplishment," Leboeuf writes.[17]

On the feeling front, sensualism describes appreciating the body for its capacity to use its senses to feel. If overindulgence and overwork in a time of capitalistic competition leads to bodily estrangement, sensualism offers an antidote by simplifying. It grounds body appreciation from sources within. This appreciation can be cultivated through activities such as physical exercise, sex, or meditation. To paraphrase the feminist writer bell hooks, removing the clutter of desire, material clutter, or incessant busyness allows us to recover our sensual capacities.[18] And what a beautiful thing. As James Baldwin wrote, "To be sensual . . . is to respect and rejoice in the force of life, of life itself, and to be present in all that one does, from the effort of loving to the breaking of bread."[19]

~

We must wrestle the contradictions of beauty culture at a societal level. Caring for and celebrating our bodies can heal us. Factory-issued beauty standards can constrain and hurt us. The pain and the pleasure take place on the same canvas. But together we can bring about a way of life that is based not on competition and coercion but on community and care, finding beauty that's spiritual and not superficial, and helps us find freedom through true agency over our bodies.

After exploring this on both sides of the Pacific, I've come to see that the care must be predicated on a reconnection with ourselves. In considering our bodies as sites of work, I realized we can also be alienated from our bodies in the same way that all workers are alienated from ownership of their labor, and for similar reasons. Reclaiming bodily integrity requires *embodiment,* defined as "awareness of our body's sensations, habits and the beliefs that inform them. Embodiment requires the ability to feel and allow the body's emotions," as Prentis Hemphill of the Embodiment Institute puts it.

This is important because the work we choose to do—or not—with and on our bodies is, like the struggle for abortion rights, a struggle for self-determination and our claim to bodily and spiritual integrity. As long as current beauty standards demand aesthetic labor (but is spun as a choice), changing the reigning beauty culture will require renegotiating the terms of this labor. Bodily autonomy is a human right and it requires collective action, among embodied people. As long as women and girls are ashamed of or critical of our bodies, with body angst boosting commerce, "it is unlikely that they can achieve the sexual agency that they need for complete and successful lives in the contemporary world," author Joan Jacobs Brumberg writes in *The Body Project,* her historical look at girls' relationships with their bodies. "Girls who do not feel good about themselves need the affirmation of others, and that need, unfortunately, almost always empowers male desire . . . Because they want to be wanted so much, they are susceptible to manipulation, to flattery, even to abuse."[20]

That's where I find the stories of the Escape the Corset women compelling: they examined why they adorned themselves and came to understand their inherent value is not defined by a man or the market or anyone but themselves. Becoming embodied, taking part in a general strike against aesthetic labor, and inspiring others along the way were therapeutic acts for them in a country that stigmatizes mental health. Their form of self-care is personal, and communal—a care that ties into a larger community—and potential lies there.

The stripped-down septuagenarian Korean ajummas are similar. They showed we can arrive at a place where we inhabit our bodies with love and appreciation and adorn ourselves in the spirit of community and self-expression. The acceptance and compassion that those women are showing themselves in their old age offers something we might aspire to our whole lives. If our connection with others can be only as deep as our connection with ourselves, having full agency to decide what we do with our bodies is a fundamental step.

On my first reporting trip to Tokyo, in 2015, I stayed in Shibuya, known for having a street crossing bursting with such density that it's common for folks to force their way through with GoPro cameras mounted on their heads, livestreaming the crush of humanity. I avoided the famous crossing on most nights but did walk a nearby pedestrian overpass every day to return to my hotel. One evening I spied a giant billboard of a young Japanese woman's face. It showed no product or logo, just a wan-looking lady with generic skies in her background, her hair pulled back in a loose ponytail and her eyes fixed in a thousand-yard stare. The copy appeared only in English: "Life is short + money."

I still chuckle when I think about this perplexing message. I still have no idea what it was selling—maybe just the collective spirit of mid-2010s capitalism? Life's ephemerality! Plus money money money!

Whatever the product, the billboard captured the anxious time we lived in when I began my stint in Asia. Sure, the world wasn't at war, fewer people were going hungry globally, the campaign was on to connect another billion to the internet. But the years marched on, and as we stared down demographic crises, fragile economies, and the existential threat of climate change, the same wheels of capitalism kept churning. Supply chains and the planet's resources buckled as we kept consuming and ordering things from home during a crippling pandemic, trying out solutions for various maladies, physical and spiritual.

In the time since I spotted the unmissable "Life is short + money" message, evidence has mounted that the economic and political philosophy undergirding my entire forty years on earth—neoliberalism—and its overreliance on individual solutions to systemic problems has failed. Our natural world is erupting in wildfires, coastal hurricanes, and bands of literal locusts in Africa. In 2020, our public health system flailed against the coronavirus. Our caregiving system hung on by a thread, with nursing homes overrun and schools shutting down, leaving parents everywhere scrambling and straining.

Existential concerns remain—as I write this, the pandemic and a land war in Europe are in the rhythm of my days. But interestingly, the COVID-19 crisis's beginnings in 2020 gave us a break from self-presentation anxieties, at least temporarily. A bigger, more pressing anxiety—survival—outranked it, and the first months of the pandemic saw the rise of a never-before-experienced laissez-faire attitude about presentation.

The places where workers get close to your face to remove

unwanted hair and touch your hands and feet were the first to shut down and the last to reopen. During the closures, my waxing artists who remove hair both "upstairs" and "downstairs" reported receiving frantic calls on their personal numbers with a range of emergencies—ingrowns, burns, scrapes—after clients tried to wax their down-there hair by themselves. "One woman cut off a piece of labia," Jodie, the owner of my go-to L.A. spa, said. "She asked me what to do and I said, '*Go to the emergency room!* You're gonna have to get part of your vagina stitched back on!'" As eyebrows grew unruly and women went without their roots retouched, our reflections in the mirror drove home how being middle class requires constant maintenance. The rich stay rich, the poor get poorer, and maintaining class status in the West and in the East is "to be constantly treading water," as culture writer Anne Helen Petersen has written.[21]

The pandemic offered a rare opportunity for people to switch the script. During lockdown, I felt a possibility of radical change, a chance to rethink how we value ourselves and to reexamine our metric for measuring the worth of human lives. We stopped wearing makeup because we didn't want to. We stopped wearing bras. Many of my friends and colleagues stopped dyeing their hair. My friend Manoush made that command decision after watching the 2020 Democratic National Convention. "One accomplished woman after another took the stage, a lot of them in their sixties and seventies, and not a single woman appeared with gray or graying hair," she observed.

Looks stopped mattering for a moment, and we learned

to survive without appearance work. Free from social requirements to adhere to beauty maintenance, many of us decided, like Bartleby, that we preferred not to. Skincare and beauty work came to feel like status handbags or restaurant openings—things we cared about before that temporarily, at least, seemed vulgar.

In place of pursuits that were literally only skin-deep, a lot of us took a dive into our inner lives, which cost a lot of energy, but zero American dollars or Korean won at all. I grew up under a "pick yourself up by the bootstraps" ethos that we could optimize and life-hack our way to anything. I wrongly believed that with enough hard work and constant movement, I could "win" meritocracy, be productive, and push past any discontentment. But when 2020 enclosed me inside the walls of my Los Angeles home and away from colleagues, my extended family, and my friends, I looked inward. The metric of "productivity" stopped mattering as much. The hustle didn't protect me, or any of us, from calamity. Nor would any blemish-free outer appearance.

Nature taught me so much during our year of stillness. I spent more time in it, just trying to pay attention. When we slowed down to pay attention, I marveled at the way plants speak by communicating in the only ways they know how: "Hi, I'm struggling and shriveling up and need water." It felt so analogous to Western societies full of burned-out, worn-out individuals. We are trying our darnedest to survive under systems of work life, family life, public health, transportation, childcare, elder care, the environment, with so little water and not enough sunlight.

But the capitalist imperative recognizes and rewards continual growth. If looking backward and getting stuck in the past produces depression, and over-focusing on the future describes anxiety, it's no wonder we're awash in anxiety. That ethos—so clearly exemplified in Korea—means we are constantly having to prove our fitness for the future.

In spring 2020, the Korean makeup line HERA shared a makeup trend forecast for a post-COVID world. The main focus was a "healthy-looking" complexion, eye makeup in neutral colors, and subtle lip gloss. The idea was to create a look both when wearing a mask and after taking it off. By spring of 2021, when vaccines were available, salons opened back up and could scarcely keep up with demand. The old ways of the capitalist grind returned without missing a beat. We spent a year ignoring our appearance; then many of us swung dramatically in the other direction. Medical spas in America reported a major run on Botox once half of the United States was fully vaccinated.[22] Today, the beauty industry is more valuable than it's ever been.[23]

In an episode of late capitalism that couldn't be more fitting for this precarious era, one early 2022 TikTok skincare trend was a K-beauty practice of slugging. It calls for smearing thick layers of Vaseline on your face and leaving it overnight, which is supposed to form a protective barrier to restore a glowy moisture to the skin. Petroleum jelly is *petroleum*, beauty critic Jessica DeFino pointed out. "I think it's really dangerous as an industry . . . to be promoting fossil fuels as the number one beauty product right now," she wrote.[24]

As the wheels of commerce started spinning again, the performance of beauty work somehow had to make up for many months of lost time. The whole experience felt like the way author Lisa Rofel described capitalism, as a "world-transforming project that has the capacity to reach into the sinews of our bodies and the machinations of our hearts."[25] The pandemic experience may have changed us individually, but not yet the systems around us.

~

A younger me felt drawn to the chaos and individualism of modern cities, and the two major cities on my reporting patch—Tokyo and Seoul—contained both. I aspired to the all-encompassing possibility they offered. But a place's strength can also be its shadow. I thought a convenient, hypermodern, individualized way of life was worth chasing, the same way a lot of us millennials believed we could each, individually, work within wavering institutions and maneuver our way past the catastrophes and keep up.

Sheet masks were not going to do the trick when my friends or family members were dying and there was no physical way to grieve together or share remembrances. I sent a box of K-beauty goodies to my ER doctor friend while she was in that period of trying to fashion a way to link two ventilators to somehow feed oxygen to eight patients gasping for air. But what she really wanted was a hug or a reason to belly laugh. The antidote to collective burnout and the crisis in our hearts could not be purchased online because the purest cure couldn't be bought and sold. The cure was connection.

When the entire world went through some version of the

same crisis at once, we were suddenly frantic to touch one another. I clung to my first nonfamilial hug after months of distance for several beats too long since I didn't know when I'd receive one like it again. I also wanted the familiar touch of beauty workers. The care and craft in their work came into sharp relief when we couldn't access them.

I would love it if the connection and comfort through the ritual of care—sometimes centered at spas and salons—remained, but the stubborn adherence to factory-issued, algorithm-juiced beauty standards did not. Beauty work should not feel compulsory. It shouldn't feel like so much work.

"When I feel like I need more grit, what I actually need is more help," the author Emily Nagoski said in a 2021 speech. Nagoski suggests connection and mutuality is the "baseline cultural change" that could address collective burnout—and, I would add, give us a break from the endless pursuit of perfection on our bodies, faces, and elsewhere. If you ask me what my dream is, it's not for everyone to believe they're beautiful but instead to believe they are worthy, flaws included. I would want, ideally, a nonpunitive meritocracy that rewards people for kindness. For helping others not-suffer by taking one another into consideration. I want us to practice the kind of self-care that is concerned about the collective and recognizes a real responsibility to one another. My mantra since repatriating to the United States and surviving a pandemic couldn't be further from "Life is short + money." It would sound more like "Life is yours + rest."

It can happen. Nothing about the way we live is inevitable. We swung from the status quo of hustle culture, which felt unsustainable, to a draconian lockdown life, which also quickly proved unsustainable. We do not need to arrive at a new place that looks like the old one. "The deep truth," the Nobel Prize–winning psychologist Daniel Kahneman said on the radio, "is that the world is much more uncertain than we feel it is."[26]

That is not fatalism, it's hope. We have an opportunity to rethink how we value ourselves and reexamine how we measure one another's worth. An opportunity to stand compassionately in our own unique, powerful bodies. To feel connected to ourselves and to each other. To be flawed and worthy.

ACKNOWLEDGMENTS

Every night at dinner I ask the girls to share one "gratitude." It can be for a person, or a moment, a creature—really anything that occurs to them—and it warms my heart to hear what they observed and feel grateful for over the course of their days. Getting to write acknowledgments is an extended version of what I would share at my dinner table, about all of you.

This book is possible only thanks to all the generous sources who let me into their thinking, curiosities, concerns, homes, line dancing classes, businesses, and everyday lives to bring this reporting to life. Thank you to every Korean woman who shared time and insight. Each became a teacher, helping the rest of us better understand.

Huge thanks also to Howard Yoon, who was game from the get-go, and Cassidy Sachs at Dutton, for seeing the vision and seeing me. Carrie Frye, for her patience and boundless writerly wisdom. Thank you also to the designers and copy editors and marketing teams at PRH, who have all touched this book with their talents.

I owe more thanks than I can say to tireless researchers, fact checkers, and interpreters Jacklyn Kim, Julie Kim, Esther Chung, and Nick Tabor in the United States, So Jeong Lee and Se Eun Gong in South Korea.

Also to the rigorous philosophers and professors who provided an academic framework for this book, notably Joanna Elfving-Hwang, Heijin Lee, So Yeon Leem, and Heather Widdows, whose 2018 book *Perfect Me* catalyzed my thinking at the most crucial point in the thinking and reporting process.

정말 고마워요 to my right-hand women during those years in Seoul: Haeryun Kang, Jihye Lee, Se Eun Gong, and my long-suffering Korean teacher, Unkyung Lee.

Thanks go to my NPR colleagues: Nishant Dahiya, Hannah Bloch, Didi Schanche, the "ops guys" Bob Duncan and Greg Dixon, Avie Schneider, Uri Berliner, Janet Woojeong Lee, Meghan Keane, Beth Donovan, the "Elise Tries" team of Claire O'Neill, Mito Habe-Evans, CJ Riculan, Bronson Arcuri. KPCC's clutchest, Fiona Ng. Bosses Edith Chapin, Margaret Lowe, Chris Turpin, and Madhulika Sikka, who sent me wandering half the planet on behalf of the network and actually ran the stories, too.

I also owe gratitude to my Reasonable Volume partners Rachel Swaby and Meghan Phillips, who held down the fort as I burrowed into the book for long stretches, and the TED team: Anna, Martha, Michelle, Colin, Oliver, Simone, David, and Corey.

Thank you to my running buddies Nate Rott and Amanda Nottke, because so many ideas are worked out on the trail, and thank you to so many big brains for their encouragement and support: My besties Liz Taylor, Skyler Stewart, Jenn Ellice, Drew Falkman, Harper Reed, Erin Baudo. Seoul-based homies JB Anton Hur, Sira Maliphol, John Delury, Raphael Rashid, Lucy Han, Misorang Seo. And fellow writers (who have big brains, too): Matt Thompson. Jenna Gibson. Kat Chow. Reeve Hamilton. Sudeep Reddy. Sarah Svoboda. Leila Fadel. Nicole Chung. David Greene. Kal Raustiala. Kaylee Domzalski. Ben Dooley. Robin Suh. Tamar Herman. Tim Leong. Laura Bicker. Victoria Kim. Ailsa Chang. Xiaowei Wang. Jake Adelstein. Robert Draper. Nicole Zhu. Danielle Keenan-Miller. Eve Rodsky. Angie Kim. Doree Shafrir. Frank Ahrens. Anna Fifield. Jean Lee. Megan Garber. Heidi Moore. Amy Fiscus. Amy Westervelt. Cedarbough Saeji. Pamela Boykoff. Alex Field. Angie Kim. Alisha Ramos. Alicia Menendez. Tim Leong. Andrew Van Tassell. Peter Blake. Alec Berg. Craig Mazin. Jacob Goldstein. Manoush Zomorodi. Eyder Peralta. Daniel Pink. Michelle Ye Hee Lee. Hannah Bae.

I'm indebted and shaped by the teachers who encouraged me the most: Sandi Shelton, Sam Ruhmkorff, Carl Coates, Caryl Gatzlaff, Kathy Blackmore, J.D. Wireman, Stacey Woelfel.

Huge thanks to my therapists, Bobbie in L.A. and Jonathan in New York, for your relentless curiosity and engagement.

Rob, you encouraged me every time I found myself on the "throne of agony" while writing this and have never stopped making me laugh, usually at your expense.

Matty, thank you for making that cross-Pacific journey and sticking it out in Seoul, despite the relentless surprises and hardships, and, for putting up with my long affliction with misusing commas. (See what I did there?)

Two of our three children were born in Korea, and that they are all girls certainly informed the way I experienced the place and shaped my thinking. Eva, Isa, and Luna, you accompanied me, whether in the womb or in my arms, for so much of this reporting and supported me as I struggled to write this book. You girls are my whole heart.

My undying gratitude goes to our nanny and domestic helper Yani, for being the nucleus of the family for seven crucial years. This book was written during the most turbulent period of my life, in the moments I could sneak between Zoom-schooling the children amid a lockdown and shuttling them to their extracurriculars, hosting five podcasts simultaneously and running a fledgling company. Yani's endless labor, patience, and grace made my work possible.

Most importantly, thank you to the family I came from— my mom and dad, and my brother Roger. I love you all so much.

Additional thanks to my beloved and now deceased friend Caesar the cat, the Daiso highlighters in Korea that sell for 1,000KRW, lightly salted almonds, Cheez-Its Extra Toasty, the Trader Joe's Bamba peanut snacks, BTS, BLACKPINK, black sugar boba milk tea popsicles, and so much "just a tad sweet" Honest Tea.

INTERVIEWS CITED

Bae Gyo-hyun, Eddie Aram Baek, Hallie Bailey, Charlotte Cho, Michelle Cho, Cho Nam Joo, Cho Young Lim, Choi Yu-jin, Helen Choo, Stephen Epstein, Alice Hahn, Jessica Hanson, Heo Jooyeon, Hong Chae-won, Charles Hsu, Michael Hurt, Jeon Hye-min, Kim Jimin, Kim Ju-duck, Kim Juhee, Katherine Yungmee Kim, Kim Mihee, Kim Minki, Yuna Kim, Elizabeth Kwon, Hye-Kyoung Kwon, Lee Chiyeon, Lee Hwajung, Kyungho Lee, Min Joo Lee, Lee Min-kyung, Sharon Heijin Lee, Lee Shieun, So Yeon Leem, Park Boram, Park Hanhee, Park Jeong-eun, Minyeong Park, Devon Price, Emily Raymundo, Seo Gwang-seok, Haein Shim, Shin Heawon, Tao Sok, James Turnbull, Rio Viera-Newton, Jenny Wang Medina, Heather Willoughby, David Yi, Yun Ahin, Yun-Kim Ji-Yeong.

BIBLIOGRAPHY

Baldwin, James. *The Fire Next Time*. New York: Vintage, 1993. First published in 1963 by The Dial Press.

Bartky, Sandra Lee. "Foucault, Femininity and the Modernization of Patriarchal Power." In *Feminist Theory Reader: Local and Global Perspectives*, 3rd ed., edited by Carole R. McCann and Seung-kyung Kim, 447–61. New York: Routledge, 2003.

———. *Femininity and Domination: Studies in the Phenomenology of Oppression*. New York: Routledge, 1990.

Berger, John. *Ways of Seeing*. New York: Penguin Books, 1977. First published in 1972.

Breen, Michael. *The New Koreans: The Story of a Nation*. New York: Thomas Dunne Books, 2017.

Brown, Brené. *Atlas of the Heart: Mapping Meaningful Connection and the Language of Human Experience*. New York: Random House, 2021.

———. *The Gifts of Imperfection: Let Go of Who You Think You're Supposed to Be and Embrace Who You Are*. Center City, MN: Hazelden Publishing, 2010.

Brumberg, Joan Jacobs. *The Body Project: An Intimate History of American Girls*. New York: Random House, 1997.

Cho, Charlotte. *The Little Book of Skincare: Korean Beauty Secrets for Healthy, Glowing Skin*. New York: William Morrow, 2015.

Cho, Michelle. "Popular Abjection & Gendered Embodiment in South Korean Film Comedy." In *Abjection Incorporated: Mediating the Politics of Violence and Pleasure*, edited by Maggie Hennefeld and Nicholas Sammond, 43–63. Durham, NC: Duke University Press, 2020.

Chung, Hae Shin. *K-Beauty: The Facts: Korea's Top Dermatologist Reveals the Insider Truth About Korean Skincare*. Zisik Books, 2020. Kindle.

Chung, Hyunback. "South Korean Women's Movement: Between Modernisation and Globalisation." In *The Routledge Handbook of East Asian Gender Studies*, edited by Jieyu Liu and Junko Yamashita, 59–74. New York: Routledge, 2019.

Cumings, Bruce. *Korea's Place in the Sun: A Modern History*. New York: W. W. Norton, 2005. Kindle.

DiMoia, John. *Reconstructing Bodies: Biomedicine, Health, and Nation-Building in South Korea Since 1945*. Stanford: Stanford University Press, 2013.

Elfving-Hwang, Joanna. "The Body, Cosmetic Surgery and the Discourse of 'Westernization of Korean Bodies." In *The Routledge Companion to Beauty Politics*, edited by Maxine Leeds Craig, 273–82. New York: Routledge, 2021.

Engeln, Renee. *Beauty Sick: How the Cultural Obsession with Appearance Hurts Girls and Women*. New York: HarperCollins, 2017.

Etcoff, Nancy. *Survival of the Prettiest: The Science of Beauty*. New York: Anchor, 2000. First published in 1999 by Doubleday.

Foucault, Michel. *Discipline and Punish: The Birth of the Prison*. New York: Vintage Books, 1979. First published in 1975 by Gallimard.

———. *The History of Sexuality*. Vol. 1, *An Introduction*. New York: Vintage, 1990. First published in 1978 by Random House.

Gill, Rosalind. *Gender and the Media*. Malden, MA: Polity Press, 2007.

Girard, René. *I See Satan Fall Like Lightning.* Maryknoll, NY: Orbis Books, 2001.

Gottschild, Brenda Dixon. *The Black Dancing Body: A Geography from Coon to Cool.* New York: Palgrave Macmillan, 2003.

hooks, bell. *All About Love: New Visions.* New York: HarperCollins, 2001. First published in 2000 by William Morrow.

Haiken, Elizabeth. *Venus Envy: A History of Cosmetic Surgery.* Baltimore: Johns Hopkins University Press, 1997.

Hong, Euny. *The Birth of Korean Cool.* New York: Picador, 2014.

Kawai, Hayao. *Dreams, Myths and Fairy Tales in Japan.* Einsiedeln, Switzerland: Daimon, 1995.

Kim, Nadia Y. *Imperial Citizens: Koreans and Race from Seoul to LA.* Stanford: Stanford University Press, 2008.

Lee, Hojung. *Tigerrabbit: An Exploration of the Asian American Experience.* Washington, DC: New Degree Press, 2022. Kindle.

Lee, Sharon Heijin. "Introduction." In *Fashion and Beauty in the Time of Asia*, edited by Sharon Heijin Lee, Christina H. Moon, and Thuy Linh Nguyen Tu, 1–20. New York: New York University Press, 2019. Kindle.

Lembke, Anna. *Dopamine Nation: Finding Balance in the Age of Indulgence.* New York: Dutton, 2021.

Nelson, Sarah M. "Bound Hair and Confucianism in Korea." In *Hair: Its Power and Meaning in Asian Cultures*, edited by Alf Hiltebeitel and Barbara D. Miller, 105–21. Albany: State University of New York Press, 1998.

Odell, Jenny. *How to Do Nothing: Resisting the Attention Economy.* Brooklyn: Melville House, 2019.

Oh, Youjeong. *Pop City: Korean Popular Culture and the Selling of Place.* Ithaca, NY: Cornell University Press, 2018.

Peiss, Kathy. *Hope in a Jar: The Making of America's Beauty Culture.* Philadelphia: University of Pennsylvania Press, 2019.

Penny, Laurie. *Sexual Revolution: Modern Fascism and the Feminist Fightback*. London: Bloomsbury, 2022.

Petersen, Helen Anne. *Too Fat, Too Slutty, Too Loud: The Rise and Reign of the Unruly Woman*. New York: Penguin, 2017.

Rofel, Lisa. *Desiring China: Experiments in Neoliberalism, Sexuality, and Public Culture*. Durham, NC: Duke University Press, 2007.

Schuman, Michael. *Confucius: And the World He Created*. New York: Basic Books, 2015.

Stanton, Elizabeth Cady. "Our Girls." In *The Selected Papers of Elizabeth Cady Stanton and Susan B. Anthony*. Vol. 3, *National Protection for National Citizens, 1873 to 1880*, edited by Ann D. Gordon, 484–513. New Brunswick: Rutgers University Press, 2003.

Storr, Will. *Selfie: How the West Became Self-Obsessed*. New York: Picador, 2017.

Tudor, Daniel. *Korea: The Impossible Country*. North Clarendon, VT: Tuttle Publishing, 2012. Kindle.

Whitefield-Madrano, Autumn. *Face Value: The Hidden Ways Beauty Shapes Women's Lives*. New York: Simon & Schuster, 2017.

Widdows, Heather. *Perfect Me: Beauty as an Ethical Ideal*. Princeton: Princeton University Press, 2018. Kindle.

Wilson, Thomas A. *Genealogy of the Way: The Construction and Uses of the Confucian Tradition in Late Imperial China*. Stanford: Stanford University Press, 1995.

Yeats, William Butler. *The Collected Poems of W. B. Yeats*. New York: Macmillan, 1976. First published 1933.

Yi, David. *Pretty Boys: Legendary Icons Who Redefined Beauty (and How to Glow Up, Too)*. New York: Houghton Mifflin Harcourt, 2021.

NOTES

Note: Works cited initially in their shortened form in the Notes are given in full in the Bibliography.

Epigraph

1. **I wonder if you are the pretty girl in question:** Zadie Smith, "An A–Z by Zadie Smith," Penguin, August 6, 2007, archived at https://web .archive.org/web/20070806051014/http://www.penguin.co.uk/nf /Author/AuthorPage/0,,0_1000049267,00.html?sym=MIS.
2. **To be born woman is to know:** Yeats, "Adam's Curse," *Collected Poems*, 78.

Introduction

1. **South Korean cosmetics exports quadrupled:** "AmorePacific, South Korea's biggest beauty firm, is struggling," *The Economist*, October 19, 2019.
2. **a cultlike following:** Nitesh Chouhan, Himanshu Vig, and Roshan Deshmukh, "K-Beauty Products Market by Product Type: Global Opportunity Analysis and Industry Forecast, 2021–2027," Allied Market Research, February 2021.
3. **Global consumers have nearly doubled:** Vanessa Grigoriadis, "The Beauty of 78.5 Million Followers: How Social Media Stars Like Addison Rae Gave the Cosmetics Industry a Makeover," *New York Times Magazine*, March 23, 2021, https://www.nytimes.com/2021 /03/23/magazine/addison-rae-beauty-industry.html.
4. **"in the form of cosmetics products":** Lee, "Introduction."

5. **the "speaking nearby" approach:** Erika Balsom, "'There Is No Such Thing as Documentary': An Interview with Trinh T. Minh-ha," Frieze, November 1, 2018, https://www.frieze.com /article/there-no-such-thing-documentary-interview-trinh-t -minh-ha.
6. **Discourse is useful:** Foucault, *History of Sexuality*, 100–101.
7. **The gender wage gap:** OECD, "The Pursuit of Gender Equality: An Uphill Battle," October 4, 2017, https://read.oecd-ilibrary.org /social-issues-migration-health/the-pursuit-of-gender-equality _9789264281318-en.
8. **"Accounts of the nation's stunning pace":** Cho, "Popular Abjection," 58.
9. **"Escape the Corset" movement:** Benjamin Haas, "'Escape the corset': South Korean women rebel against strict beauty standards," *The Guardian*, October 28, 2018, https://www .theguardian.com/world/2018/oct/26/escape-the-corset-south -korean-women-rebel-against-strict-beauty-standards.
10. **"women are broadly objectified":** Benjamin Haas, "'Escape the corset.'"

Chapter 1. Beauty Is a Beast

1. **Agencies even send actors:** Elise Hu, "Need Fake Friends for Your Wedding? In S. Korea, You Can Hire Them," NPR, August 5, 2015, https://www.npr.org/sections/parallels/2015/08/05/419419307 /fake-wedding-guests-korea-role-players.
2. **Louis Vuitton was the most popular brand:** Song Jung-a, "Luxury brands battle to stay in fashion in South Korea," *Financial Times*, June 21, 2014, https://www.ft.com/content/bffdbad8-f5f6-11e3 -83d3-00144feabdc0.
3. **Koreans spend twice as much on skincare products:** Euromonitor International data.
4. **its beauty brands number in the 8,000's:** As of 2019, the country had 7,580 beauty manufacturers. "화장품 업체수 · 품목수 · 생산실적," August 2009—March 2022, Korean Statistical Information Service.
5. **invented the cushion makeup:** "Flowerboys and the appeal of 'soft masculinity' in South Korea," BBC News, September 5, 2018, https://www.bbc.com/news/world-asia-42499809.
6. **In 1979, AmorePacific:** Rebecca Dancer, "The History of Amorepacific, a 5-Time Best of Beauty Winner," *Allure*, https:// www.allure.com/sponsored/story/history-of-amorepacific.

7. **a quarter of all South Korea's tea:** AmorePacific, "From Jeju with Love," *New York Times* (paid post), https://www.nytimes.com /paidpost/amorepacific/from-jeju-with-love.html.

8. **Not content to rest:** "Heritage Ingredients: Green Tea," AmorePacific, https://www.apgroup.com/sg/en/our-values /heritage-ingredients/green-tea/green-tea.html; "Beauty Research & Innovation: Development of New Green Tea Varieties for Preservation of Biodiversity and Skin," AmorePacific, https://www .apgroup.com/int/en/about-us/research-innovation/rnd/beauty -research-innovation/beauty-research-innovation-01.html.

9. **The use of green tea:** Oh, *Pop City*, 170.

10. **the growing Chinese beauty brand Pechoin:** Emily Lueng, "Top Trends Shaping APAC's Skin Care Industry," September 20, 2019, Euromonitor International, https://www.euromonitor.com /article/top-trends-shaping-apacs-skin-care-industry.

11. **"It does have that kind of scientific":** Raymundo interview.

12. **the eleventh biggest beauty brand globally:** Jamie Matusow and Joanna Cosgrove, "Top 20 Global Beauty Companies," Beauty Packaging, November 4, 2020, https://www.beautypackaging.com /issues/2020-10-01/view_features/top-20-global-beauty -companies-765486/.

13. **bringing in $5.3 billion:** "Amorepacific Group 2019 Annual Results," Amorepacific news release, February 5, 2020, https://www .apgroup.com/int/en/news/2020-02-05.html.

14. **Skincare know-how among contemporary Koreans:** Cho, *Little Book of Skincare*, 15.

15. **Hwahae, on its site, boasts that it's had more than 10 million:** "Hwahae Consumer Beauty Awards 2021," The Monodist, December 3, 2021, https://themonodist.com/2021/12/03/hwahae -consumer-beauty-awards-2021/.

16. **A nationalistic need for speed:** Tudor, *Korea*, 172.

17. **South Korea was poorer than sub-Saharan Africa:** Dani Rodrik, "Getting Interventions Right: How South Korea and Taiwan Grew Rich," *Economic Policy* 10, no. 20 (April 1995): 53–107.

18. **shifted rapidly from being a UN-aid-receiving nation:** Manuela V. Ferro and Akihiko Nishio, "From aid recipient to donor: Korea's inspirational development path," World Bank, December 2, 2021, https://blogs.worldbank.org/eastasiapacific/aid-recipient-donor -korea-inspirational-development-path.

19. **Going from a premodern society:** Farwa Sial, "Historicising the Aid Debate: South Korea as a Successful Aid Recipient," Developing Economics, November 12, 2018, https://

developingeconomics.org/2018/11/12/historicising-the-aid-debate
-south-korea-as-a-successful-aid-recipient/.

20. **companies spend an average of 64 percent:** "2020 년 화장품산업
분석 보고서," Korea Health Industry Development Institute, May
31, 2021, https://www.khidi.or.kr/board/view?pageNum=1&
rowCnt=10&no1=776&linkId=48857409&menuId=MENU00085&
maxIndex=00488574099998&minIndex=00002145679998&
schType=0&schText=&schStartDate=&schEndDate=&
boardStyle=&categoryId=&continent=&country=.

21. **OEM companies take over the entire process:** Myungji Lee, "베일에
싸인 'K뷰티 기술력의 본산' . . . 한국콜마 종합기술원을 가다,"
Hankyung Business, May 12, 2020, https://news.naver.com/main
/read.naver?mode=LSD&mid=sec&sid1=004&oid=050&aid=
0000053622; Baek and Park interviews.

22. **other major OEMs:** Kikuko Yano, "[화장품 컬럼] 한국이 '세계
화장품 연구소'라고 불리는 이유," Cosin, September 16, 2019,
https://cosinkorea.com/mobile/article.html?no=32593. Cosvision
Corporation is based in Daejeon (http://www.cosvision.com/).
Cosrx (http://www.cosrx.co.kr/), Coson (http://www.coson.co.kr/),
Hankook Cosmetics Manufacturing Co. (https://www.hkcosm
.com/00_main/main.jsp), and HNG (http://www.hngc.co.kr/) are
all located in Seoul.

23. **Most of the centers have decades of experience:** Myungji Lee,
"베일에 싸인 'K뷰티 기술력의 본산' . . . 한국콜마 종합기술원을
가다," *Hankyung Business*, May 12, 2020, https://news.naver.com
/main/read.naver?mode=LSD&mid=sec&sid1=004&oid=050&aid
=0000053622.

24. **Tonymoly, the brand:** Kayleen Schaefer, "What You Don't Know
About the Rise of Korean Beauty," The Cut, September 9, 2015,
https://www.thecut.com/2015/09/korean-beauty-and-the
-government.html.

25. **For as little as $20,000:** Choo interview.

26. **Many of today's K-beauty start-ups:** Baek interview.

27. **Twenty-nine-year-old Park Jeong-eun:** Jeong-eun interview.

28. **In 2019, she went on Wadiz:** "Wadiz Blazes a Crowdfunding Trail in
Korea," Red Herring, February 9, 2021, https://www.redherring
.com/startups/wadiz-blazes-a-crowdfunding-trail-in-korea/.

29. **After Unilever, a massive British consumer goods corporation:**
Hyunjoo Jin and Martinne Geller, "Unilever steps up beauty push
with $2.7 billion Carver Korea deal," Reuters, September 25, 2017,
https://www.reuters.com/article/us-carverkorea-unilever-nv

/unilever-steps-up-beauty-push-with-2-7-billion-carver-korea
-deal-idUSKCN1C00D3; Estée Lauder Companies news release,
November 18, 2019.

30. **Korea has competed with the U.S.:** Shim Woo-hyun, "S. Korea's
exports of cosmetics products ranked third in the world last year,"
Korea Herald, June 21, 2021, https://www.koreaherald.com/view
.php?ud=20210621000834.

31. **trusted to produce and package products:** Oxygen Development, for
instance, an OEM headquartered in Seoul, lists Glossier among its
clients (http://www.eyesome.co.kr/default/en/business/partner.php).

32. **To reach customers across the region:** Baek interview.

33. **The Korea Health Industry Development Institute (KHIDI):** Kim
interview.

34. **Beauty editors say when it comes to invention:** Mary-Ann Russon,
"K-beauty: The rise of Korean make-up in the West," BBC News,
October 21, 2018, https://www.bbc.com/news/business-45820671.

35. **Charlotte Cho, a key player:** Cho interview.

36. **1,259 Olive Young stores:** CJ올리브영, 2022년 전략 키워드는 '혁신
성장' . . . "건강한 아름다움을 지향하는 옴니채널 라이프스타일
플랫폼 도약의 원년 될 것," 채널CJ, December 12, 2021, https://
cjnews.cj.net/cj%EC%98%AC%EB%A6%AC%EB%B8%8C%EC%98
%81-2022%EB%85%84-%EC%A0%84%EB%9E%B5-%ED%82%A4
%EC%9B%8C%EB%93%9C%EB%8A%94-%ED%98%81%EC%8B
%A0-%EC%84%B1%EC%9E%A5-%EA%B1%B4%EA%B0%95/.

37. **twice the number of Sephoras:** Shelley E. Kohan, "Sephora to Open
over 260 New Stores in 2021 Including Kohl's Concept," *Forbes*,
February 25, 2021, https://www.forbes.com/sites/shelleykohan
/2021/02/25/sephora-to-open-over-260-new-stores-in-2021
-including-kohls-concept/?sh=26dfe51b827b.

38. **While stand-alone cosmetics stores were closing shop:** "CJ올리브영,
2022년 전략 키워드는 '혁신 성장' . . . "건강한 아름다움을 지향하는
옴니채널 라이프스타일 플랫폼 도약의 원년 될 것," 채널CJ,
December 12, 2021, https://cjnews.cj.net/cj%EC%98%AC%EB
%A6%AC%EB%B8%8C%EC%98%81-2022%EB%85%84-%EC%A0
%84%EB%9E%B5-%ED%82%A4%EC%9B%8C%EB%93%9C%EB
%8A%94-%ED%98%81%EC%8B%A0-%EC%84%B1%EC%9E%A5
-%EA%B1%B4%EA%B0%95.

39. **the last big story I covered:** Elise Hu, "South Korea, Japan Reach
Major Deal on Wartime Sex Slaves," NPR, December 28, 2015,
https://www.npr.org/2015/12/28/461304285/south-korea-japan-
reach-major-deal-on-wartime-sex-slaves.

NOTES

Chapter 2. The Birth of K-Beauty

1. **"It's when your skin is so healthy":** Lauren Valenti, "A 7-Step Guide to Glowing 'Glass Skin' from a K-Beauty Insider," *Vogue*, December 25, 2019, https://www.vogue.com/article/korean-k-beauty-glass-skin-best-products-for-clear-glowing-skin.

2. **Soko Glam's Charlotte Cho recalls:** Cho, *Little Book*, 66.

3. **In Asia, a barrage of commercials:** Widdows, *Perfect Me*, 81.

4. **While Korean marketers have promoted:** 전상희, "[wiz] 시대별 대표 피부 미인과 트랜드," 스포츠조선, September 7, 2008, *Sports Chosun*, https://sports.chosun.com/news/news_o2.htm?name=/news/entertainment/200809/20080908/89h22009.htm.

5. **Master Kong, or Confucius:** Schuman, *Confucius*.

6. **the way Han Dynasty rulers:** Wilson, *Genealogy of the Way*.

7. **Confucius's ideas emphasizing harmony:** Storr, *Selfie*, 72.

8. **the Korean people came to understand:** Odile Monod—The Monodist, "100 Years of Korean Beauty: The Birth of Modern Korean Beauty Standards (History of Korean Beauty 4)" (video), https://www.youtube.com/watch?v=QocCzJNcLxQ.

9. **A son's body:** Nelson, "Bound Hair and Confucianism," 108, 117–18.

10. **Beauty culture in the West had risen:** Peiss, *Hope in a Jar*, 45.

11. **America's mass-market beauty industry:** Peiss, *Hope in a Jar*, 97–103.

12. **"Culture tends to spread from top to bottom":** Chung Ah-young, "Tracing history of cosmetics," *Korea Times*, January 31, 2013, http://koreatimes.co.kr/www/news/culture/2013/01/135_129776.html.

13. **Pakgabun didn't come as a powder:** 손성진, "[근대광고 엿보기] 납중독 소동 일으킨 '박가분' 광고/손성진 논설고문," 서울신문, November 9, 2020, https://news.naver.com/main/read.naver?mode=LSD&mid=sec&sid1=110&oid=081&aid=0003137939; 김효정, "대한민국 1호 브랜드 화장품 '박가분' ... 역사의 뒤안길로 사라진 배경은?", 에듀동아, September 10, 2018, http://edu.donga.com/?p=article&ps=view&at_no=20180910134255250965; 이유진, 김정원, 이상문, "[옛것을 만지다](9) 백옥 피부에 대한 열망, 박가분," 레이디경향, September 4, 2014, https://news.naver.com/main/read.naver?mode=LSD&mid=sec&sid1=103&oid=145&aid=0000012533.

14. **In its heyday, Pakgabun benefited:** Hye Kyoung Kwon, "Performing Masquerade: The Politics of K-Beauty in South Korean Literary and Popular Culture from Colonialism to Neoliberalism," unpublished PhD dissertation, University of California at Los Angeles, 2019, 26–57.

15. **The roots of the company spiritually trace back:** Susan Kitchens, "Pacific Quest," *Forbes Asia*, May 8, 2006.

16. **She blasted the name of her store:** "한국의 기업가정신을 찾아서 (9) 서성환 아모레퍼시픽 창업자," *Forbes Korea*, November 23, 2016, https://jmagazine.joins.com/forbes/view/314332.

17. **In 1954, the family opened:** "The Beginning," *Straits Times*, September 24, 2015; "AmorePacific: A legacy that started in grandma's kitchen," *Korea Herald*, July 11, 2016.

18. **Suh's company produced Melody:** "AmorePacific aims to make most sales overseas," *Korea Herald*, September 25, 2013.

19. **All the fresh Western influence:** Oh, *Pop City*, 164.

20. **AmorePacific statistics show:** 김승민, "[뉴스 클립] Special Knowledge <448> 한국 화장품 100년," *JoongAng*, May 23, 2012, https://www.joongang.co.kr/article/8260419#home; 윤지원, "아모레퍼시픽 '향장' 60년 기념전 . . . 화장 변천사와 현대사 엿본다," *CNB Journal*, September 27, 2018, https://m.weekly.cnbnews.com /m/m_article.html?no=125440.

21. **Park remains infamous:** Breen, *The New Koreans*, 201–10.

22. **Korean American writer Katharine Yungmee Kim's family:** Kim interview.

23. **A government-decreed *gansobok*:** Kwon, "Performing Masquerade," 76.

24. **In 1973, the Park dictatorship:** Kang Hyun-kyung, "'Ridiculous' 1970s: Book lampoons Park Chung-hee era," *Korea Times*, February 22, 2019, https://www.koreatimes.co.kr/www/culture/2021/03/142 _264236.html.

25. **much like the subversive Modern Girl:** Kwon, "Performing Masquerade," 4, 111–38.

26. **The Factory Girls took some cues:** Kwon, "Performing Masquerade," 65.

27. **"challenge and resist the top-down hegemony":** Kwon, "Performing Masquerade," 23.

28. **the Factory Girl look spread one by one:** Kwon interview.

29. **South Korea then endured martial law:** Cumings, *Korea's Place in the Sun*, 384.

30. **the "three S" policy:** Rund Abdelfatah et al., "How Korean Culture Went Global," NPR, September 8, 2022, https://www.npr.org /2022/09/06/1121364712/how-korean-culture-went-global; Anna Fifield, "Chun Doo-hwan, Brutal South Korean Dictator, Dies at 90," *Washington Post*, November 23, 2021, www.washingtonpost .com/obituaries/2021/11/23/chun-doo-hwan-korea-dead/.

31. **the guidance of two celebrated economic advisers:** Breen, *The New Koreans*, 210.

32. **When AmorePacific's founder:** Kitchens, "Pacific Quest."

33. **the militant Park Chung-hee regime:** Yi, *Pretty Boys*, 227.

Chapter 3. Hallyu Has No Borders

1. **Hit by a currency crisis:** Andrew Pollack, "Crisis in South Korea: The Bailout," *New York Times*, December 4, 1997.
2. **Korea was barred from making:** Hong, *Birth of Korean Cool*, 96.
3. **Korean British artist Sammy Lee:** Sammy Lee, screenwriter and director, *SONG* (digital short film in possession of Lee).
4. **A Korean government council report in 1994:** Mi Sook Park, "South Korea Cultural History Between 1960s and 2012," *International Journal of Korean Humanities and Social Sciences* 1 (2016): 71–118.
5. **The newly elected Korean president:** Kim Dae-jung, "Inaugural Address by Kim Dae-Jung," February 25, 1998, Ministry of Unification, South Korea, https://unikorea.go.kr/eng_unikorea /news/speeches/?boardId=bbs_0000000000000036&mode=view &cntId=31906&category=&pageIdx=11.
6. **Samsung, the country's largest:** Breen, *The New Koreans*, 348.
7. **President Kim lifted a historic ban:** Jon Herskovitz, "S. Korea to lift ban on Japanese culture," *Variety*, October 9, 1998, https://variety .com/1998/music/news/s-korea-to-lift-ban-on-japanese-culture -1117481242/.
8. **a law to bolster the arts:** Hong, *Birth of Korean Cool*, 101; Republic of Korea, Framework Act on the Promotion of Cultural Industries (Act No. 5927 of February 8, 1999, as amended up to Act No. 11845 of May 28, 2013).
9. **the sounds of Big Bang and GFriend:** Elise Hu, "Responding to Nuclear Test, S. Korea Cranks Up the K-Pop," NPR, January 13, 2016, https://www.npr.org/sections/parallels/2016/01/13/46285 3390/responding-to-nuclear-test-s-korea-cranks-up-the-k-pop.
10. **the K-pop group BTS:** Sammy Westfall, "K-pop Icons BTS Appointed South Korean Presidential Special Envoys Ahead of U.N. General Assembly," *Washington Post*, September 14, 2021, washingtonpost.com/world/2021/09/14/bts-un-assembly/.
11. **The government goes to great lengths:** Martin Roll, "Korean Wave (Hallyu)—The Rise of Korea's Cultural Economy & Pop Culture," https://martinroll.com/resources/articles/asia/korean-wave -hallyu-the-rise-of-koreas-cultural-economy-pop-culture/.
12. **"They like to equate their identity":** Chung, *K-Beauty*, chapter 1.
13. **"The wave was about to die":** Lee interview.
14. **"The age of information technology":** John Seabrook, "Factory Girls," *The New Yorker*, October 1, 2012, https://www.newyorker .com/magazine/2012/10/08/factory-girls-2.

15. **the idea of a "global Korea":** Jojin V. John, "Globalization, National Identity and Foreign Policy: Understanding 'Global Korea,'" *Copenhagen Journal of Asian Studies* 33, no. 2 (2015): 38–57.

16. **Korea's lower-priced budget beauty brands:** Oh, *Pop City*, 168.

17. **luxury brands carve out:** Kathy Peiss, "Making Faces: The Cosmetics Industry and the Cultural Construction of Gender, 1890–1930," *Genders* 7 (1990): 143–69.

18. **When it emerged, it offered:** Oh, *Pop City*, 168.

19. **Missha brand shops passed 200:** 배정원, "'로드숍의 몰락' . . . 그 많던 미샤·더페이스샵 매장은 어디갔나," *JoongAng*, August 18, 2020, https://www.joongang.co.kr/article/23851234#home.

20. **1,190 road shops:** Oh, *Pop City*, 169.

21. **dipping to 598 by 2019:** "'로드숍의 몰락' . . . 그 많던 미샤· 더페이스샵 매장은 어디갔나," *JoongAng*.

22. **A German dermatologist developed:** Chung, *K-Beauty*, chapter 1.

23. **Korean cosmetic companies have taken this medical product:** Daniela Morosini and Jen Adkins, "The Fascinating Rise of BB Cream and Why We're Forever Hooked," Byrdie, August 25, 2021, https://www.byrdie.com/what-is-bb-cream.

24. **The cushion is a delivery system:** Ally Betker, "BB Cushion Compacts: The Korean Beauty Phenomenon Arrives Stateside," *Vogue*, May 16, 2014, https://www.vogue.com/article/korean -skincare-bb-cushion-compacts.

25. **By 2013, seven out of every ten:** Chung, *K-Beauty,* chapter 1.

26. **the company planned to open a hundred American branches:** Faye Brookman, "AmorePacific Earmarks Aritaum Stores for U.S. Expansion," *WWD*, February 1, 2017, https://wwd.com/beauty -industry-news/beauty-features/amorepacific-earmarks-aritaum -for-growth-10771428/.

27. **The South Korean survival drama** *Squid Game*: Paul Tassi, "'Squid Game' Is Now the #1 Show in 90 Different Countries," *Forbes*, October 3, 2021.

28. **In 2021, the** *Oxford English Dictionary*: Danica Salazar, "Daebak! The OED gets a K-update," *Oxford English Dictionary*, September 6, 2021, https://public.oed.com/blog/daebak-a-k-update/.

29. **BTS alone is estimated to contribute:** Stacey Vanek Smith, "How BTS Is Adding an Estimated $5 Billion to the South Korean Economy a Year," NPR, August 6, 2021, https://www.npr.org/2021 /08/06/1025551697/how-bts-is-adding-an-estimated-5-billion-to -the-south-korean-economy-a-year.

30. **spreading to the world an aspirational version of Korea:** Sharon Heijin Lee, "The (Geo)Politics of Beauty: Race, Transnationalism,

and Neoliberalism in South Korean Beauty Culture," unpublished PhD dissertation, University of Michigan, 2012, 10.

31. **She says Korean Dreams:** Lee interview.
32. **"Want a melodrama about a love triangle":** Madeleine Spence, "Chic Korea," *Air Mail*, October 16, 2021, airmail.news/issues /2021-10-16/chic-korea.
33. **"unquenchable consumerism":** Hye Kyoung Kwon, "Performing Masquerade: The Politics of K-Beauty in South Korean Literary and Popular Culture from Colonialism to Neoliberalism," unpublished PhD dissertation, University of California at Los Angeles, 2019, 144.
34. **In January 2016, *The Washington Post*:** Anna Fifield, "Young South Koreans call their country 'hell' and look for ways out," *Washington Post*, January 31, 2016, https://www.washingtonpost.com/world /asia_pacific/young-south-koreans-call-their-country-hell-and -look-for-ways-out/2016/01/30/34737c06-b967-11e5-85cd -5ad59bc19432_story.html.
35. **There's something empowering:** Kwon, "Performing Masquerade," 147.
36. **"Confucian understandings of gender":** Kwon, "Performing Masquerade," 177.
37. **Television dramas don't just transmit stories:** Oh, *Pop City*, 192.
38. **in Southeast Asia, where more than 50 percent:** US-ASEAN Business Council, "Growth Projections," July 22, 2019, https:// www.usasean.org/why-asean/growth.
39. **Cosmetics companies capitalize on the Hallyu connection:** Oh, *Pop City*, 178.
40. **star Song Hye-kyo's Laneige's TwoTone lipstick:** Park Jin-hai, "New Hallyu Dawns on 'Descendants of the Sun,'" *Korea Times*, April 3, 2016, https://www.koreatimes.co.kr/www/news/culture/2016/04 /386_201794.html.
41. **Just as the full, peach-looking:** Sophie Elmhirst, "Brazilian butt lift: behind the world's most dangerous cosmetic surgery," *The Guardian*, February 9, 2021, https://www.theguardian.com/news/2021/feb/09 /brazilian-butt-lift-worlds-most-dangerous-cosmetic-surgery.
42. **Chinese actress Zhang Yuqi:** "Chinese actress Zhang Yuqi gets plastic surgery to look exactly like Song Hye Kyo," Koreaboo, September 23, 2015, https://www.koreaboo.com/article/chinese-actress-zhang -yuqi-gets-plastic-surgery-to-look-exactly-like-song-hye-kyo.
43. **"[Hallyu] comes in as a niche":** Medina interview.
44. **By 2020, South Korea became the third largest cosmetics exporter:** "S. Korea becomes world's 3rd-largest cosmetics exporter in 2020,"

Yonhap News, June 21, 2021, https://en.yna.co.kr/view
/AEN20210621006900320.

45. **"If the argument about cultural globalization":** Cho interview.

46. **Charlotte Cho's 10 Steps:** Soko Glam, "10-Step Korean Skin Care
Routine Set (Normal Skin Type)," https://sokoglam.com
/collections/soko-glam/products/10-step-korean-skin-care
-routine-set-normal.

47. **Lee and Chang's Glow Recipe:** Cheryl Wischhover, "Korean Beauty
Has Hit the Mainstream. Now What?" BOF, June 10, 2019, https://
www.businessoffashion.com/articles/news-analysis/korean
-beauty-has-hit-the-mainstream-now-what/.

Chapter 4. Skinfirst

1. **AHC's parent company was acquired:** Unilever to buy AHC beauty
maker Carver Korea for $2.7 bn, Pulse, September 26, 2017, https://
pulsenews.co.kr/view.php?year=2017&no=645330.

2. **the extensive Mandarin training shopgirls received:** Elise Hu, "A
Chinese Tourism Boom Has South Koreans Cramming," NPR,
March 29, 2015, https://www.npr.org/sections/parallels/2015/03
/19/393752309/the-chinese-tourism-boom-has-south-koreans
-cramming.

3. **sold every three seconds:** Jessica Cruel, "This Hydrating Eye Cream
Keeps Foundation from Settling in My Smile Lines," *Allure*, June 1,
2020, https://www.allure.com/review/ahc-essential-real-eye
-cream-for-face.

4. **skin is the largest organ:** Marion Richardson, "Understanding the
Structure and Function of the Skin," *Nursing Times* 99, no. 31
(2003), 46–48.

5. **YouTube influencers, such as the pioneering Michelle Phan:** Vanessa
Grigoriadis, "The Beauty of 78.5 Million Followers: How Social
Media Stars Like Addison Rae Gave the Cosmetics Industry a
Makeover," *New York Times Magazine*, March 23, 2021, https://
www.nytimes.com/2021/03/23/magazine/addison-rae-beauty
-industry.html.

6. **"The people of the entire nation":** Chung, *K-Beauty*, chapter 3.

7. **On average, 90 percent of Korean women:** "The report on Korean
consumers' cosmetics usage patterns," Korean Ministry of Food
and Drug Safety, 2015, quoted in Chung, *K-Beauty*, chapter 3.

8. **skincare accounts for 20 percent:** Cho, *Little Book*, 132.

9. **poor translation for *brightening*:** Charlotte Cho, "What Are Korean
Skin Whitening Products and Do They Bleach Your Skin?!" Soko

Glam, February 5, 2021, https://sokoglam.com/blogs/news
/112943045-skin-whitening-explained-its-not-what-you
-think.

10. **Korean regulators define whitening:** "Enforcement Rule of the
Cosmetics Act," Ordinance of the Prime Minister No. 1182, July 29,
2015, Korean Legislation Research Institute.

11. **Korea's whitening substances and procedures:** 박소정 and 홍석경,
"K-뷰티의 미백 문화에 대한 인종과 젠더의 상호교차적 연구를
위한 시론: 화이트워싱/옐로우워싱 논쟁을 중심으로," 언론정보연구
56, no. 2 (2019), 43–78.

12. **the "alpha and omega of racial difference":** Gottschild, *Black
Dancing Body*, 190.

13. **Class-related preferences:** 박소정 and 홍석경.

14. **In premodern Japan:** Hiroshi Wagatsuma, "The Social Perception
of Skin Color in Japan," *Daedalus* 96, no. 2 (1967), 407–43.

15. **"That makeup products cannot be removed":** Chung, *K-Beauty*,
chapter 3.

16. **Korean women developed double cleansing:** Chung, *K-Beauty*,
chapter 3.

17. **Conan O'Brien yelled during his televised jjimjilbang visit:** Team
Coco, "Steven Yeun & Conan Visit a Korean Spa | CONAN on TBS"
(video), https://www.youtube.com/watch?v=k70xBg8en-4.

18. **mugwort, which is believed to help heal several ailments:** Kwang-Ok
Lee, Sue Kim, Soon-Bok Chang, and Ji-Soo Yoo, "Effects of
Artemisia A. Smoke (Ssukjahun) on Menstrual Distress,
Dysmenorrhea, and Prostaglandin F2α," *Korean Journal of Women's
Health Nursing* 15, no. 2 (2009), 150–59; Seon-Eun Baek, Sae-Byul
Jang, Kyung-Hee Choi, and Jeong-Eun Yoo, "Systematic Review of
Fumigation Therapy for Atrophic Vaginitis," *Journal of Korean
Obstetrics and Gynecology* 29, no. 1 (2016), 92–101.

19. **For a model:** Widdows, *Perfect Me*, 20.

20. **"Prepubescent girl with well-adjusted bodily esteem":** Whitefield-
Madrano, *Face Value*, 202.

21. **"It's not about finding your own path":** Elise Hu, "The All-Work,
No-Play Culture of South Korean Education," NPR, April 15, 2015,
https://www.npr.org/sections/parallels/2015/04/15/393939759
/the-all-work-no-play-culture-of-south-korean-education.

Chapter 5. Lookism

1. **their most "natural" state, when bodies are naked:** Petersen, *Too
Fat, Too Slutty, Too Loud*, 219.

2. **William Safire used the term:** "The Way We Live Now: On Language; Lookism," *New York Times*, August 27, 2000, https://www.nytimes.com/2000/08/27/magazine/the-way-we-live-now-8-27-00-on-language-lookism.html.

3. **Despite lookism being forbidden:** 이하나, "'남자인 게 스펙이네' . . . 채용 공고부터 노골적 '여성차별' 심각," 여성신문, July 6, 2016, https://www.womennews.co.kr/news/articleView.html?idxno=95525.

4. **nearly 40 percent of respondents experienced discrimination:** 조현정, "아르바이트도 '외모지상주의' . . . 10명 중 4명 '외모로 구직 차별 받아,'" *ChosunBiz*, October 24, 2017, https://biz.chosun.com/site/data/html_dir/2017/10/24/2017102401701.html.

5. **A survey of more than 900 businesses:** Matt Stiles, "In South Korea's hypercompetitive job market, it helps to be attractive," *Los Angeles Times*, June 13, 2017, https://www.latimes.com/world/asia/la-fg-south-korea-image-2017-story.html.

6. **The National Human Rights Commission:** 류주현, "C컵 이상 유인나 미모女 오세요' 정신나간 구인광고," YTN, December 10, 2015, https://www.ytn.co.kr/_ln/0103_201512101915463579.

7. **specified C as the ideal bra cup size:** 류주현, "C컵 이상 유인나 미모女 오세요' 정신나간 구인광고," YTN, December 10, 2015, https://www.ytn.co.kr/_ln/0103_201512101915463579.

8. **big firms prefer "pretty eyes":** Stiles, "In South Korea's hypercompetitive job market."

9. **"cosmetic surgery has become one of the seven credentials":** "Ministry blog suggests cosmetic surgery to win jobs," *Korea Times*, July 1, 2015, https://www.koreatimes.co.kr/www/nation/2021/12/113_182006.html.

10. **the unemployment rate among young Korean workers hovered around 10 percent:** Yon-se Kim, "[News Focus] High youth unemployment continues during Moon's term," *Korea Herald*, April 22, 2021, http://www.koreaherald.com/view.php?ud=20210422000380.

11. **Korea ranks last where gender pay equality is concerned:** OECD, "The Pursuit of Gender Equality: An Uphill Battle," October 4, 2017, https://read.oecd-ilibrary.org/social-issues-migration-health/the-pursuit-of-gender-equality_9789264281318-en.

12. **"unspoken rule against women wearing glasses":** 정혁준, "임현주 앵커가 안경 쓴 뒷 이야기를 밝혔다," HuffPost Korea, https://www.huffingtonpost.kr/entry/story_kr_5b14cbe6e4b010565aad2750.

13. **"If I could act freely":** Alexandra Stevenson, "South Korea Loves Plastic Surgery and Makeup. Some Women Want to Change That," *New York Times*, November 23, 2018, https://www.nytimes.com

/2018/11/23/business/south-korea-makeup-plastic-surgery-free
-the-corset.html.

14. **Dermatology and plastic surgery apps offer discounts:** The apps in question are BabiTalk and GangnamUnni.

15. **The surface of the body:** Lee, "Introduction."

16. **In 2007, the prototypical K-pop girl group:** Elise Hu, Janet W. Lee, and Jessica Placzek, "How Girls' Generation Shaped K-pop as We Know It," NPR, September 13, 2022, https://www.npr.org /transcripts/1122480955.

17. **Korean cultural observer T. K. Park notes:** T. K. Park and Youngdae Dim, "How Blackpink, Red Velvet, and More Are Redefining Womanhood in K-pop," MTV News, June 6, 2019, https://www .mtv.com/news/3126395/k-pop-girl-groups-womanhood-agency/.

18. **"Girls' Generation appeared":** Lee Min-kyung interview.

19. **"Family members would praise me":** Lee, *Tigerrabbit*, 54.

20. **The ancient Greeks even had a word:** Storr, *Selfie*, 54.

21. **"seemingly had less to do with the surface":** Jessica DeFino, "How White Supremacy and Capitalism Influence Beauty Standards," *Teen Vogue*, October 19, 2020, https://www.teenvogue .com/story/standard-issues-white-supremacy-capitalism -influence-beauty.

22. **the Egyptians using makeup and adornment:** "Ancient Egyptian cosmetics: 'Magical' makeup may have been medicine for eye disease," American Chemical Society news release, January 20, 2010, https://www.acs.org/content/acs/en/pressroom /newsreleases/2010/january/ancient-egyptian-cosmetics .html.

23. **the journals of American girls:** Brumberg, *Body Project*, xxi.

24. **"The idol thing":** Lee Min-kyung interview.

25. **Haein Shim, twenty-seven, recalls being in middle school:** Shim interview.

26. **unemployment climbed to as high as 20 percent:** Sharon Heijin Lee, "Beauty Between Empires: Global Feminism, Plastic Surgery, and the Trouble with Self-Esteem," *Frontiers: A Journal of Women Studies* 37, no. 1 (2016), 1–31.

27. **As feminist scholar Cho Joo-hyun writes:** "Neoliberal Governmentality at Work: Post-IMF Korean Society and the Construction of Neoliberal Women," *Korea Journal* 49, no. 3 (2009), 15–43.

28. **"The idea of competition":** Alex Taek-Gwang Lee, "The Flesh of Democracy: Plastic Surgery and Human Capital in South Korea," *Telos* 184 (2018), 209–22.

29. **"In traditional society":** 김상희, "[마이너리티의 소리] 성형수술 부추기는 사회," *JoongAng*, May 24, 2003, https://www.joongang .co.kr/article/174766#home.

30. **"It's the perfect sort of manifestation":** Medina interview.

31. **90 percent of Koreans were vaccinated:** Yonhap News, "9 out of 10 S. Korean adults received at least one vaccine shot," *Korea Herald*, October 5, 2021, http://www.koreaherald.com/view.php?ud= 20211005000932.

32. **cumulative deaths per capita forty times lower:** Our World in Data, "Cumulative confirmed COVID-19 deaths per million people," https://ourworldindata.org/explorers/coronavirus-data-explorer ?zoomToSelection=true&facet=none&pickerSort=asc &pickerMetric=location&Interval=Cumulative&Relative+to +Population=true&Color+by+test+positivity=false&country =USA~GBR~KOR&Metric=Confirmed+deaths.

33. **A former South Korean president:** Choe Sang-Hun, "Roh Moo- hyun, Ex-President of South Korea, Kills Himself," *New York Times*, May 22, 2009, https://www.nytimes.com/2009/05/23/world/asia /23korea.html.

34. **and a recent Seoul mayor:** Choe Sang-Hun, "'I'm Sorry to Everyone': In Death, South Korean Mayor Is Tainted by Scandal," *New York Times*, July 10, 2020, https://www.nytimes.com/2020/07 /10/world/asia/seoul-mayor-dead.html.

35. **a demographic researcher tried to explain:** Elise Hu, "The All- Work, No-Play Culture of South Korean Education," NPR, April 15, 2015, https://www.npr.org/sections/parallels/2015/04/15 /393939759/the-all-work-no-play-culture-of-south-korean -education.

36. **Suicide is the leading cause of death:** Yonhap News, "Suicide remains leading cause of death for S. Korean teens, youths," *Korea Herald*, April 27, 2020, http://www.koreaherald.com/view.php?ud= 20200427000687.

Chapter 6. Selfie-Surveillance

1. **a then-newfangled dating app:** Elise Hu, "Quantified Men: Tinder, Lulu and the Fallacy of Hot Dating Apps," NPR, January 7, 2014, https://www.kcur.org/2014-01-07/quantified-men-tinder-lulu -and-the-fallacy-of-hot-dating-apps.

2. **I experimented with wearing a camera:** Elise Hu, "Cool or Creepy? A Clip-On Camera Can Capture Every Moment," NPR, February 24, 2014, https://www.npr.org/sections/alltechconsidered/2014

/02/24/280733721/cool-or-creepy-a-clip-on-camera-can-capture
-every-moment.

3. **smart virtual personal assistants:** Elise Hu, "Computers That
   Know What You Need, Before You Ask," NPR, March 17, 2014,
   https://www.npr.org/sections/alltechconsidered/2014/03/17
   /290125070/computers-that-know-what-you-need-before-you-ask.

4. **a couple of tourists in Australia:** Jeff Freak and Shannon Holloway,
   "How not to get to Straddie," *Redland Times*, March 14, 2012,
   https://www.redlandcitybulletin.com.au/story/104929/how-not
   -to-get-to-straddie/.

5. **"The only solution":** Rebecca Jennings, "What would a healthy
   social media platform even look like?" Vox, September 21, 2021,
   https://www.vox.com/the-goods/22684293/facebook-antitrust
   -lawsuit-wall-street-journal-report.

6. **I created a new beat:** Anaïs Laurent, "Q&A: NPR's First 'Future
   Correspondent,' Elise Hu of Future You," NPR, May 6, 2019,
   https://www.npr.org/sections/npr-extra/2019/05/06/720696758
   /q-a-nprs-first-future-correspondent-elise-hu-of-future-you.

7. **I wore electrodes and slept in a lab:** Elise Hu, "The Military
   Discovered a Way to Boost Soldiers' Memories, and We Tried It,"
   NPR, October 22, 2019, https://www.npr.org/2019/10/22
   /769403296/video-the-military-discovered-a-way-to-boost
   -soldiers-memories-and-we-tried-it.

8. **In a Houston lab, I wore electrodes:** Elise Hu, "How Mind-
   Controlled Robot Suits Could Enhance Our Limbs," NPR, May 7,
   2019, https://www.npr.org/2019/05/07/716412296/how-mind
   -controlled-robot-suits-could-enhance-our-limbs.

9. **I wore different electrodes and zapped myself:** Elise Hu, "Higher,
   Better, Stronger, Faster—Brain Science Is Trying to Get There,"
   NPR, June 6, 2019, https://www.npr.org/2019/06/06/717486969
   /higher-better-stronger-faster-brain-science-is-trying-to-get-there.

10. **popularized based on the categories:** 실업보다 더 무서운 것, "New
    economics of tying the knot," *Korea Times*, February 5, 2012, http://
    www.koreatimes.co.kr/www/news/biz/2012/02/335_104171.html.

11. **highest educational attainment:** "Education Policy Outlook:
    Korea," OECD, November 2016, https://www.oecd.org/education
    /Education-Policy-Outlook-Korea.pdf.

12. **most working hours per week:** Kim Yon-se, "[News Focus] Korea
    has 2nd-longest working hours in OECD," *Korea Herald*, March 9,
    2021, http://www.koreaherald.com/view.php?ud=20210309000162.

13. **most wired place on earth:** Sohn Ji-young, "Korea No. 1 worldwide
    in smartphone ownership, internet penetration," *Korea Herald*,

June 24, 2018, http://www.koreaherald.com/view.php?ud=20180624000197.

14. **Koreans spend an average of four and a half hours:** Yonhap News, "S. Koreans spend more time on mobile devices in 2020: report," *Korea Herald*, January 13, 2021, http://www.koreaherald.com/view.php?ud=20210113000797.

15. **smartphone penetration is 98 percent:** "2012–2021 스마트폰 사용률 & 브랜드, 스마트워치, 무선이어폰에 대한 조사," Gallup Korea, June 8, 2021, https://www.gallup.co.kr/gallupdb/reportContent.asp?seqNo=1217.

16. **Internet addiction rehab centers:** Anna Fifield, "In South Korea, a rehab camp for Internet-addicted teenagers," *Washington Post*, January 24, 2016, https://www.washingtonpost.com/world/asia_pacific/in-south-korea-a-rehab-camp-for-internet-addicted-teenagers/2016/01/24/9c143ab4-b965-11e5-85cd-5ad59bc19432_story.html.

17. **In 1994, the birth year:** Robert D. Atkinson, Daniel K. Correa, and Julie A. Hedlund, "Explaining International Broadband Leadership," Information Technology and Innovation Foundation, May 2008, https://papers.ssrn.com/sol3/papers.cfm?abstract_id=1128203, 19, F3.

18. **Korea's broadband penetration rate was the highest:** "Broadband Policy Development in the Republic of Korea: A Report for the Global Information and Communications Technologies Department of the World Bank," Ovum Consulting, October 2009.

19. **Seoul recently installed the largest LED screens:** "Seoul steps into the future with the world's largest LED," Samsung for Business, July 23, 2020, https://insights.samsung.com/2020/07/23/seoul-steps-into-the-future-with-the-worlds-largest-led.

20. **Our "primitive" brains:** Judy Scheel, "Culture Dictates the Standard of Beauty," *Psychology Today*, April 24, 2014, https://www.psychologytoday.com/us/blog/when-food-is-family/201404/culture-dictates-the-standard-beauty.

21. **Seoul is the fourth most-surveilled city:** Paul Bischoff, "Surveillance camera statistics: Which cities have the most CCTV cameras?" comparitech, July 11, 2022, https://www.comparitech.com/studies/surveillance-studies/the-worlds-most-surveilled-cities/.

22. **we tend to exaggerate even minute fluctuations:** Etcoff, *Survival of the Prettiest*, 6.

23. **Conversely, when we look at others:** Etcoff, *Survival of the Prettiest*, 7.

24. **"A crowd-pleasing image":** Etcoff, *Survival of the Prettiest*, 4.

25. **Since the prisoner believes:** Foucault, *Discipline and Punish*, 201.

26. **a "cruel, ingenious cage":** Foucault, *Discipline and Punish*, 205.

27. **"She has to survey everything":** Berger, *Ways of Seeing*, 46.

28. **Actress Gianna Jun's look:** "YSL gets free ride on drama sensation," *Korea Herald*, March 24, 2014, http://www.koreaherald.com/view .php?ud=20140324001347.

29. **Beauty has a theatrical aspect:** Mimi Thi Nguyen, "The Right to Be Beautiful," *The Account* 6 (spring 2016), https://theaccount magazine.com/issue/spring-2016/.

30. **The human tendency to compare ourselves:** Brown, *Atlas of the Heart*, 18.

31. **comparisons are adaptive behaviors:** Leon Festinger, "A Theory of Social Comparison Processes," *Human Relations* 7, no. 2 (1954): 117–40.

32. **social media comparisons generate feelings of inferiority:** Brian A. Feinstein, Rachel Hershenberg, Vickie Bhatia, et al., "Negative Social Comparison on Facebook and Depressive Symptoms: Rumination as a Mechanism," *Psychology of Popular Media Culture* 2, no. 3 (2013): 161–70; Dian A. de Vries and Rinaldo Kühne, "Facebook and Self-Perception: Individual Susceptibility to Negative Social Comparison on Facebook," *Personality and Individual Differences* 86 (2015): 217–21; Chen Li, Dong Liu, and Yan Dong, "Self-Esteem and Problematic Smartphone Use Among Adolescents: A Moderated Mediation Model of Depression and Interpersonal Trust," *Frontiers in Psychology* 10 (2019): 2872.

33. **and correlate with depression:** Peter McCarthy and Nexhmedin Morina, "Exploring the Association of Social Comparison with Depression and Anxiety: A Systematic Review and Meta-Analysis," *Clinical Psychology and Psychotherapy* 27, no. 5 (2020): 640–71.

34. **This is especially true:** Philippe Verduyn, Nino Gugushvili, Karlijn Massar, et al., "Social Comparison on Social Networking Sites," *Current Opinion in Psychology* 36 (2020): 32–37.

35. **a virtual lipstick try-on:** "Perfect Corp. and Zamface Team Up to Bring Award-winning AI & AR-Powered Lipstick Virtual Try-on Experience to South Korean Beauty Lovers," Perfect Corp. news release, November 2, 2021, https://www.perfectcorp.com/business /news/detail/1851.

36. **one of Korea's buzziest influencers:** Debashree Dutta, "Rozy, Korea's First Virtual Influencer, Isn't Human but Humane," *Rolling Stone*, July 21, 2022, https://rollingstoneindia.com/rozy-koreas-first -virtual-influencer-isnt-human-but-humane/. rozy.

37. **"project of femininity":** Bartky, *Femininity and Domination*, 72.

38. **feminist writers such as Bartky:** Bartky, "Toward a Phenomenology of Feminist Consciousness," *Social Theory and Practice* 3, no. 4 (1975): 425–39.
39. **"a positive sense of self":** Widdows, *Perfect Me*, 217
40. **This gaze is an algorithmically determined set:** Widdows, *Perfect Me*, 126.
41. **It represents a power shift:** Gill, *Gender and the Media*, 258.
42. **leaked internal documents:** Georgia Wells, Jeff Horwitz, and Deepa Seetharaman, "Facebook Knows Instagram Is Toxic for Teen Girls, Company Documents Show," *Wall Street Journal*, September 14, 2021, https://www.wsj.com/articles/facebook-knows-instagram-is -toxic-for-teen-girls-company-documents-show-11631620739.
43. **It's in the design of our tech platforms:** Jonathan Haidt, "The Dangerous Experiment on Teen Girls," *The Atlantic*, November 21, 2021, https://www.theatlantic.com/ideas/archive/2021/11 /facebooks-dangerous-experiment-teen-girls/620767/.
44. **a "deeper form of exploitation":** Gill, *Gender and the Media*, 258.
45. **companies "are in an arms race":** "Tristan Harris warns of 'civil war for profit' business model," CNN, February 13, 2022, https://www .cnn.com/videos/business/2022/02/13/tristan-harris-warns-of -civil-war-for-profit-business-model.cnn.
46. **"inhuman, unforgiving, critical":** Widdows, *Perfect Me*, 194.
47. **"For all its talk of 'connecting people'":** DeFino, "Meta Face Is Coming," The Unpublishable, November 1, 2021, https:// jessicadefino.substack.com/p/mark-zuckerberg-face?s=r.
48. **The more we collectively work:** Widdows, *Perfect Me*, 70–95.
49. **"a collection of disparate body parts":** Quoted in Widdows, *Perfect Me*, 194.
50. **"is both a choice and not a choice at all":** Megan Garber, "The Great Novel of the Internet Was Published in 1925," *The Atlantic*, October 8, 2021, https://www.theatlantic.com/books/archive/2021/10/mrs -dalloway-virginia-woolf-internet-novel/620341/.
51. **South Korea's "improvement quarter":** "South Korean Photographer Shows Costs of Plastic Surgery," WBUR, October 20, 2015, https://www.wbur.org/hereandnow/2015/10/20/south-korea -plastic-surgery-photos.

Chapter 7. The Improvement Quarter

1. **"are making us lose touch with reality":** Susruthi Rajanala, Mayra B. C. Maymone, and Neelam A. Vashi, "Selfies—Living in the Era

of Filtered Photographs," *JAMA Facial Plastic Surgery* 20, no. 6 (2018): 443–44.

2. **the Korea Tourism Organization sprang into action:** "South Korea aims to become Asia's new medical travel hub," *Economic Times*, April 29, 2008, https://economictimes.indiatimes.com/news /international/south-korea-aims-to-become-asias-new-medical -travel-hub/articleshow/2993434.cms.

3. **In 2009, about 60,000 foreigners visited:** "2018 외국인환자 유치실적 통계분석보고서," Korea Health Industry Development Institute, November 2019, https://www.khiss.go.kr/board/view?pageNum= 4&rowCnt=10&no1=502&linkId=175529&menuId=MENU00308& schType=0&schText=&boardStyle=&categoryId=&continent=& schStartChar=&schEndChar=&country=.

4. **By 2019, the number of medical tourists:** "서울 방문 외국인환자 통계," Seoul Tourism Organization, https://medical.visitseoul.net /business.

5. **Tourists made up an estimated third:** Patricia Marx, "About Face," *The New Yorker*, March 16, 2015, https://www.newyorker.com /magazine/2015/03/23/about-face.

6. **Premier packages include perks:** Alexandra Stevenson, "Plastic Surgery Tourism Brings Chinese to South Korea," *New York Times*, December 23, 2014, https://www.nytimes.com/2014/12/24 /business/international/plastic-surgery-tourism-brings-chinese -to-south-korea.html.

7. **This "connection between popular culture":** Sharon Heijin Lee, "Beauty Between Empires: Global Feminism, Plastic Surgery, and the Trouble with Self-Esteem," *Frontiers: A Journal of Women Studies* 37, no. 1 (2016), 18–19.

8. **40 percent of all foreign cosmetic surgery patients:** "2019 외국인환자 유치실적 통계분석 보고서," Korea Health Industry Development Institute, April 7, 2021, https://www.khidi.or.kr /board/view?linkId=48855161&menuId=MENU02186.

9. **inside the subway stations:** Elise Hu, "In Seoul, a Plastic Surgery Capital, Residents Frown on Ads for Cosmetic Procedure," NPR, February 5, 2018, https://www.npr.org/sections/parallels/2018/02 /05/581765974/in-seoul-a-plastic-surgery-capital-residents-frown -on-ads-for-cosmetic-procedure.

10. **South Korea leads the world:** Sanghoo Yoon and Young A. Kim, "Cosmetic Surgery and Self-Esteem in South Korea: A Systematic Review and Meta-Analysis," *Aesthetic Plastic Surgery* 44, no. 1 (2020): 229–38.

11. **South Korea has twice as many plastic surgeons:** International Society of Aesthetic Plastic Surgery, "ISAPS International Survey on Aesthetic Cosmetic Procedures, Performed in 2018," https://www.isaps.org/wp-content/uploads/2019/12/ISAPS-Global-Survey-Results-2018-new.pdf, 32.

12. **"surgical specialization, diagnostic tests":** DiMoia, *Reconstructing Bodies*, 202.

13. **One in four Korean mothers:** 김희선, "어머니 25% "딸에게 성형수술 권한 적 있다," 한경닷컴, October 1, 2007, https://www.hankyung.com/news/article/2007100183898.

14. **One in three women:** "외모와 성형수술에 대한 인식," Gallup Korea.

15. **A 2019 study showed that the average age:** Hyunlye Kim, Young A. Kim, and Duckhee Chae, "Factors Affecting Acceptance of Cosmetic Surgery Among Undergraduate Students," *Journal of the Korean Contents Association* 17, no. 1 (2017), 455–64.

16. **59 percent of men:** "외모와 성형수술에 대한 인식—1994/2004/2015/2020년" Gallup Korea, February 2, 2020, https://www.gallup.co.kr/gallupdb/reportContent.asp?seqNo=1097.

17. **66 percent of women:** "외모와 성형수술에 대한 인식—1994/2004/2015/2020년" Gallup Korea, February 2, 2020, https://www.gallup.co.kr/gallupdb/reportContent.asp?seqNo=1097.

18. **Each contestant on the show got a nickname:** Marx, "About Face."

19. **According to a 2021 survey:** 김한솔, "바비톡, 인기 있는 성형 조사 결과 '필러·보톡스' 큰 비중 차지," 인사이트, March 30, 2021, https://www.insight.co.kr/news/331413.

20. **Half of all East Asian women:** Harry S. Hwang and Jeffrey H. Spiegel, "The Effect of 'Single' vs. 'Double' Eyelids on the Perceived Attractiveness of Chinese Women," *Aesthetic Surgery Journal* 34, no. 3 (2014), 374–82.

21. **most popular and common cosmetic surgery:** Summer Kim Lee, "'Don't Touch Your Face,'" Vice, April 17, 2020, https://www.vice.com/en/article/3a8gjb/korean-beauty-eui-jip-hwang-photography-new-visions.

22. **part of the three-pack:** 송지혜, "수능 수험생 겨냥 '찜찜한' 성형 상술," *JoongAng*, November 18, 2010, https://www.joongang.co.kr/article/4675049#home.

23. **The next most popular surgery:** Marx, "About Face."

24. **some researchers connected the eyelid and nose procedures:** Lauren E. Riggs, "The Globalization of Cosmetic Surgery: Examining BRIC and Beyond," unpublished master's thesis, University of San Francisco, 2012, 180–82.

25. **"Shifting beauty ideals"**: Joanna Elfving-Hwang and Jane Park, "Deracializing Asian Australia? Cosmetic Surgery and the Question of Race in Australian Television," *Continuum: Journal of Media & Cultural Studies* 30, no. 4 (2016), 397-407.

26. **As early as the first Korean dynasty**: Eric P. H. Li, Hyun Jeong Min, and Russell W. Belk, "Skin Lightening and Beauty in Four Asian Cultures," in *Advances in Consumer Research,* vol. 35, ed. Angela Y. Lee and Dilip Soman (Duluth, MN: Association for Consumer Research), 444-49.

27. **The "privileged classes did not toil"**: Lee Hyo-won, "The Complex Culture and History Behind 'K-beauty,'" *Nikkei Asia*, March 1, 2018, https://asia.nikkei.com/NAR/Articles/The-complex-culture-and-history-behind-K-beauty.

28. **In 1896, after performing a procedure**: Yukio Shirakabe and Mia Shirakabe, "Pioneer Doctors Who Made the History of Japanese Aesthetic Surgery," *Advances in Plastic & Reconstructive Surgery* 3, no. 3 (2019): 286–90.

29. **He described the single eyelid as a "defect"**: Shirakabe and Shirakabe, "Pioneer Doctors Who Made the History of Japanese Aesthetic Surgery."

30. **In February 1895, an unnamed special correspondent**: Kat Chow, "Is Beauty in the Eye(Lid) of the Beholder?" NPR, November 17, 2014, https://www.npr.org/sections/codeswitch/2014/11/17/363841262/is-beauty-in-the-eye-lid-of-the-beholder.

31. **The American and European militarization**: Kat Chow, "Is Beauty in the Eye(Lid) of the Beholder?"

32. **It was also on the rise in the United States and Europe**: Haiken, *Venus Envy*, 131–32.

33. **"More critical than the surgery itself"**: DiMoia, *Reconstructing Bodies*, 180.

34. **The double eyelid surgery was popularized**: Laura Kurek, "Eyes Wide Cut: The American Origins of Korea's Plastic Surgery Craze," *Wilson Quarterly*, fall 2015, https://www.wilsonquarterly.com/quarterly/transitions/eyes-wide-cut-the-american-origins-of-koreas-plastic-surgery-craze.

35. **"a plastic surgeon's paradise"**: DiMoia, *Reconstructing Bodies*, 178.

36. **he considered natural monolids a defect**: Kurek, "Eyes Wide Cut."

37. **"occidental eye"**: D. Ralph Millard, "The Oriental Eyelid and Its Surgical Revision," *American Journal of Ophthalmology* 57, no. 4 (1964), 646–49.

38. **As Nadia Y. Kim writes**: Kim, *Imperial Citizens*, 53; DiMoia, *Reconstructing Bodies*.

39. **Korean Society of Plastic and Reconstructive Surgeons:** Yog Bae Kim, "The History and Future of Plastic and Reconstructive Surgery," *Archives of Plastic Surgery* 42, no. 5 (2015): 515–16.

40. **influenced in part by cultural exchange:** Steve Glain, "Cosmetic Surgery Goes Hand in Glove with the New Korea," *Wall Street Journal*, November 23, 1993.

41. **"while the early surgical practices":** Elfving-Hwang, "The Body," 280.

42. **Koreans' decisions to "go Anglo":** Glain, "Cosmetic Surgery."

43. **Or in Korea, the movie star Hwang Shin-hye:** 정서희, "황신혜, 컴퓨터 미인은 다르네 . . . 시공간 멈춰버린 듯한 동안 비주얼," SPOTV NEWS, December 17, 2021, http://www.spotvnews.co.kr /news/articleView.html?idxno=459970.

44. **Since the 2000s:** "외모와 성형수술에 대한 인식—1994/2004/2015/ 2020년," Gallup Korea, February 2, 2020, https://www.gallup.co.kr /gallupdb/reportContent.asp?seqNo=1097.

45. **Researcher Joanna Elfving-Hwang points out:** "The Body," 280.

46. **Starting in the late 1990s:** So Yeon Leem, "Gangnam-Style Plastic Surgery: The Science of Westernized Beauty in South Korea," *Medical Anthropology* 36, no. 7 (2017): 657–71.

47. **The market research firm TrendMonitor:** 채성숙, "[트렌드모니터] 올해도 저마다의 '새해 계획'을 세우고, '운세'를 보는 사람들," 매드타임스, January 21, 2021, http://www.madtimes.org.

48. **In the early aughts, doctors:** Leem, "Gangnam-Style Plastic Surgery," 658.

49. **The surgery involves shaving:** Marx, "About Face."

50. **In 2014, a clinic exhibited:** Marx, "About Face."

51. **and lays out three conditions:** Widdows, *Perfect Me*, 5.

52. **these fixes are sold and internalized:** Cressida J. Heyes, "Cosmetic Surgery and the Televisual Makeover: A Foucauldian Feminist Reading," *Feminist Media Studies* 7, no. 1 (2007): 17–32.

53. **Studies indicate cosmetic surgery:** David J. Castle, Roberta J. Honigman, and Katharine A. Phillips, "Does Cosmetic Surgery Improve Psychosocial Wellbeing?" *Medical Journal of Australia* 176, no. 12 (June 2002): 601–604.

54. **the effect on overall "psychological well-being":** Tilmann von Soest, Ingela Lundin Kvalem, Helge E. Roald, and Knut C. Skolleborg, "The Effects of Cosmetic Surgery on Body Image, Self-Esteem, and Psychological Problems," *Journal of Plastic, Reconstructive & Aesthetic Surgery* 62, no. 10 (2009): 1238–44.

55. **Psychological outcomes are mixed:** Melissa Dittmann, "Plastic Surgery: Beauty or Beast?" *Monitor on Psychology* 36, no. 8 (2005), https://r4dn.com/what-is-the-monitor-on-psychology/.

56. **the pleasure wears off:** Lembke, *Dopamine Nation*, 53–54.
57. **perfectionism can be both self-destructive *and* addictive:** Brown, *Gifts of Imperfection*, 76.
58. **"If the metric":** Lee interview.
59. **Self-esteem in modern capitalist societies:** Thomas Lemke, "Foucault, Governmentality, and Critique," *Rethinking Marxism* 14, no. 3 (2002): 49–64.

Chapter 8. The New Modern

1. **"*neoliberal multiculturalism*":** Jodi Melamed, "The Spirit of Neoliberalism: From Racial Liberalism to Neoliberal Multiculturalism," *Social Text* 24, no. 4 ((89) winter 2006): 1–24.
2. **a sterile, recognizably similar aesthetic:** Kyle Chayka, "Welcome to Airspace: How Silicon Valley helps spread the same sterile aesthetic across the world," The Verge, August 3, 2016, https://www.theverge.com/2016/8/3/12325104/airbnb-aesthetic-global-minimalism-startup-gentrification.
3. **Eve Peyser, in a *New York Times* op-ed:** "The Instagram Face-Lift," April 18, 2019, https://www.nytimes.com/2019/04/18/opinion/instagram-celebrity-plastic-surgery.html.
4. **The "natural" Korean face:** Joseph Kim, "The Changing Face of South Korea," *Wall Street Journal*, September 24, 2014, https://www.wsj.com/articles/BL-KRTB-6638.
5. **free or heavily discounted surgeries:** Choe Sang-Hun, "South Korean Plastic Surgeons Help Northern Defectors Erase Their Scars," *New York Times*, October 24, 2015, https://www.nytimes.com/2015/10/25/world/asia/south-korean-plastic-surgeons-help-northern-defectors-erase-their-scars.html.
6. **an eerie resemblance to one another:** Neetzan Zimmerman, "Plastic Surgery Blamed for Making All Miss Korea Contestants Look Alike," Gawker, April 25, 2013, https://www.gawker.com/plastic-surgery-blamed-for-making-all-miss-korea-contes-480907455.
7. **This phenomenon made the rounds:** Sharon Heijin Lee, "Beauty Between Empires: Global Feminism, Plastic Surgery, and the Trouble with Self-Esteem," *Frontiers: A Journal of Women Studies* 37, no. 1 (2016), 1.
8. **The American blog Jezebel:** Dodai Stewart, "Plastic Surgery Means Many Beauty Queens, But Only One Kind of Face," Jezebel, April

25, 2013, https://jezebel.com/plastic-surgery-means-many-beauty
-queens-but-only-one-480929886.

9. **"a mindless 'manga' aesthetic":** Elfving-Hwang, "The
   Body," 278.

10. **It is "practical to dream":** Autumn Whitefield-Madrano, "Only
    Women Are Named Hope," New Inquiry, June 22, 2016, https://
    thenewinquiry.com/only-women-are-named-hope/.

11. **The goal is always to look "younger":** Widdows, *Perfect Me*,
    13, 25.

12. **"These days, there are so many accidents":** Marx, "About Face."

13. **The number of complaints about botched procedures:** —> 심은혜,
    "'마스크 덕'에 늘어난 성형수술, 부작용 책임은 '누가,'" 우먼타임스,
    June 18, 2021, https://www.womentimes.co.kr/news/articleView
    .html?idxno=52925.

14. **up from 71 complaints in 2010:** 민정혜, "성형수술 부작용
    피해구제건수 3배↑ 소비자원, 최근 5년 자료 분석," 데일리메디,
    June 18, 2013, https://www.dailymedi.com/detail.php?number=
    769547.

15. **Figures from the international open access journal:** Rod J. Rohrich,
    Ira L. Savetsky, and Yash J. Avashia, "Assessing Cosmetic Surgery
    Safety: The Evolving Data," *Plastic and Reconstructive Surgery—
    Global Open* 8, no. 5 (May 2020): e2643.

16. **Of the hundreds of millions of Botox treatments given:** Timothy R.
    Coté, Aparna K. Mohan, Jacquelyn A. Polder, et al., "Botulinum
    Toxin Type A Injections: Adverse Events Reported to the US Food
    and Drug Administration in Therapeutic and Cosmetic Cases,"
    Journal of the American Academy of Dermatology 53, no. 3 (2005):
    407–15.

17. **As cultural critic Haley Nahman observes:** Nahman, "#45:
    Rage against self-checkout," Maybe Baby, March 14, 2021,
    https://haleynahman.substack.com/p/45-rage-against-self
    -checkout?s=r.

18. **The technological gaze "invites you":** Widdows, *Perfect Me*, 126.

19. **"While fixing individuals":** Widdows, *Perfect Me*, 150.

20. **Under the theory of French philosopher René Girard:** Girard, *I See
    Satan Fall Like Lightning*, 7–18.

21. **"We assume that desire is objective":** Girard, *I See Satan Fall Like
    Lightning*, 9.

22. **The platforms, writes Geoff Shullenberger:** "The Scapegoating
    Machine," New Inquiry, November 30, 2016, https://
    thenewinquiry.com/the-scapegoating-machine/.

Chapter 9. Free Size Isn't Free

1. **Korea has nearly the lowest obesity rate:** OECD, "Non-Medical Determinants of Health: Body Weight," https://stats.oecd.org /Index.aspx?DataSetCode=HEALTH_STAT.

2. **the starting point for plus-size:** Maxine Builder, "One Size Fits All in South Korea, As Long as That Size Is Small," Racked, November 3, 2015, https://www.racked.com/2015/11/3/9645610/south-korea -plus-size-women.

3. **It's "easy to lose sight":** James Turnbull, "Revealing the Korean Body Politic, Part 3: Historical precedents for Korea's modern beauty myth," Grand Narrative, January 4, 2013, https://thegrandnarrative.com/2013/01/04/y-line-y라인-glamor -글래머/.

4. **Just as the face has a "magic ratio":** Stephen Epstein and Rachael M. Joo, "Multiple Exposures: Korean Bodies and the Transnational Imagination," *Asia-Pacific Journal* 10, issue 33, no. 1 (2012), https:// apjjf.org/2012/10/33/Stephen-Epstein/3807/article .html#http://article.joinsmsn.com/news/article/article.asp?total _id=4498402&ctg=1200.

5. **In Korea, legs are the third most popular place:** 장윤서, "한국인 보톡스 선호 부위 1위 '사각턱,'" *ChosunBiz*, November 21, 2019, https://biz.chosun.com/site/data/html_dir/2019/11/21 /2019112102497.html.

6. **"women's legs became a showpiece item":** Epstein and Joo, "Multiple Exposures."

7. **legs function as a marketing tool:** Epstein and Joo, "Multiple Exposures."

8. **In 2012, the Thai government:** Epstein and Joo, "Multiple Exposures."

9. **celebrity endorsements make up more than half of all ads:** Vivienne Leung, Kimmy Cheng, and Tommy Tse, "Insiders' Views: The Current Practice of Using Celebrities in Marketing Communications in Greater China," *Intercultural Communication Studies* 27, no. 1 (2018): 96–113.

10. **"Where K-pop stars excel":** John Seabrook, "Factory Girls," *The New Yorker*, October 1, 2012, https://www.newyorker.com/magazine /2012/10/08/factory-girls-2.

11. **"I think a lot of young, female entertainers":** Claire Lee, "Feminist novel becomes center of controversy in South Korea," *Korea Herald*, March 27, 2018, http://www.koreaherald.com/view.php?ud= 20180327000799.

12. **A psychological process called perceptual narrowing:** Lisa Scott, Olivier Pascalis, and Charles Nelson, "A Domain-General Theory of the Development of Perceptual Discrimination," *Current Directions in Psychological Science* 16, no. 4 (2007): 197–201.

13. **Korea's abundant dating and marriage matchmaking companies:** "행복을 매칭하는 듀오, 결혼 기업 '부동의 1위,'" 한경경제, January 8, 2020, https://www.hankyung.com/economy/article /2020010806381.

14. **One of the oldest and most established:** Joo-hyun Cho, "Neoliberal Governmentality at Work: Post-IMF Korean Society and the Construction of Neoliberal Women," *Korea Journal* 49, no. 3 (2009), 34.

15. **To find their "ideal" weight in kilograms:** 정승엽, 조현수, 주다빈, "'살찌느니 죽겠어요' . . . 10대 건강 위협하는 '프로아나 신드롬' [이슈 컷]," Yonhap News, March 24, 2021, https://www.yna.co.kr/view /AKR20210323128200797.

16. **"arms and legs that look like they could break":** 굿네이버스_official, "[미디어 아동권리옹호 토론회] '미디어에도 어린이보호구역이 필요합니다,'" https://www.youtube.com/watch?v=Gmn6ECexzZM.

17. **By the time of her debut:** Won Ho-jung, "Park Bo-ram on way to being 'Celepretty,'" *Korea Herald*, April 24, 2015, http://www .koreaherald.com/view.php?ud=20150424000924.

18. **In the video for "Beautiful":** Stone Music Entertainment, "박보람 (Park Boram)—예뻐졌다 (Feat. Zico of Block B) (BEAUTIFUL) MV," August 7, 2014, https://www.youtube.com/watch?v=uFogEwzH4a0.

19. **"I Became Pretty" climbed up the Korean charts:** 송오정, "'싶으니까' 박보람, 직접 답한 신곡 인터뷰 공개 . . . 음원 발매와 동시 차트인," 톱스타뉴스, April 29, 2022, https://www.topstarnews.net/news /articleView.html?idxno=652492.

20. **Park became a spokesmodel for a diet drink:** "Park Bo Ram Promotes Healthy Life Style with 'Super Body' MV," Soompi, May 15, 2015, https://www.soompi.com/article/731929wpp/park-bo -ram-promotes-healthy-life-style-with-super-body-mv.

21. **Korea's consumption of diet drugs:** "Koreans Overdose on Diet Pills," *Chosun Ilbo*, March 27, 2010, http://english.chosun.com/site /data/html_dir/2010/03/27/2010032700362.html.

22. **A 2017 Korean Health Ministry survey:** "청소년건강행태온라인조사 제 13차(2017) 주요결과," 질병관리본부 질병예방센터 건강영양조사과, November 2, 2017, https://www.moe.go.kr /boardCnts/view.do?boardID=294&boardSeq=72430&lev=0 &searchType=null&statusYN=C&page=37&s=moe&m=050201 &opType=N; 김수진, "그것이 알고싶다, '나비약과 뼈말라족' 편 봉송,"

스타뉴스, October 23, 2021, https://m.star.mt.co.kr/view.html?no
=2021102221333751380&ref=; 김소연, "'몸에서 콩알탄 터지는
느낌'... 식욕억제제 '나비약' 부작용 고백한 배우," 스타투데이,
October 24, 2021, https://www.mk.co.kr/star/hot-issues/view
/2021/10/1006009/; 이슬비,식약처 "식욕억제제는 의존성 있는
마약류," 헬스조선, January 27, 2021, https://m.health.chosun.com
/svc/news_view.html?contid=2021012701122.

23. **Korean lawmaker Nam In-soon, who brought up the abuse:** 우정현,
"[2021 국감]남인순 의원 "마약류 식욕억제제 오남용 심각"...
마약관리 인력 확충하고 '마약류통합관리시스템 사후관리'
강화해야," 메디컬헤럴드, October 20, 2021, http://www
.mediherald.com/news/articleView.html?idxno=66053.

24. **Phentermine production in Korea:** Hyun-Sic Jo, Sheng-Min Wang,
and Jung Jin Kim, "Recurrent Psychosis After Phentermine
Administration in a Young Female: A Case Report," *Clinical
Psychopharmacology and Neuroscience* 17, no. 1 (2019): 130–33,
https://www.cpn.or.kr/journal/view.html?doi=10.9758/cpn
.2019.17.1.130.

25. **Fen-phen was pulled from American pharmacy shelves:** Marlene
Cimons, "2 Diet Drugs Tied to Heart Problems Taken Off Market,"
Los Angeles Times, September 16, 1997, https://www.latimes.com
/archives/la-xpm-1997-sep-16-mn-32755-story.html; Gina Kolata,
"How Fen-Phen, a Diet 'Miracle,' Rose and Fell," *New York Times*,
September 23, 1997, https://www.nytimes.com/1997/09/23
/science/how-fen-phen-a-diet-miracle-rose-and-fell.html.

26. **In total, four prescription appetite-suppressing substances:** Kwak
Sung-sun, "3.3 million Koreans took psychotropic appetite
suppressants last year," *Korea Biomedical Review*, February 19, 2021,
http://www.koreabiomed.com/news/articleView.html?idxno=10484.

27. **can induce psychotic disorder and dependence:** Ji-Ae Yun, Wu-Ri
Park, Je-Chun Yu, and Kyeong-Sook Choi, "A Case of
Phendimetrazine-Induced Psychotic Disorder and Dependence,"
Journal of Korean Neuropsychiatric Association 52, no. 5 (September
2013): 402–5.

28. **when the Korean Ministry of Food and Drug Safety monitored the
web:** "의료용 마약류 식욕억제제 온라인에서 판매.구매 모두
안돼요!," 식품의약품안전처, November 25, 2021, https://www
.mfds.go.kr/brd/m_99/view.do?seq=45949&srchFr=&srchTo
=&srchWord=&srchTp=&itm_seq_1=0&itm_seq_2=0&multi_itm
_seq=0&company_cd=&company_nm=&page=7.

29. **Lawmaker Jung Choun-sook proposed legislation:** "마약류 관리에
관한 법률 일부개정법률안," 의안정보시스템, July 1, 2021, http://

likms.assembly.go.kr/bill/billDetail.do?billId=PRC
_B2Z1O0T6A1J0X1T3Y4D7A3Y5P7K6U3.

30. **noting psychotropic appetite suppressants:** 정춘숙, "[보도자료]
정춘숙 의원, '항정약 처방전 거짓 기재 처벌' 마약류관리법 개정안
발의," Naver Blog, July 8, 2021, https://blog.naver.com/chounsook
_jung/222424591703.

31. **The rise of eating disorders across East Asia:** Kathleen Pike and
Patricia Dunne, "The Rise of Eating Disorders in Asia: A Review,"
Journal of Eating Disorders 3 (2015): 33, https://jeatdisord
.biomedcentral.com/articles/10.1186/s40337-015-0070-2#ref-CR125.

32. **overall expansion of capitalistic pursuits:** Jan Jindy Pettman,
"Gendering Globalization in Asia Through Miracle and Crisis,"
Gender, Technology and Development 7, no. 2 (2003): 171–87.

33. **"In sum":** Pike and Dunne, "Rise of Eating Disorders."

34. **The spread of eating disorders across the region closely tracked:**
Peter Marcotullio, "Asian Urban Sustainability in the Era of
Globalization," *Habitat International* 25, no. 4 (2001): 577–98.

35. **Japan led the pack:** Marcotullio, "Asian Urban Sustainability in the
Era of Globalization," 581.

36. **It seems factors unique to living in Korea:** Safia Jackson, Pamela
Keel, and Young Ho Lee, "Trans-Cultural Comparison of
Disordered Eating in Korean Women," *International Journal of
Eating Disorders* 39, no. 6 (2006): 498–502.

37. **And in a study comparing college women:** Jaehee Jung and Gordon
Forbes, "Body Dissatisfaction and Disordered Eating Among
College Women in China, South Korea, and the United States:
Contrasting Predictions from Sociocultural and Feminist
Theories," *Psychology of Women Quarterly* 31, no. 4 (2007): 381–93.

38. **As the rest of the world:** Sung Il Park, Young Gyu Cho, Jae Heon
Kang, et al., "Sociodemographic Characteristics of Underweight
Korean Adults: Korea National Health and Nutrition Examination
Survey, 2007–2010," *Korean Journal of Family Medicine* 34, no. 6
(2013): 385–92.

39. **percentage of underweight Korean women:** Sung Il Park, Young
Gyu Cho, Jae Heon Kang, et al., "Sociodemographic
Characteristics of Underweight Korean Adults."

40. **female societal empowerment led to backlash:** Tess Hellgren,
"Explaining Underweight BMI and Body Dissatisfaction Among
Young Korean Women," unpublished research paper, Harvard
University, 2011, archived at https://web.archive.org/web
/20210513151849/http://expose.fas.harvard.edu/issues/issue_2012
/hellgren.html.

41. **Seventy-four percent of South Korean women attend college:** Yang Hyunsoo, "Gender equality: Korea has come a long way, but there is more work to do," OECD, October 25, 2021, https://www.oecd.org/country/korea/thematic-focus/gender-equality-korea-has-come-a-long-way-but-there-is-more-work-to-do-8bb81613/.

42. **"It happened in the 1980s":** Penny, *Sexual Revolution*, 142.

43. **Further, Sandra Lee Bartky and others:** Summarized in Jung and Forbes, "Body Dissatisfaction."

44. **As Europe industrialized:** Jung and Forbes, "Body Dissatisfaction."

45. **Those in collectivist cultures:** Jaehee Jung and Seung-Hee Lee, "Cross-Cultural Comparisons of Appearance Self-Schema, Body Image, Self-Esteem, and Dieting Behavior Between Korean and U.S. Women," *Family and Consumer Sciences Research Journal* 34, no. 4 (2006): 350–65; **"internal states from external expectations":** Jackson et al., "Trans-Cultural Comparison of Disordered Eating," 500.

46. **A 2000 study by Woo Mee Park:** Woo Mee Park, "Comparative Study on the Satisfaction with and Perception About Their Bodies by Korean and American Female Students," *Journal of the Korean Society of Clothing and Textiles* 24, no. 5 (2000): 736–47.

47. **A systematic review by Jon Arcelus:** Jon Arcelus, Michelle Haslam, Claire Farrow, and Caroline Meyer, "The Role of Interpersonal Functioning in the Maintenance of Eating Psychopathology: A Systematic Review and Testable Model," *Clinical Psychology Review* 33, no. 1 (2013): 156–67.

48. **The "plus-sized" in South Korea:** 신지후 and 이우진, "살찐 게 죄?" 어딜가든 마주치는 한국인의 비만 혐오," *Hankook Ilbo*, May 19, 2018, https://www.hankookilbo.com/News/Read/201805181414793690%20.

49. **Online, they are the target:** 신지후 and 이우진, "회사 · 식당 어딜가든 삐딱한 시선 . . ."살찐게 죄인가요?,'" *Hankook Ilbo*, March 6, 2018, https://www.hankookilbo.com/News/Read/201803060444108118.

50. **national broadcaster Arirang TV:** Epstein and Joo, "Multiple Exposures."

51. **Outcry over that particular Sulli segment:** Epstein and Joo, "Multiple Exposures."

52. **Sulli was the most googled person:** "Sulli is officially the most Googled person in Korea this year," KPopLove, December 14, 2017, https://kpoplove.koreadaily.com/sulli-most-googled-korea/.

53. **By 2019, she faced a nonstop barrage:** Haeryun Kang, "How a K-pop star's death reveals the truth about our society," *Washington Post*,

October 15, 2019, https://www.washingtonpost.com/opinions /2019/10/15/how-k-pop-stars-death-reveals-truth-about-our -society/.

54. **Sulli's manager found her dead:** Jacey Fortin, "Sulli, South Korean K-Pop Star and Actress, Is Found Dead," *New York Times*, October 14, 2019, https://www.nytimes.com/2019/10/14/arts/music/sulli -dead.html.

55. **her death was described as a "social homicide":** Louise Oualid, "Cyber Bullying: K-Pop singer Sulli's social homicide," The Forum, January 1, 2020, http://www.theforumcuf.com/news/articleView .html?idxno=218.

56. **As such, as sociologist Cho Joo-hyun argues:** Cho Joo-hyun, "Neoliberal Governmentality at Work: Post-IMF Korean Society and the Construction of Neoliberal Women," *Korea Journal* 49, no. 3 (2009), 16.

57. **Some K-pop writers have noted:** T. K. Park and Youngdae Dim, "How Blackpink, Red Velvet, and More Are Redefining Womanhood in K-pop," MTV News, June 6, 2019.

58. **"Well-being is derived from valuing":** Widdows, *Perfect Me*, 60.

59. **British health psychologist Nichola Rumsey:** Nichola Rumsey, "The challenges of living with an unusual appearance: What do we know, why don't we know more and where do we go from here?" AboutFace, May 19, 2020, https://aboutfaceyork.com/2020/05 /the-challenges-of-living-with-an-unusual-appearance/.

60. **"We can't stop the cycle":** Anne Helen Petersen, "The Millennial Vernacular of Fatphobia," Culture Study, May 23, 2021, https:// annehelen.substack.com/p/the-millennial-vernacular-of -fatphobia?s=r.

61. **Myriad devastating consequences:** Dianne Neumark-Sztainer, Susan Paxton, Peter Hannan, et al., "Does Body Satisfaction Matter? Five-Year Longitudinal Associations Between Body Satisfaction and Health Behaviors in Adolescent Females and Males," *Journal of Adolescent Health* 39, no. 2 (2006): 244–51.

62. **Beyond the time and energy suck:** Sandra Aamodt, "Why dieting doesn't usually work," TED, June 2013, https://www.ted.com/talks /sandra_aamodt_why_dieting_doesn_t_usually_work?referrer =playlist-the_logic_of_loving_yourself.

63. **The global weight-loss industry was valued at $255 billion:** "Global Weight Loss Products and Services Market Report 2021: A $377.3 Billion Market by 2026 with 8% CAGR Forecast During 2021– 2026," ResearchAndMarkets.com news release, July 30, 2021, https://www.businesswire.com/news/home/20210730005355/en

/Global-Weight-Loss-Products-and-Services-Market-Report-2021
-A-377.3-Billion-Market-by-2026-with-8-CAGR-Forecast-During
-2021-2026—-ResearchAndMarkets.com.

64. **Mass media promoting [impossible] ideals:** Bae Guk-nam,
"Controversy About Son Ye-jin's Body: What Is the Problem?"
Entermedia, July 2, 2012, translated at https://thegrandnarrative
.com/2012/07/04/korean-media-male-gaze-son-ye-jin/.

Chapter 10. Escape the Corset

1. **Off-line, tens of thousands:** Seulki Lee, "'Escaping the corset,'"
Taipei Times, February 20, 2019, https://www.taipeitimes.com
/News/feat/archives/2019/02/20/2003710047.
2. **Kim announced in his deep baritone:** "Kim Jong Un's 2018 New
Year's Address," National Committee on North Korea, January 1,
2018, https://www.ncnk.org/node/1427.
3. **History-making inter-Korean talks:** Choe Sang-Hun, "North Korea
to Send Olympic Athletes to South Korea, in Breakthrough," *New
York Times*, January 8, 2018, https://www.nytimes.com/2018/01
/08/world/asia/north-korea-south-olympics-border-talks.html.
4. **The two Koreas agreed:** Choe Sang-Hun, "North and South Korean
Teams to March as One at Olympics," *New York Times*, January 17,
2018, https://www.nytimes.com/2018/01/17/world/asia/north
-south-korea-olympics.html.
5. **By February, a North Korean delegation:** Motoko Rich, "Olympics
Open with Koreas Marching Together, Offering Hope for Peace,"
New York Times, February 9, 2018, https://www.nytimes.com/2018
/02/09/world/asia/olympics-opening-ceremony-north-korea.html.
6. **In March, for the first time:** Steven Lee Myers and Jane Perlez, "Kim
Jong-un Met with Xi Jinping in Secret Beijing Visit," *New York Times*,
March 27, 2018, https://www.nytimes.com/2018/03/27/world/asia
/kim-jong-un-china-north-korea.html; James Reinl, "The fragile
diplomatic dance between US and North Korea," Al Jazeera,
September 21, 2018, https://www.aljazeera.com/news/2018/9/21
/the-fragile-diplomatic-dance-between-us-and-north-korea.
7. **By late April:** David E. Sanger and Choe Sang-Hun, "Korea Talks
Begin as Kim Jong-un Crosses to South's Side of DMZ," *New York
Times*, April 26, 2018, https://www.nytimes.com/2018/04/26
/world/asia/korea-kim-moon-summit.html.
8. **Women were in "total rebellion":** E. Tammy Kim, "#KoreaToo," *New
York Review of Books*, March 7, 2019, https://www.nybooks.com
/articles/2019/03/07/koreatoo/.

9. **largest women's rallies the country had ever known:** Claire Lee, "Largest ever women's rally protests spy-cam pornography," *Korea Herald*, May 20, 2018, http://www.koreaherald.com/view.php?ud= 20180520000165.

10. **a thirty-four-year-old man stabbed:** Steven Borowiec, "A woman's slaying in Seoul's tony Gangnam district stirs emotions in South Korea," *Los Angeles Times*, May 21, 2016, https://www.latimes.com /world/asia/la-fg-south-korea-woman-killed-20160521-snap-story .html.

11. **the man passed over six men:** 임정요, "Murder suspect admits he is misogynist," *Korea Herald*, May 18, 2016, http://www.koreaherald .com/view.php?ud=20160518000866.

12. **He told police that women had "belittled" him:** Ock Hyun-ju, "Gangnam murder was not a hate crime: police," *Korea Herald*, May 22, 2016, http://www.koreaherald.com/view.php?ud= 20160522000287.

13. **there was something all too familiar:** Elise Hu, "Violent Crimes Prompt Soul-Searching in Korea About Treatment of Women," NPR, July 6, 2016, https://www.npr.org/sections/parallels/2016/07 /06/484135201/violent-crimes-prompt-soul-searching-in-korea -about-treatment-of-women.

14. **"It was misogyny that killed her":** Farz Edraki, "Escape the corset," ABC News (Australia), December 20, 2019, https://www.abc.net .au/news/2019-12-20/south-korean-women-escape-the-corset /11611180?nw=0&r=HtmlFragment.

15. **"I survived, only by coincidence":** Hu, "Violent Crimes Prompt Soul-Searching."

16. **"What happened to you happened to me":** Kim, "#KoreaToo."

17. **a prominent theater director:** Lee Kyung-min, "Renowned play director resigns over #MeToo claim," *Korea Times*, February 19, 2018, http://www.koreatimes.co.kr/www/nation/2018/02/113 _244348.html.

18. **a famous poet:** Kim Jae-heun, "Poet Ko Un to leave Suwon," *Korea Times*, February 18, 2018, http://www.koreatimes.co.kr/www /nation/2018/02/113_244348.html.

19. **and a liberal provincial governor:** Choe Sang-Hun, "Korean Political Star Falls as #MeToo Campaign Grows, *New York Times*, March 5, 2018, https://www.nytimes.com/2018/03/05/world/asia /me-too-south-korea-ahn-hee-jung.html.

20. **On the two-year anniversary:** "South Korean women protest in Seoul over hidden sex cameras," BBC, July 7, 2018, https://www .bbc.com/news/world-asia-44751327.

21. **Participants wore red but donned hats:** "South Korean women protest in Seoul."

22. **clothing store dressing rooms:** Laura Bicker, "South Korea's spy cam porn epidemic," August 3, 2018, https://www.bbc.com/news/world-asia-45040968.

23. **public bathrooms:** Bicker, "South Korea's spy cam porn epidemic."

24. **at school:** "School principal arrested for allegedly installing hidden camera in women's bathroom," Yonhap, October 29, 2021, https://www.koreatimes.co.kr/www/nation/2021/10/251_317883.html?fl.

25. **in hospitals:** Josh Taylor, "South Korea: woman reportedly kills herself after being secretly filmed by doctor," *The Guardian*, October 1, 2019, https://www.theguardian.com/world/2019/oct/02/south-korea-woman-kills-herself-after-being-secretly-filmed-by-doctor-reports.

26. **on buses:** Haeryun Kang, "My Life Isn't Your Porn: Why South Korean Women Protest," Korea Exposé, June 10, 2018, https://www.koreaexpose.com/south-koreas-biggest-womens-protest-in-history-is-against-spycam-porn/.

27. **from schoolteachers:** 위성욱, "폰에 '무더기 몰카' 교사, 年2000명 찾는 수련원서도 일했다," *JoongAng*, July 9, 2020, https://n.news.naver.com/mnews/article/025/0003016243?sid=102; 김민기, "女기숙사·화장실서 116명 찍었다 . . . 그 몰카 교사에겐 700개 파일," 조선일보, July 29, 2021, https://www.chosun.com/national/national_general/2021/07/29/HXYQZZJ4RJFZNNDFEOMAJFFREM/.

28. **to doctors:** Josh Taylor, "South Korea: woman reportedly kills herself"; 임현정, "여성환자 진료중 '최대한 안 보겠다'던 의사 . . . 몰카 찍었다," 머니투데이, December 1, 2021, https://news.mt.co.kr/mtview.php?no=2021100110212346574.

29. **to civil servants:** 박효주, "'여성 몰카 123회' 보건소 공무원 '집유' . . . "코로나 스트레스," 머니투데이, May 3, 2022, https://news.mt.co.kr/mtview.php?no=2022050314205733185; 신진호, "구청 화장실에 몰카, 동료 여직원도 찍은 9급 공무원의 최후," *JoongAng*, November 13, 2020, https://www.joongang.co.kr/article/23919820#home; 이기진, "'2시간 일찍 출근, 성실한줄 알았는데' . . . 화장실 몰카 공무원 집유," 동아일보, February 10, 2021, https://www.donga.com/news/Society/article/all/20210210/105372504/1.

30. **The overwhelming majority of the content:** Claire Lee, "'Isu station' assault case triggers online gender war in South Korea," *Korea Herald*, November 18, 2018, http://www.koreaherald.com/view.php?ud=20181118000177.

31. **It's almost always captured by men:** Heather Barr, "'My Life Is Not Your Porn,'" Human Rights Watch, June 16, 2019, https://www.hrw.org/report/2021/06/16/my-life-not-your-porn/digital-sex-crimes-south-korea.

32. **"Spycam porn" is its own genre:** Haeryun Kang, "The First Rally Against South Korea's Spycam Porn Epidemic," Korea Exposé, May 22, 2018, https://koreaexpose.com/south-korea-spycam-porn-epidemic/.

33. **Human Rights Watch calls molka a form of sexual violence:** Heather Barr, "'My Life Is Not Your Porn.'"

34. **crimes of this type jumped sixfold:** Haeryun Kang, "My Life Isn't Your Porn."

35. **a jury awarded sportscaster Erin Andrews:** Daniel Victor, "Erin Andrews Awarded $55 Million in Lawsuit Over Nude Video at Hotel," *New York Times*, March 7, 2016, https://www.nytimes.com/2016/03/08/business/media/erin-andrews-awarded-55-million-in-lawsuit-over-nude-video-at-hotel.html.

36. **police did manage to arrest a *woman*:** "S. Korean woman given rare jail term for spycam crime," Agence France-Presse, August 13, 2018, https://www.yahoo.com/news/korean-woman-given-rare-jail-term-spycam-crime-053313799.html.

37. **In the streets, women chanted:** Korea Exposé, Twitter post, May 21, 2018, 12:36 p.m., https://twitter.com/KoreaExpose/status/998543028406009858.

38. **The May rally was repeated:** E. Tammy Kim, "#KoreaToo."

39. **An estimated 300,000 Korean women:** Chung, "South Korean women's movement," 70.

40. **accompanied them with a Korean hashtag:** 게이했어요, Twitter post, July 31, 2018, 1:13 p.m., https://twitter.com/COICCC/status/1024281784232501248.

41. **a mesmerizing video called "I am not pretty":** Lina bae, "I am not pretty" (video), June 4, 2018, https://www.youtube.com/watch?v=Zq51xKG-hyU (no longer available as of May 4, 2022).

42. **CNN and the BBC both featured clips:** Sophie Jeong, "Escape the corset: How South Koreans are pushing back against beauty standards," CNN, January 12, 2019, https://www.cnn.com/style/article/south-korea-escape-the-corset-intl/index.html; Laura Bicker, "Why women in South Korea are cutting 'the corset,'" BBC, December 10, 2018, https://www.bbc.com/news/worldasia-46478449.

43. **As Yun-Kim told NPR in 2019:** Anthony Kuhn, "South Korean Women 'Escape the Corset' and Reject Their Country's Beauty

Ideals," NPR, May 6, 2019, https://www.npr.org/2019/05/06
/703749983/south-korean-women-escape-the-corset-and-reject
-their-countrys-beauty-ideals.

44. **Many are boycotting marriage and motherhood:** Beh Lih Yi, "No
sex, no babies: South Korea's emerging feminists reject marriage,"
Reuters, January 19, 2020, https://www.reuters.com/article
/us-southkorea-women-rights/no-sex-no-babies-south-koreas
-emerging-feminists-reject-marriage-idUSKBN1ZJ02Z.

45. **South Korea's fertility rate fell:** "S. Korea's total fertility rate hits
record low of 0.92 in 2019," Yonhap, August 26, 2020, http://www
.koreaherald.com/view.php?ud=20200826000726.

46. **By 2020, its rate was the lowest:** "South Korea's fertility rate falls to
lowest in the world," Reuters, February 24, 2021, https://www
.reuters.com/article/us-southkorea-fertility-rate/south-koreas
-fertility-rate-falls-to-lowest-in-the-world-idUSKBN2AO0UH.

47. **At this rate, Koreans will be extinct:** Kim Dong-seop, "Koreans 'to
Become Extinct in 2750,'" *Chosun Ilbo*, August 25, 2014, http://
english.chosun.com/site/data/html_dir/2014/08/25
/2014082500859.html?_ga=1.138289013.437630734.1408766762.

48. **reportedly assaulted:** Claire Lee, "'Isu station' assault case triggers
online gender war in South Korea."

49. **dissidents would often shave their heads:** "Why are South Korean
politicians shaving their heads?" BBC, September 17, 2019, https://
www.bbc.com/news/world-asia-49723871.

50. **One collective head-shaving:** Elise Hu, "A Year After Ferry Disaster,
South Koreans Await Answers," NPR, April 15, 2015, https://www
.npr.org/sections/parallels/2015/04/15/398214127/a-year-after
-deadly-ferry-disaster-s-koreans-still-awaiting-answers.

51. **An San, Korea's three-time gold medalist:** Jing Yu Young, "She just
won her third gold medal in Tokyo. Detractors in South Korea are
criticizing her haircut," *New York Times*, July 30, 2021, https://
www.nytimes.com/2021/07/30/sports/olympics/an-san-hair.html.

52. **She calls herself fat:** Gyo-hyun interview.

53. **the country has yet to affirm LGBTQ + rights:** "Joint Letter to South
Korea's National Assembly Calling for the Immediate Passage of a
Comprehensive Anti-Discrimination Law," Human Rights Watch,
December 20, 2021, https://www.hrw.org/news/2021/12/20
/joint-letter-south-koreas-national-assembly-calling-immediate
-passage-comprehensive.

54. **One study found transgender people:** Andrew Flores, Ilan Meyer,
Lynn Langton, and Jody Herman, "Gender Identity Disparities in
Criminal Victimization," Williams Institute, March 2021, https://

williamsinstitute.law.ucla.edu/publications/ncvs-trans
-victimization/.

55. **the Ministry of Economy and Finance:** 서영빈, "92년생, 82년생, 72
년생, 62년생, 52년생 김지영," 통계데이터센터, August 10, 2020.

56. **In 2016, feminists successfully campaigned:** Isabella Steger, "An epic
battle between feminism and deep-seated misogyny is under way
in South Korea," Quartz, October 23, 2016, https://qz.com/801067
/an-epic-battle-between-feminism-and-deep-seated-misogyny-is
-under-way-in-south-korea/.

57. **In 2019, Korea's highest court:** Yoongjung Seo, "South Korea to
legalize abortion after 66-year ban," CNN, April 11, 2019, https://
www.cnn.com/2019/04/11/health/south-korea-abortion-ban
-ruling-intl/index.html.

58. **The girl group Mamamoo:** "Dungeons and dimples: how to speak
K-pop," *The Economist*, August 12, 2021, https://www.economist
.com/1843/2021/08/12/dungeons-and-dimples-how-to-speak-k-pop.

59. **Translation rights sold in roughly twenty countries:** Alexandra
Alter, "Just an Average Woman. That's the Savage Point," *New York
Times*, April 10, 2020.

60. **"If we women all go through these experiences":** Elise Hu, "South
Korean Bestseller 'Kim Jiyoung, Born 1982' Gives Public Voice to
Private Pain," NPR, April 19, 2020, https://www.npr.org/2020/04
/19/835486224/south-korean-bestseller-kim-jiyoung-born-1982
-gives-public-voice-to-private-pain.

61. **youth unemployment had hovered around 10 percent:** Kim Yon-se,
"High youth unemployment continues during Moon's term," *Korea
Herald*, April 22, 2021, http://www.koreaherald.com/view.php?ud=
20210422000380.

62. **women earn 68 cents:** OECD, Gender wage gap (indicator), https://
data.oecd.org/earnwage/gender-wage-gap.htm, accessed on May 5,
2022.

63. **occupy only 5 percent of corporate board seats:** "Boards appointing
women as new law requires diversity," *JoongAng Daily*, March 8,
2021, https://koreajoongangdaily.joins.com/2021/03/08/business
/industry/women-female-women-power/20210308194700337.html.

64. **women's representation in the legislature:** World Bank, "Proportion
of seats held by women in national parliaments (%)," https://data
.worldbank.org/indicator/SG.GEN.PARL.ZS, accessed on May 5,
2022.

65. **nearly 90 percent of victims of violent crimes:** "Secure society for
women," *Korea Times*, September 6, 2021, https://www.koreatimes
.co.kr/www/opinion/2021/11/202_315104.html.

66. **some 79 percent of South Korean men in their twenties:** Choe Sang-Hun, "The New Political Cry in South Korea: 'Out with Man Haters,'" *New York Times*, January 1, 2022, https://www.nytimes .com/2022/01/01/world/asia/south-korea-men-anti-feminists.html.

67. **Women's suicide rates spiked:** Hawon Jung, "A vicious anti-feminist backlash stuns South Korea," *Globe & Mail*, January 22, 2022, https://www.theglobeandmail.com/opinion/article-a-vicious-anti -feminist-backlash-stuns-south-korea/.

68. **And in 2021, distressed Korean men:** Jung, "A vicious anti-feminist backlash stuns South Korea."

69. **vowing to get rid of the Ministry of Gender Equality and Family:** Darcie Draudt, "The South Korean Election's Gender Conflict and the Future of Women Voters," Council on Foreign Relations, February 8, 2022, https://www.cfr.org/blog/south-korean -elections-gender-conflict-and-future-women-voters.

70. **He also slammed a post-2018 law:** Jo He-rim, "Feminism is one aspect of humanism, Yoon says," *Korea Herald*, March 3, 2022, http://www.koreaherald.com/view.php?ud=20220302001019.

71. **not a single presidential candidate:** Yim Hyun-su, "Once neglected, young women emerge as an important voting bloc," *Korea Herald*, March 6, 2022, http://www.koreaherald.com/view.php?ud= 20220306000064.

72. **a majority of men in their twenties:** 이서희, "2050 여성은 이재명에, 2030 남성은 윤석열에 쏠렸다," 한국일보, March 9, 2022, https:// m.hankookilbo.com/News/ReadA2022030917160002669; Victoria Kim, "What's size got to do with it? Mocking a man's manhood spurs a reverse #MeToo in South Korea," *Los Angeles Times*, June 11, 2021, https://www.latimes.com/world-nation/story/2021-06-11 /whats-size-got-to-do-with-it-the-pinching-hand-anti-feminist -backlash-drive-up-the-fever-pitch-of-south-koreas-gender-wars.

73. **a struggle between the past and the future:** Youngmi Kim, "After reading The Bronze Garden by Young-Mi Choi," Edinburgh Forum on Korea, https://blogs.ed.ac.uk/edinburghforumonkorea /young-mi-choi/.

Chapter 11. Child's Play

1. **Sungshin Women's University surveyed 288 elementary-aged girls:** 김주덕, "초등학생들의 화장품 사용 실태에 관한 연구," 예술인문사회 융합 멀티미디어 논문지 7, no. 5 (2017), 381–93.

2. **"The age in which children do makeup":** Ju-duck interview.

3. **Another study bears this out:** 전민희, "'나만 화장 안 해 왕따됐어' 초2 딸 어떻게 할까요," *JoongAng*, May 6, 2019, https://www .joongang.co.kr/article/23459382#home.

4. **The cosmetics are kid-safe:** Min Joo Kim and Simon Denyer, "Lipstick in kindergarten? South Korea's K-beauty industry now targets those barely able to read," *Washington Post*, February 16, 2019, https://www.washingtonpost.com/world/asia_pacific /lipstick-in-kindergarten-south-koreas-k-beauty-industry-now -aims-for-the-super-young/2019/02/14/af02c6d0-136d-11e9-ab79 -30cd4f7926f2_story.html; Chiyeon interview.

5. **"I watch my mom":** 김자매, Twitter post, January 19, 2019, 5:30 p.m., https://twitter.com/12345678_____9/status /1086677413319168002.

6. **A YouTube video of a seven-year-old:** Lime Tube[라임튜브], "엄마처럼 화장하고 싶어요! 파랑마법사 매니큐어와 립크레용 어린이 화장품을 선물해 주세요 |프린세스 핑크 공주 화장놀이 LimeTube & Toy 라임튜브" (video), April 21, 2017, https://www .youtube.com/watch?v=WIff4D1Gjv0.

7. **These brands are selling appearance labor:** Lee, "Introduction."

8. **A study by the consumer-advocacy group:** Jieun Choi, "The K-beauty Nation Begins to Question Its Obsession with Beauty," *Korea Exposé*, November 16, 2018, https://koreaexpose.com /south-korean-women-question-beauty-obsession-remove-corset/.

9. **School uniforms marketed for girls:** Claire Lee, "How teen feminism is changing school uniforms in South Korea," *Korea Herald*, October 21, 2018, http://www.koreaherald.com/view.php ?ud=20181021000211.

10. **"I think, in general, school uniforms":** Lee, "How teen feminism is changing school uniforms in South Korea."

11. **When the Gender Minister at the time:** Lee, "How teen feminism is changing school uniforms in South Korea."

12. **This "should ring alarm bells":** Widdows, *Perfect Me*, 64–65.

Chapter 12. Of Marketing and Men

1. **13 percent of the world's skincare products for men:** Euromonitor International data.

2. **Men's lip balm in South Korea:** Hwajung interview.

3. **the country's market for male skincare grew by 25 percent:** Euromonitor International data.

4. **Nearly half of South Korean respondents:** Hwajung interview.

5. **Three out of four Korean men said they use skincare products:** GlobalData Q4 2021 Global Consumer Survey.

6. **A Gangnam clinic told the newspaper *Hankyung*:** 안혜원, "'차은우 눈·서강준 코 갖고 싶어요'" . . . 성형시장 '큰손' 이젠 남성," 한경경제, December 8, 2021, https://www.hankyung.com/economy/article /202112083165g.

7. **he'd expand public healthcare to cover hair treatment:** "South Korea should fund hair loss treatment, says election hopeful in bald bid for power," *The Guardian*, January 6, 2022, https://www .theguardian.com/world/2022/jan/06/south-korean-presidential -hopeful-says-state-should-pay-for-hair-loss-treatment.

8. **A 2020 Gallup Korea poll showed:** "외모와 성형수술에 대한 인식—1994/2004/2015/2020년," Gallup Korea, April 9, 2020, https://www.gallup.co.kr/gallupdb/reportContent.asp?seqNo=1097.

9. **"generally being a lil cutie":** Lauren Strapagiel, "Here's Why Boys All Over Social Media Are Proudly Calling Themselves 'Softboys,'" BuzzFeed News, April 16, 2019, https://www.buzzfeednews.com /article/laurenstrapagiel/heres-everything-you-need-to-know -about-the-history-and.

10. **The origins of flowerboys can be traced:** Natalie Morin, "What K-Pop's Beautiful Men Can Teach Us About Masculinity," Refinery29, May 12, 2020, https://www.refinery29.com/en-us /2020/05/9674149/kpop-male-singers-masculinity.

11. **In music, the legendary K-pop mogul:** Tamar Herman, "SM Entertainment A&R Chris Lee Talks 'Cultural Technology' & Creating K-Pop Hits," *Billboard*, August 5, 2019, https://www .billboard.com/music/music-news/sm-entertainment-ar-chris-lee -talks-cultural-technology-creating-k-pop-hits-8526179/.

12. **said Korean music should be marketed as cultural commodities:** *Explained*, Netflix show written by Joe Posner, Vox Media, 2018. Netflix, https://www.netflix.com/watch/80216753?trackId= 255824129.

13. **Lee had witnessed the rise of MTV:** Hannah Waitt, "The History of Kpop, Chapter 4: How Lee Soo Man's First Big Fail Resulted in Korea's Modern Pop Star System," MoonROK, July 14, 2014, http:// www.moonrok.com/history-k-pop-chapter-4-how-lee-soo-mans -first-big-fail-resulted-koreas-modern-pop-star/.

14. **He spent years surveying girls:** David Yi, "How K-Pop Empowered Men Everywhere to Embrace Make-Up," *Esquire*, June 21, 2021, https://www.esquire.com/style/grooming/a36743526/k-pop -influence-mens-makeup-bts/.

15. **K-pop audiences are "predominantly made up of girls":** Roald Maliangkay, "The Effeminacy of Male Beauty in Korea," *The Newsletter* (International Institute for Asian Studies), no. 55 (autumn/winter 2010), https://www.iias.asia/sites/default/files /nwl_article/2019-05/IIAS_NL55_0607.pdf.

16. **giving off an availability to a reciprocal relationship with fans:** Shorenstein APARC, "SUHO, Leader of EXO, on the Korean Wave (Hallyu)," May 26, 2022, https://www.youtube.com/watch ?v=-fXGcYgAHT8.

17. **"As the socioeconomic status of women rises":** Jaeil Kim, WoongHee Han, DongTae Kim, and Widya Paramita, "Is beauty in the eye of the beholder? Gender and beauty in the cosmetic sector: A comparative study of Indonesia and Korea," *Marketing Intelligence & Planning* 31, no. 2 (March 2013): 127–40.

18. **"one of the most popular icons in Korean pop culture":** Kim et al., "Is beauty in the eye of the beholder?" 137.

19. **"perhaps the most culturally significant teen trend":** "Softboys," Quartz, April 21, 2020, https://qz.com/emails/quartz-obsession /1842285/softboys/.

20. **"The way they (K-pop stars)":** "Flowerboys and the appeal of 'soft masculinity' in South Korea," BBC, September 5, 2018, https:// www.bbc.com/news/world-asia-42499809.

21. **fans had a "twink gay fetish":** "K-Pop Twitter Flames YouTube's h3h3 for Calling Fans 'Gay,'" CCN, December 9, 2019, https://www.ccn .com/k-pop-twitter-flames-youtubes-h3h3-for-calling-fans-gay/.

22. **"And young men are obliging":** Brianna Holt, "Film showed women that softboys are the emotionally intelligent men they wanted all along," Quartz, December 19, 2019, https://qz.com/1772566 /film-changed-the-softboy-trend-now-it-fights-toxic-masculinity/.

23. **The Face Shop hired Kwon Sang-woo:** "권상우, 화장품 '더 페이스 샵' 모델," 스포츠조선, June 17, 2004, https://entertain.naver.com/read ?oid=076&aid=0000003983.

24. **Missha signed the mega-heartthrob:** 오미영, "미샤 원빈과 모델계약," 파이낸셜뉴스, August 30, 2004, https://n.news.naver .com/mnews/article/014/0000139458?sid=101.

25. **"I think Korea is a trailblazer":** "Flowerboys and the appeal of 'soft masculinity.'"

26. **"Just put the long-legged *oppa*":** Quoted in Xiaomeng Li, "How Powerful Is the Female Gaze? The Implication of Using Male Celebrities for Promoting Female Cosmetics in China," *Global Media and China* 5, no. 1 (2020): 55–68.

27. **"the emergence of a 'soft' male ideal":** Kam Louie, "Popular Culture and Masculinity Ideals in East Asia, with Special Reference to China," *Journal of Asian Studies* 71, no. 4 (2012): 929–43.

28. **Gen Z's ease with gender fluidity:** Sarah Todd, "Gen Z consumers are making companies bend to their will," Quartz, April 5, 2020, https://qz.com/1832884/what-is-gen-z-spending-its-money-on/.

29. **A member of BTS said he once ate only chicken breasts:** "Dungeons and dimples: how to speak K-pop," *The Economist*, August 12, 2021, https://www.economist.com/1843/2021/08/12/dungeons -and-dimples-how-to-speak-k-pop.

30. **Even if this pressure led to the extinction:** Widdows, *Perfect Me*, 251.

31. **"For women, beauty work is compulsory":** Sharon Heijin Lee interview.

Chapter 13. The Wisdom of Ajummas

1. **the signs of aging confer honor:** Seong-min Hong, "The significance of the aging body and caring of the aged in Confucian society" (in Korean). Summarized in Elfving-Hwang, "Old, Down, and Out? Beauty Work, Agency, and Between-Women Sociality Among Elderly South Korean Women," *Journal of Aging Studies* 38 (2016): 6–15.

2. **She interviewed twenty senior women:** Elfving-Hwang, "Old, Down, and Out?" 12–13.

3. **they are outliving men by an average of four and a half years:** "World Health Statistics Overview: 2019," World Health Organization, 2, https://apps.who.int/iris/bitstream/handle /10665/311696/WHO-DAD-2019.1-eng.pdf.

4. **"The ageing body both as an object":** Elfving-Hwang, "Old, Down, and Out?" 14.

5. **"The Japanese fairy tales tell us":** Kawai, *Dreams, Myths and Fairy Tales*, 129.

6. **"Again, the recipe says":** Stanton, "Our Girls," 496.

7. **For proof of how much youthfulness is valued:** Widdows, *Perfect Me*, 80–81.

8. **Thirty-five percent of the cosmetics market:** "Global cosmetics market worth €181 billion, L'Oreal dominates," Consultancy.uk news release, November 18, 2015, https://www.consultancy.uk/ news/2810/cosmetics-market-worth-181-billion-loreal-dominates.

9. **"The number-one thing I hear":** Autumn Whitefield-Madrano, "Only Women Are Named Hope," New Inquiry, June 22, 2016, https://thenewinquiry.com/only-women-are-named-hope/.

Conclusion

1. **The message that "all women are beautiful":** TedX Talks, "Body Positivity or Body Obsession? Learning to See More & Be More | Lindsay Kite | TEDxSaltLakeCity" (video), November 6, 2017, https://www.youtube.com/watch?v=uDowwh0EU4w&t=152s.
2. **"As an individual I cannot":** Widdows, *Perfect Me*, 211.
3. **"While many women (and some men)":** Engeln, *Beauty Sick*, 117.
4. **"living paycheck to paycheck":** Nahman, "#59: Beauty anxiety," Maybe Baby, June 20, 2021, https://haleynahman.substack.com/p/59-beauty-anxiety?s=r.
5. **You "take on a much gloomier view":** Elise Hu and Clare Marie Schneider, "You aren't lazy. You just need to slow down," NPR, September 24, 2021, https://www.npr.org/2021/09/24/1039676445/laziness-does-not-exist-devon-price.
6. **"When you see a beautiful painting":** Jessica DeFino, "Beauty Isn't Superficial," The Unpublishable, October 12, 2021, https://jessicadefino.substack.com/p/topicals-mental-health-spotline.
7. **For transgender women, appearing femme:** Hari Nef, "The aesthetics of survival," TED, April 2016, https://www.ted.com/talks/hari_nef_the_aesthetics_of_survival?language=en.
8. **The worldwide medical aesthetic market:** "Medical Aesthetics Market Research Report [2022–2028]," MarketWatch, February 21, 2022, https://www.marketwatch.com/press-release/medical-aesthetics-market-research-report-2022-2028-industry-size-share-growth-rate-business-strategies-industry-revenue-opportunities-future-trends-leading-players-update-analysis-and-forecast-2022-02-21.
9. **As author Jenny Odell pointed out:** Odell, "Introduction."
10. **The philosopher Martin Hägglund has argued:** Meagan Day, "True to Life: An Interview with Martin Hägglund," Jacobin, May 28, 2019, https://jacobin.com/2019/05/this-life-martin-hagglund-review-interview.
11. **"letting these costs become an integral part":** Engeln, *Beauty Sick*, 117.
12. **"This is the intimate edge":** Laurie Penny, "Model Behavior," New Inquiry, May 30, 2012, https://thenewinquiry.com/model-behavior/.
13. **other studies show the opposite:** John Swaddle and Innes Cuthill, "Asymmetry and Human Facial Attractiveness: Symmetry May Not Always Be Beautiful," *Proceedings of the Royal Society B* 261, no. 1360 (1995): 111–16.

14. **They risk reinforcing the long-standing norm:** Kaila Prins, "3 Reasons Why Body-Positive Ad Campaigns Are Less Empowering Than You Think," Everyday Feminism, May 5, 2015, https://everydayfeminism.com/2015/05/problem-with-body-positive-ads/.

15. **"body neutrality says, 'all bodies are bodies'":** Jessica DeFino, "'Acne Neutrality' May Be a Better Confidence-Boosting Benchmark Than 'Acne Positivity,'" Fashionista, November 5, 2019, https://fashionista.com/2019/11/acne-skin-positivity-neutrality.

16. **The work of Céline Leboeuf:** Céline Lebouef, "What Is Body Positivity? The Path from Shame to Pride," *Philosophical Topics* 47, no. 2 (2019): 113–28.

17. **"For many of us, participating":** Leboeuf, "What Is Body Positivity?" 125.

18. **To paraphrase the feminist writer bell hooks:** hooks, *All About Love*, 218.

19. **"To be sensual":** Baldwin, *The Fire Next Time*, 43.

20. **"it is unlikely that they can achieve the sexual agency":** Brumberg, *The Body Project*, 212.

21. **"constantly treading water":** Anne Helen Petersen, "No One Told Me Being Middle Class Meant Wearing My Retainer Forever," Culture Study, April 18, 2021, https://annehelen.substack.com/p/no-one-told-me-being-middle-class-846?s=r.

22. **Medical spas in America reported a major run on Botox:** Anna Rahmanan, "These Cosmetic Procedures Have Been on the Rise During the Pandemic," Huffington Post, April 27, 2021, https://www.huffpost.com/entry/cosmetic-procedures-pandemic_l_608049e3e4b047b9f8b594e9.

23. **Today, the beauty industry is more valuable:** Reilly Roberts, "2022 Beauty Industry Trends & Cosmetics Marketing: Statistics and Strategies for Your Ecommerce Growth," Common Thread Collective, March 5, 2022, https://commonthreadco.com/blogs/coachs-corner/beauty-industry-cosmetics-marketing-ecommerce.

24. **Petroleum jelly is *petroleum*:** Jessica DeFino, "Please Stop Slugging," The Unpublishable, January 18, 2022, https://jessicadefino.substack.com/p/the-glow-life-podcast-jessica-defino?s=r.

25. **a "world-transforming project":** Lisa Rofel, *Desiring China*, 15.

26. **"The deep truth":** "Daniel Kahneman: Why We Contradict Ourselves and Confound Each Other," *On Being* with Krista Tippett, October 5, 2017, https://onbeing.org/programs/daniel-kahneman-why-we-contradict-ourselves-and-confound-each-other/.

INDEX